# DAVID KING

*Corinne — All the best from*
*David King*
*28/04/09*

# RED STAR OVER RUSSIA

## A VISUAL HISTORY OF THE SOVIET UNION FROM 1917 TO THE DEATH OF STALIN

## POSTERS, PHOTOGRAPHS AND GRAPHICS FROM THE DAVID KING COLLECTION

TATE PUBLISHING

# COMMUNISTS NEVER SLEEP

*Page 1:* "Workers of the World, Unite!" Gouache on paper. Artist unknown (signed "N.Sh."), Leningrad, mid-1920s.
*Pages 2/3:* Barge haulers on the Volga, circa 1900.
*Pages 4/5:* Tsar Nicholas II, Tsarina Alexandra Feodorovna and their eldest daughters, Olga and Tatiana, on a boating trip in 1909.
*Pages 6/7:* Yakov Shteinberg's photograph of the newly-formed People's Militia attacking the Petrograd police headquarters during the first days of the February Revolution, 1917.
*Page 8: Oktyabr* (October). Sergei Chekhonin's cover design for an album of photomontages covering the early years of Soviet power. Petrograd, 1921.
*Pages 10/11:* The Bolsheviks come to power. A meeting of Sovnarcom (Council of Peoples' Commissars) in Petrograd, early 1918.
*Front row, left to right:* Moisei Uritsky, Leon Trotsky, Yakov Sverdlov, Grigorii Zinoviev and Mikhail Lashevich. Uritsky was assassinated by an SR (Socialist Revolutionary) later that year. Sverdlov died suddenly in 1919. Lashevich committed suicide in 1928. Zinoviev was executed after the Moscow Show Trial of 1936. Trotsky was murdered in Mexico in 1940.

*Please note: The Bolsheviks adopted the new-style Gregorian calendar on February 18, 1918, replacing the old-style Julian calendar which was thirteen days behind. Thus May Day took place on April 18 (old calendar) in tsarist times.*
*Saint Petersburg's name was changed to Petrograd in the First World War as part of a protest against everything German. It became Leningrad after Lenin's death, but reverted to Saint Petersburg after the collapse of the Soviet Union in 1991.*

## RED STAR OVER RUSSIA

*Red Star Over Russia* is a fast-forward visual history of the Soviet Union. It is a heavy bombardment of posters, photographs, graphics and text depicting the revolutionary upheavals of 1917, the Civil War that followed, the defeat of the Bolsheviks and their ideals in the wake of the catastrophic rise of Stalinism, through to the heroic struggle and ultimate victory of the Russian people against the Nazi invaders in the Great Patriotic War. The book closes with Stalin's last years, the intrigue surrounding his death, and the ascendancy of Nikita Khrushchev.

The subsequent "period of stagnation", when Leonid Brezhnev was in charge, was generally as dull and sluggish on the visual front as it was politically, and for this reason has been left out. So too have the final years of collapse under Mikhail Gorbachev and Boris Yeltsin.

The reader/viewer must be careful; the journey is a dangerous one. In the four decades covered, tens of millions of Russians suffered the consequences of three wars, two famines and a totalitarian dictator. After Lenin's death, Stalin wielded such power that at any moment of his choosing, the life of the ordinary citizen, let alone the high-ranking communist, could be turned into a nightmare of arrest, interrogation and torture, followed by harsh years in the Gulag or execution.

The stories of some of the men and women who saw their early revolutionary struggles transformed into almost unspeakable tragedy are recorded here, alongside hundreds of examples of indelible images created by the designers, artists and photographers who shaped the iconography of the first workers' state. Much of this work, highly-skilled but often anonymous, is little known or long forgotten. In Stalin's Russia, the applause could still be ringing in a person's ears as they faced the firing squad.

## CHAOS

As I write this, my top floor studio is in chaos. Thousands of Russian photographs and graphics, unused or about to be used, are piled high on trestle tables or scattered all over the floor. Nearly one hundred recently-framed posters are waiting to be transported to Tate Modern to be shown in the latest of a series of displays of material from my collection. Stalagmites of books and albums, early Soviet newspapers and journals, have formed in my Russian library, making access almost impossible. Up and down the stairs, boxes of even more photographs, fallen in the fray of frenetic decision making, wait in vain to be re-filed.

It has taken me four decades to assemble the 250,000 artefacts in the collection and two more years to plan, design and write this book. It will

*Opposite page:* This modestly-produced Bolshevik poster with its bizarre typography, crudely printed in seven different Cyrillic typefaces on poor quality paper, is of the utmost rarity. Distributed by Red Guards on the night of the October Revolution it states:

"From the Military-Revolutionary Committee of the Petrograd Soviet of Workers' and Soldiers' Deputies.
TO THE CITIZENS OF RUSSIA.
The Provisional Government has been overthrown. State power has passed into the hands of the organ of the Petrograd Soviet of Workers' and Soldiers' Deputies, the Military Revolutionary Committee, the leadership of the Petrograd proletariat and garrison. The cause for which the people have been fighting: the immediate offer of a democratic peace, the abolition of the landlords' property rights over the land, the workers' control of production, the creation of a government of the Soviets – this cause has been secured.
LONG LIVE THE WORKERS', SOLDIERS' AND PEASANTS' REVOLUTION!
The Military-Revolutionary Committee of the Petrograd Soviet of Workers' and Soldiers' Deputies.
25 October 1917. 10 o'clock in the morning."

The claim that the Bolshevik's seizure of power had already happened was somewhat premature. The poster is datelined "25 October 1917. 10 o'clock in the morning" and the storming of the Winter Palace didn't take place until much later that night. The poster thus underlines the rock-solid confidence that Lenin and Trotsky had in their plans for the successful overthrow of the old regime.

Отъ Военно - Революціоннаго Комитета при Петроградскомъ Совѣтъ Рабочихъ и Солдатскихъ Депутатовъ.

# Къ Гражданамъ Россіи.

Временное Правительство низложено. Государственная власть перешла въ руки органа Петроградскаго Совѣта Рабочихъ и Солдатскихъ Депутатовъ Военно-Революціоннаго Комитета, стоящаго во главѣ Петроградскаго пролетаріата и гарнизона.

Дѣло, за которое боролся народъ: немедленное предложеніе демократическаго мира, отмѣна помѣщичьей собственности на землю, рабочій контроль надъ производствомъ, созданіе Совѣтскаго Правительства — это дѣло обезпечено.

ДА ЗДРАВСТВУЕТЪ РЕВОЛЮЦІЯ РАБОЧИХЪ, СОЛДАТЪ И КРЕСТЬЯНЪ!

Военно-Революціонный Комитетъ
при Петроградскомъ Совѣтѣ
Рабочихъ и Солдатскихъ Депутатовъ.

25 октября 1917 г. 10 ч. утра.

take another six months to box it all up and send it to storage, no doubt. So here are some notes, anecdotes and memories of how this chaos of collecting came about, documenting the vision of communism in a world of sleepless nights.

## WHERE'S TROTSKY?

My first visit to the Soviet Union took place in the deep mid-winter of 1970. It was a particularly dark and snowbound February in Moscow and the temperature often plummeted to thirty below zero. Sometimes my Nikon F2 cameras would protest at the cold and freeze up and then I would have to return to the hotel and defrost them on the radiators for half an hour. About to do this one evening, I opened the door to my room and interrupted someone leafing through my notebooks. It didn't matter, I had nothing to hide and in a way was rather expecting it. He said sorry in English and left, empty-handed. I remember being glad it wasn't the 1930s.

Everyone was very nice to me, especially after I had mentioned in a telephone call to London that the food wasn't up to much. It used to take three or four hours in those days to get an overseas connection, which you had to do through the Russian operator. The next day attentive questions were put to me about the kind of food I liked. It was rather disarming.

I was visiting Russia that first time to research and photograph two large visual features on the life of Lenin for the London *Sunday Times Magazine*. The revolutionary museums in those days were sensational and very popular. Their echoing halls were filled with acres of paintings, sculptures, banners, posters, photographs and large-format commemorative albums, brilliantly designed, from the 1920s, 30s and 40s.

The one figure who I was most interested in finding out about, however, was nowhere to be seen. So I spent a lot of time asking, "Yes, but where's Trotsky?" or "That's very interesting, but what about Trotsky?" Feeble attempts were made in the official photo archives to drag out even one picture of the co-leader of the Russian Revolution. There was nothing. They had totally wiped him out, and as I was soon to find out, legions of others too.

## YESSUS CHRISTUS

My great grandfather was my earliest link with Russia. He was an engineer for the Great Western Railway (GWR). They got the contract to build the Russian rail network in tsarist times because the GWR gauge (the width between the rails) was wider than that used by other railway companies and it gave the trains a smoother ride. When the railways were nationalised in Britain after the war, the GWR tracks were narrowed to the uniform measure but the Russians continue to use the wide gauge to this day. That is the reason why all the rail equipment has to be changed on reaching the Russian border.

On the dresser in my grandmother's kitchen there used to be a heavy lead cosh. When I was a child my father told me darkly that it had been issued to my great grandfather in Russia to beat off the wolves in the forests when he and his fellow railwaymen were constructing the lines. Let's hope that was all it was used for.

★ ★ ★ ★ ★

I remember my first journey on the night train to Leningrad back in the winter of 1970 and remember thanking my great grandfather, wherever he was, for the comfortable ride in the warm train with its red star on the front of the engine and a samovar in every carriage. In the early hours of the morning it made an unscheduled stop at a lamp-lit wayside halt. Perhaps a hundred peasants, mainly elderly women, struggled to get on board (illegally of course) with sacks of homegrown produce to sell (also illegally) at the station in Leningrad which, like other Soviet stations, had become an unofficial market.

When the peasant women who had successfully clambered inside saw me they became filled with wonderment at the sight of my beard: "Why is he so young that he has a beard? He must be from the tundra. Yes, that's it, he is from the tundra!" said one, stroking the hair on my face. "No, no," said another, "He is Yessus Christus! Yessus Christus! Christ is risen!" and everyone of them crossed themselves in the gently moving carriage and started to sing hymns in those beautiful little girls' voices given only to the Russian peasant woman.

## PLANNED ECONOMY

Even as a child I detested capitalism. I thought it was unfair. I also loathed religion and the monarchy. I found the clothes they dressed up in sinister and frightening. When my uncle, who was a socialist, taught me about the true nature of the ruling class I agreed with him that it clearly had to be overthrown. I used to dream, like all children, how life would be in the 21st century. If anyone had told me that there would still be inequality, racism, kings, queens and religious maniacs stalking the planet I would have considered them crazy.

At my first school in the late 1940s in London, the geography teacher, whose name was Mrs Raines, was, I realise now, a Stalinist. Whatever the subject of the lesson, it would always get back to the "collectivisation of agriculture in the Russian Steppes" and the "planned economy".

I fell in love with Russian names; Nadezhda, Natalya, Tatiana. Likewise, I found Soviet place names indescribably romantic. I pored for hours over the atlas; Volochanka, Kolymskaya, Petropavlovsk, Suntar. But my dream city was on the Irtysh river – Semipalatinsk. How I longed to go there. Stalin's name was everywhere; Stalinabad, Stalingrad, Stalino, Stalinsk, Mount Stalin, the Stalin Glacier. All those names disappeared in the Soviet Union, of course, after de-Stalinisation but there is still a Stalingrad on the map – an area in the north east of Paris.

★ ★ ★ ★ ★

Chelyabinsk, 1970. An industrial city on the eastern slopes of the Urals in western Siberia. The airport. Hot dry sun. Saturday afternoon. The terminal building is little more than a shed. On the runway, waiting for the plane which has been delayed. A battered wooden fence separates us would-be passengers from the locals who have come to watch the aeroplanes landing (rare) and taking off again (even rarer).

Everything is quiet, expectant, except for the slight sound of the clip-clop of hooves on concrete; the locals have arrived on horseback. Tough horses, short and squat. But their riders are even tougher, Mongolian looking, in black leather outfits welded to their bodies as if they haven't been able to take them off for thirty years.

In the distance, fifty-nine factory smokestacks (I counted them twice). The Chelyabinsk Tractor Factory, the largest in the world, another of Stalin's gigantic industrialisation projects, once home to the "Stalinets-60", one of the best caterpillar tractors ever made.

The pride on the horseriders' faces in the late afternoon sun as they watch the silver aircraft, Cyrillic "CCCP" emblazened on its fuselage, slowly thundering towards us on the tarmac.

## MURDERS IN MEXICO

I returned to London in great excitement. I was weighed down with suitcases full of photographs and albums on Lenin and the Russian Revolution but I had a new plan; to search for Trotsky, to document his life in pictures. I wanted to show that no amount of political falsification, no amount of photographic retouching, could extinguish the memory of the twentieth century's inspirational revolutionary genius. Much had been written about Trotsky in the West, but as a designer/photographer I wanted his story to reach out to a much wider audience.

The *Sunday Times Magazine*, in those days a hotbed of creative activity, once again saw the point of the project. Much detective work followed, but I started as ever in the old *Sunday Times* photo library. It was run by a man named Wally Squires. He had worked there forever. The preservation of photographs was very low on the agenda for newspapers in those days. Whenever Wally opened the library's green metal boxes and found an old sepia print, slightly torn and rough at the edges, he would say, "Oh, no one will ever want that any more," and throw it in the bin. Fortunately his spring cleaning, which went on throughout the year, hadn't got to the box marked "T". Inside there were at least six great images of Trotsky from the Civil War that hadn't been disturbed for thirty years. The work had begun.

I traced many of the comrades and ex-comrades still surviving who had known or worked with Trotsky and most of them produced interesting photographs. Many Trotskyist groups existed at that time and each one willingly helped me, with the proviso, "Don't mention where you got this information from or they won't see you." I travelled all over Europe, the United States and to Coyoacán, the suburb of Mexico City where Trotsky and his wife, Natalya, spent their last years together before his assassination by a Stalinist agent in 1940.

Today, their house is a museum but in 1971 it was still lived in by his grandson, Estaban Volkov and his wife and their three young daughters. I remember the children so well. Each one bore a strong resemblance to their great grandfather and they all displayed the most astonishing intelligence, even though the eldest could not have been more than about ten years old. Estaban brought out some battered manilla envelopes containing rare pictures from Trotsky's Mexican years to lend for the project.

☆ ☆ ☆ ☆ ☆

Another person who supplied me with great photographs was Jean van Heijenoort. We arranged to meet on the steps of the New York Public Library. "I will be wearing a red scarf," he told me. Van Heijenoort was one of Trotsky's longest-serving political secretaries during his exile. He had lived through the nightmare of Stalinist assassinations and political intrigues that blighted the European Trotskyist movement in the 1930s. He was a brilliant mathematician, a Trotskyist and a very sweet man.

In 1986, aged 73, he came to a shocking end, eerily reminiscent of those earlier years. He shared a turbulent marriage with his fourth wife, who was Mexican. She disliked living in America, while the climate of Mexico City didn't suit him. So they lived separately. One day he received an urgent message that he must fly down to Mexico immediately to see her, no reason given. This he did. She greeted him at her house. He was tired after the flight. They talked for a while and then he asked if he could lie down on the sofa in the living room and take a nap. This he did. She left the room. While he was asleep, she re-entered with a gun in her hand and shot him dead. Then she turned the gun on herself.

## MR ROTHSTEIN

Someone helpfully suggested to me in 1971 that it might be worth contacting Andrew Rothstein, a famous British Stalinist whose Russian father, Theodore, had been a friend of Lenin. Andrew Rothstein had written a number of polemical pamphlets in the 1930s attacking Trotsky. Perhaps he might be able to give me some leads on visual material.

I dialled his number and told him about the work that I was doing. There was a short silence of, maybe, disbelief followed by a blistering reply in his strong Scottish accent: "Trotsky? Mr Trotsky? I've got NOTHING on Mr Trotsky" and he slammed down the phone.

Over twenty years later, I got a frantic telephone call: "We must see you urgently. We have something for you. It's very important. Can we come round immediately? We need money." Over the years I have had quite a few phone calls like this, so of course I said yes. About ten minutes later two British communists arrived in business suits. One of them was carrying a shoebox. "Open this. We need cash immediately. We have to pay the printer today or the paper won't come out."

It was like a scene from the great 1941 film noir, "The Maltese Falcon". Taking the role of Sidney Greenstreet, I feverishly untied the string, paused, and slowly lifted the lid. Whatever was inside was carefully wrapped in straw. What was revealed was as rare as the legendary bird but, unlike in the film, this was not a fake. There, in perfect condition, was a porcelain mug on which was painted a portrait of Trotsky as leader of the Red Army by Mikhail Adamovich in 1923; and it had been donated to their newspaper in order to raise money by – Andrew Rothstein. It had lain hidden under his bed for over seventy years.

## STRIKE!

The *Sunday Times Magazine* ran the Trotsky feature over fifteen pages plus cover on September 19, 1971. One and a half million copies were printed but the issue never hit the streets. The weekend it was due to appear there was an industrial dispute and most of the copies were subsequently pulped. The few that survived have become some of the rarest issues in the magazine's history. I recall some Trotskyists at the time blaming the strike, only half-jokingly, on Stalinists at the printshop who had objected to the subject matter.

Michael Rand, the visionary art director of the magazine who kept the rest of us from going totally out of control in those days, suggested that I should turn the feature into a book. The distinguished writer and novelist, Francis Wyndham, agreed to write the text and the first photographic biography of Trotsky was published in 1972 by Penguin Books with a print run of 25,000 copies.

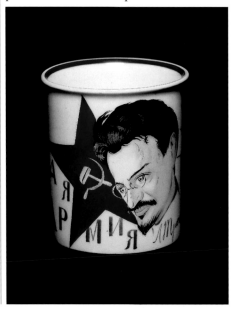

*Right:* Two photographs showing the porcelain mug portraying Leon Trotsky as leader of the Red Army, painted by Mikhail Adamovich in 1923.

Francis was amazed when he first saw the vast number of pictures there were to choose from: "Far from Trotsky being expunged from history, it turns out there are more photographs of him than there are of Marilyn Monroe!"

## WORKING LIBRARY

During the 1970s I decided to expand the collection and visually document every important aspect of Soviet history (particularly regarding alternatives to Stalinism) and include material from communist movements everywhere. This high-flown objective was made easier by the global dissemination of photographs and printed matter by the Communist International in the 1920s and 30s, the Soviet's major propaganda machine. Vast amounts of material reached the West in those days and could still be found, unloved and unwanted, in the world's secondhand bookshops forty years later.

This archaeological quest coincided with a long partnership with the designer and artist Judy Groves, producing posters, books, magazines, newspapers, museum catalogues and exhibitions, mainly on political subjects. When designing posters for leftist political organisations such as the Anti-Apartheid Movement or the Anti-Nazi League, we used our knowledge of the work of revolutionary designers from the past to produce powerful imagery whilst coping with overnight deadlines, low production costs and bootleg printing.

## HOPE AGAINST HOPE

Cheryomushkinskaya, 1977. Visiting Nadezhda Mandelstam in her tiny one room flat. A little bed in the corner, an icon above it, and a small bottle of Valium on the little bedside table. She was raised as a child in Moscow in tsarist times by an English governess. She speaks English with a precise Victorian humour: "Must I Mister you?" she asks when we meet. "So you come from that green little island so faraway." We sit having lemon tea at the little green table in her minute kitchen. She was a student during the Revolution: "We marched around with flags. We had a lovely time. We were young and we were idiots." We talked about the Russian avant-garde: "That Tatlin! He was in our group. He was always trying to invent things... a monument... and a glider that never could fly. He even tried to build a stove once in his kitchen. It caught fire and burnt down his flat. What a fool!"

"I have to thank Mr Khrushchev for my little home. Before that, for twenty five years, I had nothing." That was painfully the case. Her husband, the poet and writer Osip Mandelstam, was one of the literary martyrs of the twentieth century. Vilified for years by Stalinist hacks and tormented by ill health, in 1933 he was denounced for writing "the prose of a lackey" and never found work again. One night he recited his secret poem about Stalin to a small group of friends ("... the Kremlin mountineer... with fat grubs for fingers... and his cockroach whiskers"). One of them informed on him and he was arrested. Osip and Nadezhda were sentenced to three years internal exile in Voronezh.

On May Day, 1938, Mandelstam was arrested again and the following winter he died in a transit camp near Vladivostock. His works were banned. For a quarter of a century after his death, Nadezhda continued to be victimised by the Stalinist authorities. Forced into poverty, sometimes all she had was a quarter of a room to live in, divided from the other occupants by old curtains. But determined that her late husband's work would not be lost forever, she memorised all his poetry, in the hope that things might change, that some day his work might be published again.

⭐ ⭐ ⭐ ⭐ ⭐

Travelling on a Soviet bus far from Moscow in 1987. A vast white abstract expressionist snowstorm. The landscape reaps the whirlwind. Sudden appearances of traditional wooden Russian architecture, cupolas hugely commanding in the snowdrifts. Parallel lines of speeding telegraph wires, zigzagging in black on white. Once again my cameras freeze up.

Now the road is long, straight and empty. Forests of silver birch trees on either side. It's about two hours before dark. Out of the dirty windows of the bus I see an old peasant woman walking down the road alone. She has a sack on her back. Dressed to stay alive. Bast shoes. The bus moves on past her. She is left behind in the distance. No buildings, no turnings left or right for perhaps the next twenty kilometres. Just dense, dark, unwelcoming forest. The old peasant woman walking on and on...

## SOVIET WOMEN

Moscow, November 7, 1977: The night of the sixtieth anniversary of the Russian Revolution. Western communists standing around in the hotel lobby. Some animatedly swapping stories about the Red Square parade they had attended that morning, others in deep discussion on how best to approach the tasks ahead. Suddenly a desperate middle-aged Russian woman, messed-up clothes, drunk and haggard, staggers in through a side door, slurring to the crowd: "Who wants my body? Who will pay thirty dollars for my body? Will someone take my body? Give me thirty dollars for my body!" The communists turn away sheepishly as the hotel staff bundle her off down a corridor.

⭐ ⭐ ⭐ ⭐ ⭐

A discussion with a Moscow primary school teacher the following day. The school runs beautifully, her pupils are happy and love their work and there are no shortages on the education front. There is only one thing that she finds a bit of a bore in her job; once every three weeks it is her turn on the teachers' rota to stay up all night alone on sentry duty, guarding the school against the constant threat of a Chinese invasion.

## IN THE BASEMENTS

There used to be a famous socialist secondhand bookseller in Zurich. I visited his shop one day but was disappointed to find that it bore little relation to the interesting catalogues he had been publishing for years. I asked him where all his Russian material had gone. He replied, "Oh, that!... it should still be here, I think it's in the basement, but it's a bit difficult down there." I said that's Okay, can we have a look.

An iron spiral staircase led down into darkness; black on black. Knowing the way, the bookman went down first with a small torch and I followed. In the basement he asked me to stand still in the middle of the room while he searched for the light switch. The single 15-watt bulb made a slight difference but the brick-walled basement didn't look likely to give away any secrets. "So where are the photographs?" I asked, trying to hide my disappointment. "You are standing on them," came the friendly reply. "They've been down here for years, nobody's interested in them, take what you want."

I looked down. The floor was covered with original Russian pho-

*Above:* Mugshots of the poet Osip Mandelstam taken by Stalin's secret police. Mandelstam was to die in captivity eight months later on December 27, 1938. His wife Nadezhda devoted the rest of her life to the preservation of his poetry.

tographs from the 1920s and 30s; fine prints, captioned on the back by Soviet photographers, of great industrialisation projects and social documentation, including the fabulous picture of the fliers, Shura Kuvshinova and Tonya Kamenskaya, reproduced on pages 254/5.

⭐ ⭐ ⭐ ⭐ ⭐

Basements, too, have played a part, usually sinister, in Soviet politics. The victims of Stalin were often shot in the back of the head on the stairs to the basement of the Lubyanka, the once feared secret police headquarters in the centre of Moscow, and in her memoir, *Into the Whirlwind*, Evgenia Ginzberg recalls her experience of being literally walled up in the darkness of a basement prison for weeks on end. The two volumes of her life under Stalin's terror are the greatest books ever written on the subject.

There is another basement in the heart of Moscow, however, that holds many secrets without being in the least bit sinister. The Lenin Museum closed its doors in 1992 after the collapse of Soviet power, but remarkably it continues in a sort of self-imposed exile far from the public's gaze. A small side door close to Red Square leads to a labyrinth of offices and studios housing the contents of the museum. Over eighty years of political documentation and Leninalia are still studied there by a highly-trained, knowledgeable and friendly group of directors and staff. But in the ill-lit basement, again reached by spiral staircase, lies a breathtaking collection of giant paintings and sculptures of Lenin, Stalin and their comrades that once took pride of place in the great halls of the museum. As is so often the case, the drama of seeing art under these conditions, stacked together in great long racks, far exceeds most of the tasteful layouts that museum curators normally offer the public. It used to be said that communists never sleep, but Soviet power lives on in the basement.

## IN THE MAUSOLEUM

It's Sunday morning in Moscow and I decide to visit Lenin in his mausoleum. In Soviet times the queues were, of course, legendary. You might have had to wait in line for eight hours. Now it is only a question of how long Lenin will have to wait in the mausoleum before he receives a proper burial.

I walk through Red Square and enter through the double doors underneath the large Cyrillic "LENIN" and descend into the red and black depths of the marble building. The armed guards are as motionless as ever, except for their eyes which search me for signs that I might be the provocateur who could earn them a medal. I turn into the crypt, mystically lit by diffused natural light, where Lenin lies suffocated in his sarcophagus, designed by the great god of architecture, Melnikov.

He looks the same as ever; waxen faced, yellow of complexion, school masterish. It feels strange to be alone and face-to-face with the corpse of someone who died eighty years ago and is still wearing the same suit.

"A Spectre is Haunting Europe, the Spectre of Communism". A poster of Lenin, artist unknown (signed "V.Shch"), circa 1924. The slogan is taken from the first line of the Manifesto the Communist Party (Marx and Engels, 1848).

## PROVOCATION

It was an offence under Soviet law, and still is, to import or export almost anything except the most innocuous souvenirs and gifts without official permission. All forms of printed matter and photography were felt to be particularly suspect at the customs...

⭐ ⭐ ⭐ ⭐ ⭐

1984. The night before I left Leningrad I visited a photographer and his friend, a scientist. I had been researching the life of the late Maria Yudina, the distinguished Russian concert pianist. The photographer had been related to her in some way. He was a nice person and his photographs were very funny. All taken in the zoo, they were allegorical pictures intending to subvert Kremlin bureaucrats. At least, that's what he said.

The evening passed pleasantly but I could see that the scientist was agitated. He said he was an expert on the darkest days of Stalin's Great Terror, that he had information nobody else knew. Many people in Soviet times said that, of course, but sometimes it was true. We drank quite a bit of vodka. The evening ended. I was putting on my coat in the hall when the scientist came straight out with it: "I've got sixty one rolls of microfilm in this bag. It is a lifetime's scientific research and I can't get it published here. I know people in France who will publish it. Will you take it for me?"

I gasped. "You want me to take sixty one rolls of microfilm to the West?"

"Yes. It's my last hope, my last chance. You must do this for me." There were tears in his eyes.

"I can't. The customs will find it."

"Please, please, take it. It's my only hope. It's not illegal, it's pure science." At Soviet customs, pure science was definitely illegal.

"If I take that stuff and the customs find it, which they will, they might just put me on a plane but they will certainly come knocking on your door."

He was in tears now: "Please, here it is, you have to take it."

⭐ ⭐ ⭐ ⭐ ⭐

Leningrad airport is a pleasant place, not very big, and it was a crisp sunny morning. There was the usual massive queue for departures; fur coats, fur hats, fur everything. Passport control was a long desk manned by seven operatives in a row. A small door beyond them led to the departure area. The line moved swiftly, passports were hardly glanced at. Until mine.

"King, David," said the first operative. Instead of returning my passport he passed it on to his next in line who repeated, "King, David." Then he passed it on, and so on down the row. The passport went through the departure door, but I didn't. There was a lot of staring from the other passengers. I was taken out of the queue and escorted into a side room, empty except for a bare table and three rather gormless guards. We all waited in silence. I started to think about the scientist, and I wondered if they were thinking about him too.

Soon an exceptionally beautiful woman commissar hurriedly entered the room. She was about twenty-seven, tall with long dark hair. She spoke perfect English: "What have you got in your bags?"

"Nothing much. Books, clothes, one or two presents, some photographs, film..."

"Film? What film?"

"Oh, you know, just photographs I've taken."

"How much film?"

"Not a lot, see for yourself."

"How many rolls of film?"

"Fifteen." That's 540 negatives. I waited for trouble.

"What have you been doing here?"

I lowered my voice: "I have been researching the life of Maria Yudina, the great Russian pianist. I have copied many photographs of Yudina because I wish to publish a book on her in the West."

Now she lowered her voice and her eyes went deep: "You know about Marushya? You knew her? Are you related? I love Marushya. She is my favourite pianist of all. I love her. Have you got all her records? Did you meet her? Are you related to her?" I replied that I wasn't related to her and sadly had never met her because she died in 1969, but that I had all her records.

She quietly spoke again: "Make a wonderful book on Marushya, please, make a wonderful book."

Then she turned sharply to the gormless guards: "Let him through," she ordered in Russian: "He studies Yudina!"

## THINGS MISSED

One afternoon many years ago I rang the doorbell of a rather strange Russian bookdealer in New York whose premises were quite near the wonderful Strand Bookstore. After a few minutes the door slowly opened.

"You see, David, there is a God!"

"Excuse me?" I replied.

"It has been so many years since you have been here and I was just saying to my wife... David is coming to see us today!"

We talked like this for a little while and then I told him what I was looking for: an incredibly rare large-format album published in Moscow in 1934 on the Red Army, designed by Alexander Rodchenko. His face drained of blood. "Please come in to the kitchen," he stuttered. Spread out on the kitchen table was a large amount of brown wrapping paper, in the middle of which, looking as if it had just landed from outer space, sat the Red Army album with its gleaming red and gold cover. I think it was the first time I had ever seen a copy. It glowed. "There is a slight problem, David," the bookdealer continued, "You see... I have just sold it today for sixty dollars to someone in California... there is nothing I can do."

The hand of God seems to play a rather large part in book collecting. I was mindlessly wandering down a side street in Paris one afternoon when I came across a secondhand bookshop, "Librairie des Cinq Continents". I was surprised to see some Russian books in the window, so I went in. The shop was full of dusty shelves of decaying volumes but empty of clientele. The owner, an elderly French gentleman wearing a black beret and pince nez, sat behind a desk at the far end of the room. There wasn't much of interest on the shelves, mainly 1950s Russian reprints, but then... I couldn't believe it!

On the top of a bookcase just in front of me, at shoulder height, was the Russian catalogue for the Soviet pavilion at the 1925 Musee des Arts Decoratif exhibition in Paris, in perfect condition with its fine typographical cover (also designed by Alexander Rodchenko). Insanely rare.

I was about to pick it up when, suddenly, a very long arm came flying over my shoulder from behind and grabbed the book. The shop had been empty. Bewildered, I looked round just in time to see a long raincoat paying the black beret 200 francs in cash.

## GLASNOST

Two events of world-shattering importance changed everything as the twentieth century closed – the arrivals of both Mikhail Gorbachev and the internet. Suddenly Russia's doors were thrown open and all at once the world's media wanted visual material from my collection ("Have you got any pictures of someone called Lenin?"). It became possible for Soviet and former Eastern bloc citizens to travel to the West without difficulty for the first time and this led to many close collaborations previously unimaginable. In the words of my great friend from Budapest, the historian and Kremlinologist, Dr. Miklos Kun: "It was our dream!" His inside knowledge of the Stalin era is total (his grandfather was the Hungarian revolutionary, Bela Kun). Miklos surely took Isaak Babel's advice to heart: "You must know everything."

## THIS IS CAPITALISM

Moscow can be a pretty tough city, often when you are least expecting it. Vladimir invited me to his flat, far beyond Yugo-Zapadnaya at the end of the Metro. He lived in a multi-storey shoebox, one of many built in Khrushchev's time in the microdistricts that litter the outskirts of the city; cultural deserts built to ease the post war housing shortages.

Vladimir's flat was a cultural oasis. He asked me if I would like to see his library: "It's through that door." I tried to open it; it wouldn't budge. He said don't worry, just keep on pushing, so I did. Eventually I managed to squeeze in. Floor to ceiling; books. Row after row, shelf upon shelf of Russian avant-garde paperbacks, heavy Stalinist photographic albums, huge runs of newspapers, magazines and literary journals from the 1920s and 30s. The gangways between them were also piled up to shoulder height with books; that's why it was so difficult to get in. Vladimir said it's okay, just climb over them to see what you want. And one mustn't forget the dust. After a memorable few hours spent in this labyrinth of Bolshevik and Stalinist print production, I return, deep in thought, to the Metro.

★ ★ ★ ★ ★

In the Metro. The train is almost empty; it's night and I'm at the end of the line. I choose a corner seat at the far end of the carriage from the few other passengers. The lights are bright and the doors slam shut; but not before four huge men dressed in combat gear, maybe in their early twenties, burst into the carriage. Suddenly the standing area of the exit space next to me is transformed into a tornado of violence. I have been ringside, photographing Muhammad Ali destroying yet another luckless opponent but I have never seen anything like this. The four thugs are punching each other to pulp. Heads, fists, boots, the vile crunch of knuckle in face, boot in stomach; and I am stuck in the corner, centimetres away from certain death. One of them is getting the worst of it; he doesn't seem to have much brain, but what brain he does have is seeping out of his eyes, down his nose, out of his ears, mouth, teeth. His face has become an object of disgusting filth.

With all the groaning and the pain of killing each other, they don't seem to have noticed me. I'm on the wrong side of sixty, with glasses and a heart condition; if they see me I've had it. I take my only chance. They are flailing around on top of each other in the opposite corner. I leap out of my seat and dive to the far end of the carriage. As luck would have it, they don't notice, too busy with the massacre. The Metro train clatters on; it never seems to stop.

I slump down between two men, honest workers in their early forties, noticeably shocked and horrified at the spectacle. A fattish middle-aged mother wrapped up in her Russian winter padded overcoat is gripped by disbelief. The train screams to a halt at the station and the doors fly open. All four crash out of the carriage onto the platform, still fighting.

The doors slam shut again, the train roars on through the tunnel as if nothing has happened. The honest workers make eye contact: "Things have changed. This should not happen in our Metro. This is what happens under capitalism. This is capitalism. This would not have happened in the Soviet Union."

*David King, London, 2008*

*Opposite page:* A quasi-religious portrait of Vladimir Ilych Ulyanov (Lenin), made in Petrograd by Smolikov in 1922, using the first six paragraphs of the Bolshevik leader's 1918 Constitution for the Russian Socialist Federative Soviet Republic.
*Overleaf:* The People's Militia on patrol during the first days of the February Revolution in Petrograd 1917. Photograph by Yakov Shteinberg.

# Владимир Ильич УЛЬЯНОВ (ЛЕНИН).

**Портрет, выступающий на фоне текста первых 6 глав Конституции РСФСР.**

*Работа акад. Смоликова).*

# „ИЗВѢСТІЯ"

## 28-го февраля 1917 г.

### Газеты не выходятъ.

### Событія идутъ слишкомъ быстро.

### Населеніе должно знать, что происходитъ.

---

## Отъ Временнаго Комитета Гос. Думы.

Временный Комитетъ членовъ Государственной Думы при тяжелыхъ условіяхъ внутренней разрухи, вызванной мѣрами стараго правительства, нашелъ себя вынужденнымъ взять въ свои руки возстановленіе государственнаго и общественнаго порядка. Сознавая всю отвѣтственность принятаго имъ рѣшенія, Комитетъ выражаетъ увѣренность, что населеніе и армія помогутъ ему въ трудной задачѣ созданія новаго правительства, соотвѣтствующаго желаніямъ населенія и могущаго пользоваться его довѣріемъ.

Предсѣдатель Государственной Думы
**М. РОДЗЯНКО.**

27-го февраля 1917 г.

### Первые шаги Исполнительнаго Комитета.

Въ два часа ночи на 28-е февраля Исполнительный Комитетъ Государственной Думы выпустилъ нижеслѣдующее воззваніе:

«Временный Комитетъ Государственной Думы обращается къ жителямъ Петрограда, а также съ призывомъ во имя общихъ интересовъ щадить государственныя и общественныя учрежденія и приспособленія, какъ-то: телеграфъ, водопроводъ, электрическія станціи, трамваи, а также тѣлеграфный желѣзныхъ агентовъ и учрежденій. Равнымъ образомъ Комитетъ Государственной Думы поручаетъ охранять гражданъ заводы и фабрики, какъ работающихъ на оборону такъ и общаго назначенія. Необходимо помнить, что порча и уничтоженіе учрежденій и имущества, не приноси никому пользы, причиняетъ огромный вредъ, какъ государству такъ и всему населенію, ибо всѣмъ одинаково нужна вода, свѣтъ и пр. Недопустимы также посягательства на жизнь и здоровье, а равнымъ образомъ имущества частныхъ лицъ. Пролитіе крови и разгромъ имущества наметатъ пятно на совѣсть людей совершившихъ эти дѣянія и можетъ принести вредъ того начинаніе бѣдствіе всему населенію столицы.

27 февраля 1917 г. Предсѣдатель Государственной Думы Михаилъ Родзянко».

### Исполнительный Комитетъ Гос. Думы.

27-го февраля ровно въ полночь окончательно организовался Исполнительный Комитетъ Государственной Думы въ слѣдующемъ составѣ:

- М. В. Родзянко.
- А. Ф. Керенскій.
- Н. С. Чхеидзе.
- В. В. Шульгинъ.
- П. Н. Милюковъ.
- М. А. Карауловъ.
- А. И. Коноваловъ.
- И. И. Дмитрюковъ.
- В. А. Ржевскій.
- С. И. Шидловскій.
- Н. В. Некрасовъ.
- В. Н. Львовъ.

### Полк. Энгельгардъ.

По предложенію Исполнительнаго Комитета Государственной Думы обязанности коменданта возставшихъ Петроградскихъ гарнизона принялъ на себя членъ гос. Государственной Думы Б. А. Энгельгардъ, вступившій въ должность въ началѣ 1-го часа ночи.

### Задачи Исполнительнаго Комитета Государственной Думы.

Временный Комитетъ Гос. Думы такъ опредѣляетъ свои задачи:

Онъ стремится установить связь между офицерами и нижними чинами. Чувствуется настоятельная потребность въ организаціи воинскихъ массъ, имѣющихъ лучшихъ стремленій, но она не организованныхъ: слишкомъ быстро идутъ событія.

Поэтому офицеры приглашаются оказывать всемѣрное содѣйствіе Государственной Думѣ въ этомъ тяжеломъ трудѣ.

Порядокъ поддерживается членами Государственной Думы и автомобильными отрядами.

Принятыя мѣры къ охранѣ арсенала и монетнаго двора, Петропавловской крѣпости. Взята временными отрядами единственная крѣпость гауптвахты и освобождены всѣ политическіе заключенные, томившіеся въ казематахъ, въ томъ числѣ и 19 солдатъ арестованныхъ по послѣдней дни, вышедшихъ на свободу.

Несмотря на глубокое различіе политическихъ и соціальныхъ взглядовъ членовъ...

### Рѣчь М. В. Родзянко къ юнкерамъ Артиллерійскаго училища.

Передъ полуднемъ Таврическаго дворца выстроились юнкера Михайловскаго артиллерійскаго училища, къ которымъ вышелъ М. В. Родзянко.

Начальникъ училища генералъ сломался...

### Рѣчь Родзянко къ Преображенцамъ.

### Рѣчь М. В. Родзянко къ лейбъ-гренадерамъ.

### Рѣчь М. В. Родзянко 9-му запасному кавалерійскому полку.

### Обращеніе командира къ своему полку.

---

## Къ населенію Петрограда и Россіи

## Отъ Совѣта Рабочихъ Депутатовъ

Старая власть довела страну до полнаго развала, а народъ до голоданія. Терпѣть дальше стало невозможно. Населеніе Петрограда вышло на улицу, чтобы заявить о своемъ недовольствѣ. Его встрѣтили залпами. Вмѣсто хлѣба царское правительство дало народу свинецъ.

Но солдаты не захотѣли итти противъ народа и возстали противъ правительства. Вмѣстѣ съ народомъ они захватили оружіе, военные склады и рядъ важныхъ правительственныхъ учрежденій.

Борьба еще продолжается; она должна быть доведена до конца. Старая власть должна быть окончательно низвергнута и уступить мѣсто народному правленію. Въ этомъ спасеніе Россіи.

Для успѣшнаго завершенія борьбы въ интересахъ демократіи народъ долженъ создать свою собственную властную организацію.

Вчера 27 февраля въ столицѣ образовался Совѣтъ Рабочихъ Депутатовъ—изъ выборныхъ представителей заводовъ и фабрикъ, возставшихъ воинскихъ частей, а также демократическихъ и соціалистическихъ партій и группъ.

Совѣтъ Рабочихъ Депутатовъ, засѣдающій въ Государственной Думѣ, ставитъ своей основной задачей организацію народныхъ силъ и борьбу за окончательное упроченіе политической свободы и народнаго правленія въ Россіи.

Совѣтъ назначилъ районныхъ комиссаровъ для установленія народной власти въ районахъ Петрограда.

Приглашаемъ все населеніе столицы немедленно сплотиться вокругъ Совѣта, образовать мѣстные комитеты въ районахъ и взять въ свои руки управленіе всѣми мѣстными дѣлами.

Всѣ вмѣстѣ общими силами будемъ бороться за полное устраненіе стараго правительства и созывъ учредительнаго собранія, избраннаго на основѣ всеобщаго, равнаго, прямого и тайнаго избирательнаго права.

*Совѣтъ Рабочихъ Депутатовъ.*

---

## П. Н. Милюковъ въ первомъ запасномъ полку.

28 февраля утромъ П. Н. Милюковъ былъ приглашенъ офицерами перваго запаснаго полка, стоящаго на Охтѣ (Новочеркасскій), прибыть въ помѣщеніе полка.

П. Н. Милюковъ прибылъ въ сопровожденіи нѣсколькихъ офицеровъ полка съ командирами во главѣ.

П. Н. Милюковъ вышелъ...

*Top:* Troops pose for the camera on the Liteiny Prospekt, Petrograd, during the first days of the February Revolution, 1917. Their hastily-produced flag reads "Down with the Monarchy – Long Live the Democratic Republic". The shop front in the background advertises "Watches, Gold and Silver". The photograph was taken by Viktor Bulla.

Three years of devastation, food shortages and massive inflation caused by Tsarist Russia's disastrous involvement in the First World War had brought the country to the point of collapse. The International Women's Day demonstration in Petrograd on February 23, 1917 (March 8, new calendar) sparked a spontaneous uprising that spread first across the city and then across the land.

By February 25, tens of thousands of striking workers had been joined in mass street demonstrations by disaffected soldiers returning from the horrors of the frontline. Their collective protests would swiftly lead to the end of 300 years of Romanov rule.

On February 26, Nicholas II was forced to dissolve the old Tsarist Duma. A Provisional Government of timid bourgeois liberals was formed which uneasily found itself exercising dual power with the much more radical Petrograd Soviet of Workers' and Soldiers' Deputies. Democracy flourished.

*Centre:* The People's Militia arresting a Tsarist secret police chief in Petrograd during the February Revolution. The unidentified militia leader, dressed in a leather jacket, can be seen in both photographs, as well as directing the attack on the police headquarters from the running board of the vehicle in the photograph on the previous page. All three pictures were taken by the famous Petrograd photojournalist Yakov Shteinberg.

*Opposite page:* A special one-page edition of the newspaper *Izvestia* (News) published by the Committee of Petrograd Journalists, February 28, 1917. It leads with the latest news from the Provisional Committee of the State Duma and an unenthusiastic statement from its chairman, Mikhail Rodzianko. A much more forceful bulletin is also included from the Soviet of Workers' Deputies. Greeting with excitement the overthrow of the old order, "which was leading the country to total destruction", it calls for a people's government, "wherein lies the salvation of Russia". It urges the people to create their own state organisations, unite around the Soviet and form local committees.

Tsar Nicholas II abdicated on March 2, 1917. Five days later the Provisional Government ordered his arrest. Commissars were dispatched to the railway station at Mogilev where the now former Tsar was lying low in his imperial train.

According to the newspapers *Rannee Utro* (Early Morning) and *Russkoe Slovo* (Russian Word), the commissars entered the station at 3pm on March 8. They negotiated with members of the imperial staff and at 4.50pm Nicholas Romanov gave himself up in silence and without resistance. A reporter on the spot described the scene: "Looking ashen, the Tsar saluted, fingered his moustache as was his habit, and returned to his train to be taken by escort to Tsarskoe Selo where his wife was already under arrest. His entourage stood in silence on the platform as the train pulled out of the station. Other onlookers saluted the commissars."

Months of uncertainty for the Romanov family were to follow. Attempts were made by the Provisional Government for the British to take them but King George V, the former Tsar's cousin, wanted nothing of it; he was too fearful that what had happened in Russia might soon take place at home.

*Top:* The religious fanatic, mystic and libertine Grigorii Rasputin is shown wielding his influence in a postcard satirising the "House of the Russian former Tsar", published in 1917.

*Right:* Happier times in Saint Petersburg. Nicholas and Alexandra dressed for the Costume Ball in the Winter Palace, February 1903. The theme was 17th century. He wears a gold brocade kaftan. She wears a brocade dress with silver decorations.

*Left:* Kaiser Wilhelm II and Tsar Nicholas II parading with crack troops from the Alexander Regiment of the Prussian Grenadier Guards in Bjorko, 1905.

The Kaiser is dressed in Russian uniform whilst the Tsar is wearing the field uniform of the Prussian Grenadiers. Nine years later the cousins would be at war with one another.

*Overleaf:* By order of the Provisional Government, the imperial train was impounded at Peterhof following the Tsar's arrest. Built in 1896–7, the train had seven carriages for the Tsar's living quarters, a kitchen carriage and two more for the servants and luggage. Extreme luxury in the baroque style was the dominant theme of the train's interior.

By contrast, Peterhof station was decorated with a suprematist-influenced artwork incorporating a double-headed eagle tumbling to the ground. The slogan reads: "The Imperialist War and the Collapse of the Autocracy".

The overthrow of the old regime allowed for the long-awaited return of Russia's political exiles. The Bolsheviks organised a spectacular reception for Lenin's arrival in Petrograd on the night of April 3, 1917. Thousands converged on the Finland Station to witness their hero, surrounded by flags and banners in red and gold, proclaim that "the worldwide socialist revolution has already dawned".

Nikolai Sukhanov, the distinguished chronicler of the Russian Revolution was at the scene: "The throng in front of the Finland Station blocked the whole square, making movement impossible... awe-inspiring outlines of armoured cars thrust up from the crowd... a strange monster – a mounted searchlight – beamed upon the bottomless void of darkness tremendous strips of the living city, the roofs, many-storeyed houses, columns,

wires, tramways and human figures."

Unfortunately, no photographs were taken of Lenin's return and, according to Sukhanov, his speech from the top of an armoured car could only be heard in snatches amid the din: "... shameful imperialist slaughter... lies and frauds... capitalist pirates..." Five visual variations of Lenin's tumultuous homecoming can be seen here.

*Top left: Krasnaya Niva* (Red Field) magazine announced on October 31, 1926, that a massive bronze sculpture of Lenin weighing in at 4000 kilos was to be unveiled in Finland Station Square. The statue was "the fruit of a collective artistic endeavour" between Vladimir Shchuko, G.Gelfreykh and the sculptor Sergei Evseyev, who can all be seen in the photograph taken at the artist's studio.

*Top right:* A typically wild steel engraving by Pyotr

Staronosov from an album entitled *The Life of Lenin,* published in Moscow in 1936.

*Above left:* The event depicted in a work of early socialist realism, circa1930, artist unknown.

*Above right:* Lenin portrayed by the actor Vasilii Nikandrov on the cover of a promotional booklet for Sergei Eisenstein's 1927 film "Oktyabr" (October).

*Opposite page:* Rudolf Frentz's cover for *Krasnaya Niva,* January 23, 1927, showing Evseyev's sculpture in place at Finland Station Square where it still resides.

*Overleaf:* May Day celebrations in Palace Square, Petrograd, 1917. The banners read: "Long Live the Democratic Republic!" and "Long Live Socialism." Political demonstrations on May Day in tsarist times had been illegal.

КРАСНАЯ НИВА

*соединяйтесь!*

4

Открытие памятника В. И. Ленину у Финляндского вокзала (Ленинград)

УПРАВ. ПЕТРОГР. УѢЗДН. ВОИН. НАЧАЛЬН.

ДА ЗДРАВСТВУЕТЪ ДЕМОКРАТИЧЕСКАЯ РЕСПУБЛИКА!

17

Всенародный праз
18-го Апрѣля 1917 г. в

Да Здравствуетъ
СОЦIАЛИЗМЪ

РАБ. ОБ. МАСТЕРО___ ИНСТИТ.

___икъ 1-го Мая

Петроградъ    Дворцовая пл__щадь.

The Provisional Government's general sluggishness and seeming inability to end the war and push through badly-needed social reforms led to a summer of extreme unrest in Petrograd. In June, Alexander Kerensky, the war minister, had ordered a disastrous offensive against the German army. The ill-equipped Russian troops suffered terrible defeat. Thousands of soldiers deserted the front for the capital where they joined angry workers in a new wave of mass street protests. The organised political parties could only look on helplessly at this uncontrolled outburst of popular resentment against the government.

*Left:* At 2pm on July 4, 1917, the photographer Viktor Bulla was working in his third floor studio on the corner of Nevsky Prospekt and Sadovaya in Petrograd when he heard the first of many bursts of gunfire in the street below. Startled, he rushed to the window and saw hundreds of demonstrators running for their lives, under attack from Provisional Government troops. Many others were lying on the ground, either shot dead or writhing in agony. Bulla carefully positioned his plate camera, focused on the horrific scene and shot one of the most famous documentary photographs of the twentieth century.

Sixteen people were killed that afternoon in what had been, up to that point, a peaceful demonstration. Six hundred and fifty more were wounded of which forty died later in hospital. Since then the photograph has been printed literally millions of times. Its dynamic overhead composition became the visual embodiment of the Russian Revolution (even though it was shot in July and not October).

The Bulla studio had been handed down to Viktor and his brother Alexander by their father, Karl Karlovich, a famous photographer in Saint Petersburg at the turn of the century who retired to Estonia before the Revolution. Viktor made many famous documentary photographs of the revolutionary period but was arrested in 1937, at the height of Stalin's terror, on trumped-up charges of moral degeneracy and spying for Germany. He died in the Gulag in 1944. Alexander had already been arrested in the early 1930s and spent five years as a convict in the Stalin Belomor Canal slave labour camp. He died shortly after his release.

The studio, disused for decades, is now the junk room of a rather depressing post-Soviet department store. It is still possible, however, to replicate the composition of Viktor Bulla's photograph from the same third floor window. Where in 1917 there were demonstrators in the streets, now there are traffic jams.

Following the spontaneous mass uprisings of the "July Days", Alexander Kerensky, now prime minister of the Provisional Government, proceeded to crack down on all his political opposition. The printing plant of *Pravda* (Truth), the Bolsheviks' newspaper, was smashed up and there were raids on numerous other left-wing addresses throughout the city. Trotsky, recently returned from exile in New York and now a leading member of the Bolsheviks, was jailed and Lenin and Zinoviev were forced to flee to a hut in the Gulf of Finland.

*Top:* The satirical journal, *Pugach* (Screech Owl), lampoons the Bolshevik leader in hiding, falsely accusing him of being a German agent. "Lenin reading his own newspaper" runs the headline and the caption reads, "The truth – not to be found in Pravda – is that I got two million from Wilhelm! But even that's not the whole truth. If they knew, I'd hang!"

*Above:* As is often the case, the caricature barely resembled the much more sinister reality; Lenin had disguised himself with a wig and shaved his face to escape the attentions of Kerensky's secret police. The photograph, needed for his passport for the escape to Finland, was taken on July 29 by the station master at the Razliv border.

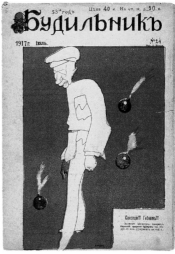

Kerensky's next act was to appoint the hard-line General Lavr Kornilov as his military chief. A battle for power between them ensued. In August, Kornilov tried to stage a counter-revolutionary coup that failed spectacularly. As his troops marched on Petrograd, 14,000 workers came out on the streets to confront them. The troops threw down their weapons without a fight. In September, the Bolsheviks won a majority in the Petrograd Soviet and Trotsky, released from jail, became its chairman. "All Power to the Soviets" and "Peace, Bread and Land" became the key slogans of the Bolsheviks. The stage was set for a new revolution.

*Left:* A Socialist Revolutionary poster designed by Lev Brodoty in 1917. Up until September the Socialist Revolutionaries, along with the Mensheviks, had been the strongest elements in the Soviets. They called for the distribution of all land to the peasantry and viewed the war with disgust. The poster portrays a peasant (with scythe), a worker (with hammer) and an intellectual (with scroll). The letters on the banner read "S-R" in Cyrillic. It is perhaps the only Russian revolutionary poster in existence that symbolically features a member of the intelligentsia in a positive light (albeit in third place).

*Top:* Kerensky caricatured on the cover of the satirical journal *Budilnik* (Alarm Clock), July 1917. The caption reads, "Sensation!!! We Are Dying!!! War minister Comrade Kerensky has sold himself to the bourgeoisie for 275 roubles and 85 kopeks." The drawing is by Dmitrii Moor.

*Overleaf:* Forty eight hours before the start of the Great October Revolution, a detachment of Red Guards from the Putilov Steel Works, who were to play a key role in the storming of the Winter Palace, take aim for the photographer Yakov Shteinberg. They have named their armoured car "Lieutenant Schmidt" after the hero of the 1905 Revolution.

Отдѣльные номера въ Петроградѣ и провинціи ПЯТНАДЦАТЬ (15) коп.

Огонекъ

№ 16 – 1917 г.

Рисунокъ для журнала «Огонекъ» худ. О. Ф. АМОСОВОЙ.

Olga Amosova's cover for *Ogonyek* (Little Lamp), April 30, 1917. Amosova studied art in Rome from 1911 to 1914 and contributed many illustrations to the journal before the Revolution.

The Bolsheviks found *Ogonyek* politically "harmful". During the Revolution sailors from the Baltic fleet closed it down along with other "bourgeois" publications.

отдѣльные нумера въ Петроградѣ и провинціи **ТРИДЦАТЬ (30)** коп. на станц., жел. дор. **35** коп.

**Огонекъ**

**№43–1917**г.

Рисунокъ для журнала „Огонекъ" худ. О. Ф. АМОСОВОЙ.

Protracted negotiations with the Bolsheviks to reopen *Ogonyek* meant that its less than sympathetic October Revolution issue appeared four weeks late. Amosova once again supplied the cover. *Ogonyek* was closed down again during the Civil War. It was relaunched as a pro-Bolshevik reportage magazine on April 1, 1923 and has continued in one form or another ever since.

КЪ ГРАЖДАНАМЪ РОССІИ!

Временное правительство низложено. Дѣло, за
которое боролся народъ: немедленное предложеніе
демократическаго мира, отмѣна помѣщичьей собственности на землю, рабочій контроль надъ
производствомъ, созданіе Совѣтскаго правительства—это дѣло обезпечено.

Да здравствуетъ
революція рабочихъ, солдатъ и крестьянъ!
Хлѣбъ—голоднымъ!
Землю—крестьянамъ!
Заводы—рабочимъ!
Миръ—народамъ!

Военно-Революціонный Комитетъ
при Петроградскомъ Совѣтъ
Рабочихъ и Солдатскихъ Депутатовъ
25 октября 1917 г. 10 ч. утра.

ТМР з. 589—30.000

*Above:* A handbill published by the
Military Revolutionary Committee of
the Petrograd Soviet of Workers' and
Soldiers' Deputies datelined 10am on
October 25, 1917. Like the poster
reproduced on page 13, it is headlined
"To the Citizens of Russia" and
continues: "The Provisional
Government has been overthrown. The
causes that the people have been fighting
for are now within reach: an immediate
and democratic peace, the abolition of
landowners' property rights, workers'
control of production, a government
based on the soviets." It finishes with a
flourish: "Long live the workers',
soldiers' and peasants' revolution! Bread
for the hungry! Land to the peasants!
Factories to the workers! Peace to the
peoples!"

This leaflet, like many others at the time,
was published from the building shown
in the photograph on the right. It was
taken by Pyotr Otsup during the days of
the October Revolution. Red Guards,
soldiers and sailors can be seen on duty
in front of the Smolny Institute,
formerly an expensive girls' school and
since September 1917 the headquarters
of the All-Russian Congress of Soviets.
Here could be found the offices of Lenin
and Trotsky as well as countless other
high-ranking leaders of the Bolsheviks
and other revolutionary parties. Every
major resolution, vote and decision
concerning the October Revolution and
the final overthrow of the Provisional
Government took place within these
walls.

Вл. Ил. Ульянов (Н. Ленин.)
Председатель сов. народных комиссаров.

LENIN

The distinguished portrait photographer Moisei Nappelbaum was called into the Smolny Institute by the Bolsheviks in January 1918 to take the first pictures of Lenin since the formation of the world's first workers' state.

*Top left:* Nappelbaum's most famous portrait of Lenin was to be printed in millions of copies.

*Top centre:* A variation on the original with the photographer's trademark brush strokes on the negative giving the portrait a more painterly effect.

*Top right:* Vasilii Emirov used Nappelbaum's photograph, reversing it from left to right, as the basis for his painting of the Chairman of the Soviet of

People's Commissars in 1918.

*Above left:* A Milanese artist's rendering from the late 1920s, taken from the Nappelbaum photo but replacing Lenin's formal Russian attire with a more casual Italian look.

*Above centre:* A composite print entitled "Leaders of the Proletarian Revolution" published by Nappelbaum in November 1918. From the top can be seen Lenin, Zinoviev, Lunacharsky, Trotsky, Kamenev and Sverdlov (bottom right).

*Above right:* Another famous portrait of Lenin by Nappelbaum taken at the January sitting.

*Opposite page:* Moisei Nappelbaum's striking

photograph of Leon Trotsky taken in 1919 when the founder and leader of the Red Army in the Civil War was at the height of his popularity and power.

*Overleaf:* The vanguard of the Revolution. Fully-armed Bolshevik sailors from the cruiser "Aurora" at the time of the October insurrection. During the storming of the Winter Palace blank shells were fired from the ship to frighten off Kerensky and those still supporting the Provisional Government.

Lenin to Trotsky (in a quiet moment after the seizure of power): "... from persecution and a life underground, to come so suddenly into power... it makes you feel giddy."

Trotsky

Rudolf Frentz's painting "October Night". Frentz was director of agitational propaganda at the People's Commissariat of Enlightenment, Petrograd, from 1919 to 1925.

Viktor Bulla's powerful photographic portrait of Lenin, taken in the Moscow Kremlin, early March, 1919.

№ 208.
Пятница,
27 октября 1917 г.

**ИЗВѢСТІЯ**

ЦѢНА:
въ Петроградѣ **15** коп.
на ст. жел. д. **18** коп.

## Центральнаго Исполнительнаго Комитета
### и Петроградскаго Совѣта
## Рабочихъ и Солдатскихъ Депутатовъ.

Адресъ конторы: Лиговка, Сайкинъ пер., д. № 6. Телефонъ № 218-41.
Адресъ редакціи: Смольный Институтъ, 2-й этажъ комната № 14А. Телефонъ № 38-89.

# Декретъ о мирѣ,

## принятый единогласно на засѣданіи Все-россійскаго Съѣзда Совѣтовъ Рабочихъ, Солдатскихъ и Крестьянскихъ Депутатовъ 26 октября 1917 г.

Рабочее и крестьянское правительство, созданное революціей 24—25 октября и опирающееся на Совѣты Рабочихъ, Солдатскихъ и Крестьянскихъ Депутатовъ предлагаетъ всѣмъ воюющимъ народамъ и ихъ правительствамъ начать немедленно переговоры о справедливомъ демократическомъ мирѣ.

Справедливымъ или демократическимъ миромъ котораго жаждетъ подавляющее большинство истощенныхъ, измученныхъ и истерзанныхъ войной рабочихъ и трудящихся классовъ всѣхъ воюющихъ странъ—миромъ, котораго самымъ опредѣленнымъ и настойчивымъ образомъ требовали русскіе рабочіе и крестьяне послѣ сверженія царской монархіи,—такимъ миромъ правительство считаетъ немедленный миръ безъ аннексій (т. е. безъ захвата чужихъ земель, безъ насильственнаго присоединенія чужихъ народностей) и безъ контрибуцій.

Такой миръ предлагаетъ Правительство Россіи заключить всѣмъ воюющимъ народамъ немедленно, выражая готовность сдѣлать безъ малѣйшей оттяжки тотчасъ-же всѣ рѣшительные шаги впредь до окончательнаго утвержденія всѣхъ условій такого мира полномочными собраніями народныхъ представителей всѣхъ странъ и всѣхъ націй.

Подъ аннексіей или захватомъ чужихъ земель Правительство понимаетъ сообразно правовому сознанію демократіи вообще, и трудящихся классовъ въ особенности всякое присоединеніе къ большому или сильному государству малой или слабой народности безъ точно, ясно и добровольно выраженнаго согласія и желанія этой народности, независимо отъ того, когда это насильственное присоединеніе совершено, независимо также отъ того, насколько развитой или отсталой является насильственно присоединяемая или насильственно удерживаемая въ границахъ даннаго государства нація. Независимо, наконецъ, отъ того, въ Европѣ или въ далекихъ заокеанскихъ странахъ эта нація живетъ.

Если какая бы то ни была нація удерживается въ границахъ даннаго государства насиліемъ, если ей, вопреки выраженному съ ея стороны желанію—все равно, выражено ли это желаніе въ печати, въ народныхъ собраніяхъ, въ рѣшеніяхъ партій или въ возмущеніяхъ и возстаніяхъ противъ національнаго гнета—не представляется права свободнымъ голосованіемъ, при полномъ выводѣ войска присоединяющей или вообще болѣе сильной націи, рѣшить безъ малѣйшаго принужденія вопросъ о формахъ государственнаго существованія этой націи, то присоединеніе ея является аннексіей, т. е. захватомъ и насиліемъ.

Продолжать эту войну изъ-за того, какъ раздѣлить между сильными и богатыми націями захваченныя ими слабыя народности, Правительство считаетъ величайшимъ преступленіемъ противъ человѣчества и торжественно заявляетъ свою рѣшимость немедленно подписать условія мира, прекращающаго эту войну на указанныхъ, равно справедливыхъ для всѣхъ безъ изъятія народностей условіяхъ.

Вмѣстѣ съ тѣмъ Правительство заявляетъ, что оно отнюдь не считаетъ вышеуказанныхъ условій мира ультимативными, т. е. соглашается разсмотрѣть и всякія другія условія мира, настаивая лишь на возможно болѣе быстромъ предложеніи ихъ какой бы то ни было воюющей страной и на подобнѣйшей ясности, на безусловномъ исключеніи всякой двусмысленности и всякой тайны при предложеніи условій мира.

Тайную дипломатію Правительство отмѣняетъ, со своей стороны выражая твердое намѣреніе вести всѣ переговоры совершенно открыто передъ всѣмъ народомъ, приступая немедленно къ полному опубликованію тайныхъ договоровъ, подтвержденныхъ или заключенныхъ правительствомъ помѣщиковъ и капиталистовъ съ февраля по 25 октября 1917 года. Все содержаніе этихъ тайныхъ договоровъ, поскольку оно направлено, какъ это въ большинствѣ случаевъ бывало къ доставленію выгодъ и привилегій русскимъ помѣщикамъ и капиталистамъ, къ удержанію или увеличенію аннексій великороссовъ, Правительство объявляетъ безусловно и немедленно отмѣненнымъ.

Обращаясь съ предложеніемъ къ правительствамъ и народамъ всѣхъ странъ начать немедленно открытые переговоры о заключеніи мира. Правительство выражаетъ съ своей стороны готовность вести эти переговоры, какъ посредствомъ письменныхъ сношеній, по телеграфу, такъ и путемъ переговоровъ между представителями разныхъ странъ или на конференціи таковыхъ представителей. Для облегченія такихъ переговоровъ Правительство назначаетъ своего полномочнаго представителя въ нейтральныя страны.

Правительство предлагаетъ всѣмъ правительствамъ и народамъ всѣхъ воюющихъ странъ немедленно заключить перемиріе, причемъ со своей стороны, считаетъ желательнымъ, чтобы это перемиріе было заключено не меньше, какъ на три мѣсяца, т. е. на такой срокъ, въ теченіе котораго вполнѣ возможно, какъ завершеніе переговоровъ о мирѣ съ участіемъ представителей всѣхъ безъ изъятія народностей, или націй, втянутыхъ въ войну или вынужденныхъ къ участію въ ней, такъ равно и созывъ полномочныхъ собраній народныхъ представителей всѣхъ странъ для окончательнаго утвержденія условій мира.

Обращаясь съ этимъ предложеніемъ мира къ правительствамъ и народамъ всѣхъ воюющихъ странъ, временное рабочее и крестьянское правительство Россіи обращается также въ особенности къ сознательнымъ рабочимъ трехъ самыхъ передовыхъ націй человѣчества и самыхъ крупныхъ участвующихъ въ настоящей войнѣ государствъ, Англіи, Франціи и Германіи. Рабочіе этихъ странъ оказали наибольшія услуги дѣлу прогресса и соціализма и великіе образцы чартистскаго движенія въ Англіи, рядъ революцій, имѣвшихъ всемірно-историческое значеніе, совершенныхъ французскимъ пролетаріатомъ, наконецъ, въ геройской борьбѣ противъ исключительнаго закона въ Германіи и образцовой для рабочихъ всего міра длительной, упорной дисциплинированной работѣ созданія массовыхъ пролетарскихъ организацій Германіи. Всѣ эти образцы пролетарскаго героизма и историческаго творчества служатъ намъ порукой за то, что рабочіе названныхъ странъ поймутъ лежащія на нихъ теперь задачи освобожденія человѣчества отъ ужасовъ войны и ея послѣдствій, — ибо эти рабочіе всесторонней рѣшительной и беззавѣтно энергичной дѣятельностью своей помогутъ намъ успѣшно довести до конца дѣло мира и вмѣстѣ съ тѣмъ дѣло освобожденія трудящихся и эксплоатируемыхъ массъ населенія отъ всякаго рабства и всякой эксплоатаціи.

Lenin's Decree on Peace (to end the war with Germany), dated October 26, 1917, makes headline news in *Izvestia*, now firmly edited along Bolshevik lines. After long and difficult negotiations, the punitive Treaty of Brest-Litovsk was signed on March 3, 1918. Russia ceded Poland, parts of the Baltic and allowed independence for Ukraine and Finland.

# ДЕКРЕТЪ О ЗЕМЛѢ

## Съѣзда Совѣтовъ Рабоч. и Солдат. Депутатовъ.

### (Принятъ на засѣданіе 26-го октября въ 2 часа ночи).

1) Помѣщичья собственность на землю отмѣняется немедленно безъ всякаго выкупа.

2) Помѣщичьи имѣнія, равно какъ всѣ земли удѣльныя, монастырскія, церковныя со всѣмъ ихъ живымъ и мертвымъ инвентаремъ, усадебными постройками и всѣми принадлежностями переходятъ въ распоряженіе волостныхъ земельныхъ Комитетовъ и уѣздныхъ Совѣтовъ Крестьянскихъ Депутатовъ впредь до Учредительнаго Собранія.

3) Какая бы то ни была порча конфискуемаго имущества, принадлежащаго отнынѣ всему народу, объявляется тяжкимъ преступленіемъ, караемымъ революціоннымъ судомъ. Уѣздные Совѣты Крестьянскихъ Депутатовъ принимаютъ всѣ необходимыя мѣры для саблюденія строжайшаго порядка при конфискаціи помѣщичьихъ имѣній, для опредѣленія того, до какого размѣра участки и какіе именно подлежатъ конфискаціи для составленія точной описи всего конфискуемаго имущества и для строжайшей революціонной охраны всего переходящаго къ народу хозяйства на землѣ со всѣми постройками, орудіями, скотомъ, запасами продуктовъ и проч.

4) Для руководства по осуществленію великихъ земельныхъ преобразованій впредь до окончательнаго ихъ рѣшенія Учредительнымъ Собраніемъ долженъ повсюду служить слѣдующій крестьянскій наказъ, составленный на основаніи 242 мѣстныхъ крестьянскихъ наказовъ редакціей «Извѣстія Всероссійскаго Совѣта Крестьянскихъ Депутатовъ» и опубликованный въ номерѣ 88 этихъ «Извѣстій» (Петроградъ, номеръ 88, 19 августа 1917 г.).

## О землѣ.

Вопросъ о землѣ можетъ быть разрѣшенъ только всенароднымъ Учредительнымъ Собраніемъ.

Самое справедливое разрѣшеніе земельнаго вопроса должно быть таково:

1) Право частной собственности на землю отмѣняется навсегда; земля не можетъ быть ни продаваема, ни покупаема, ни сдаваема въ аренду либо въ залогъ, ни какимъ либо другимъ способомъ отчуждаема. Вся земля: государственная, удѣльная, кабинетская, монастырская, церковная, поссесіонная, майоратная, частновладѣльческая, общественная и крестьянская и т. д. отчуждается безвозмездно, обращается во всенародное достояніе и переходитъ въ пользованіе всѣхъ трудящихся на ней.

За пострадавшими отъ имущественнаго переворота признается лишь право на общественную поддержку на время, необходимое для приспособленія къ новымъ условіямъ существованія.

2) Всѣ нѣдра земли: руда, нефть, уголь, соль и т. д., а также лѣса и воды, имѣющіе общегосударственное значеніе переходятъ въ исключительное пользованіе государства. Всѣ мелкіе рѣки, озера, лѣса и проч. переходятъ въ пользованіе общинъ, при условіи завѣдыванія ими мѣстными органами самоуправленія.

Lenin's Decree on Land, a typographical poster from the Congress of Soviet Workers' and Soldiers' Deputies, datelined October 26 (1917) at 2am. This historic decree, a hugely popular act, transferred the ownership of all landholdings throughout Russia from the landlords and the church to peasant land committees.

*Right and opposite page:* Five early editions (in French, Russian, German and English) of the left-wing American journalist John Reed's eyewitness account of events in Petrograd in 1917. *Ten Days that Shook the World,* first published in New York in 1919, was billed by its British publisher Martin Lawrence as the "Epic of the Bolshevik Revolution that Lenin read three times."

Reed's masterpiece is written in a hectic *cinema verité* style that brilliantly captures the contrast between the chaos and intrigue of those creating or attempting to sabotage the Revolution and the ordinary citizens of Petrograd who were trying with some difficulty to continue their lives undisturbed.

The cover of the first Russian edition *(opposite page, top left)* was designed by Sergei Chekhonin.

The German edition with the rifle and flag was designed in 1927 by John Heartfield, who was to become legendary for his anti-Nazi photomontages in the 1930s.

John Reed returned to Russia in 1919 to work in the secretariat of the Communist International but he died of typhus a year later. His ashes were placed in the Kremlin Wall. Stalin's name hardly appears in Reed's book. This became a source of great embarrassment to the future dictator so, during his reign, the book was banned.

*Top:* Isaak Brodsky's line drawing of John Reed at the Second Congress of the Communist International, 1920. Brodsky made many such sketches of delegates at the conference for later use in a monumental painting depicting Lenin's speech at the opening ceremony. Brodsky's technical ability put him in the forefront of Socialist Realist painters in the 1930s.

JOHN REED
10 JOURS QUI ÉBRANLÈRENT LE MONDE

*Overleaf:* Baltic sailors, loyal to the Bolsheviks, carefully checking documentation at a roadblock in Petrograd during the October Revolution. Thus began almost seventy five years of obsessive Soviet bureaucratic controls. Photograph by Yakov Shteinberg.

*Top:* Red Guards on patrol in the streets of Petrograd during the October Revolution. In the background of Yakov Shteinberg's photograph, echoing depictions of the Holy Trinity, one notice advertises "Icons and Iconostases", another reads "Made to order".

*Above left:* An optimistic postcard welcoming the dawn of a new year and a new age of enlightenment.

*Above right:* On the back of the same postcard, sign language for the deaf and mute surrounds three mystical symbols with the inscription "Faith, Hope and Love" written in Cyrillic, a repeat of the headline on the front of the card.

*Above centre:* Revolutionary iconoclasm. The destruction of the Alexander III monument in Moscow, 1918.

*Opposite page:* Alexander Kerensky in exile, caught on camera in a Paris courtyard by a press photographer in 1922. He had fled from Russia soon after the Bolshevik Revolution, living first of all in Berlin before settling in Paris. He moved to the USA in 1940. The Soviets had often planned to kill him, even as late as the 1950s, but they had to make do with stealing a part of his archives instead. He died in London in 1970 and is buried in Putney Vale cemetery.

After months of internal exile, first in Tsarskoe Selo and then Tobolsk in the Urals, the former Tsar Nicholas and his family were moved by the Bolsheviks to their final destination, the Ipatiev House in Ekaterinburg, on April 30, 1918. They were put to death in the basement a few weeks later on July 16.

*Right:* The firing squad that killed the former Tsar and his family.

*Below, left and right:* Happier days at Tsarskoe Selo. The former Tsar's five children pose for the camera with their heads shaven after measles in the spring of 1917. Their father's popularity decreased even further after his abdication and to large sections of his former loyal subjects he became known as "Nicholas the Bloody".

*Opposite page:* Yakov Yurovsky, commandant of the Ipatiev House during the Romanovs' captivity, enjoying a cup of tea. He joined the Bolsheviks in 1905. For some years he ran a successful photographic studio in Ekaterinburg and after the Revolution he signed up with the Cheka (Lenin's secret police). He organised and took part in the execution of the former Tsar and his family, as well as the subsequent disposal of the bodies, which were laid in a pit and drenched in sulphuric acid to render them unrecognisable. Yurovsky remained proud of his role in the assassination all his life, and left a detailed description of the event before his death in 1938.

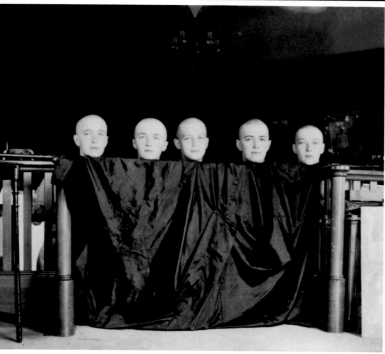

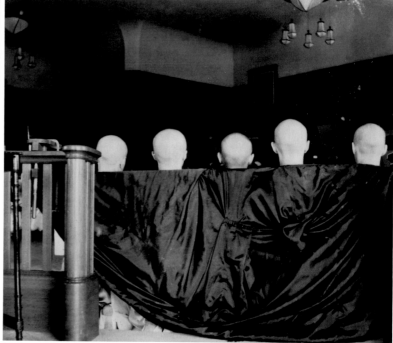

*Above:* The Ipatiev House at the time of the former Tsar's incarceration, showing the stockade-like wooden fence surrounding the residence and two armed Bolshevik sentries on duty outside.

*Right:* The stairs leading down to the basement where the assassination took place in a small back room. The shooting lasted for two or three minutes.

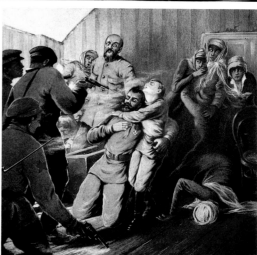

*Above:* A French artist's gruesome re-enactment in pastel of the execution made for an album entitled *Histoire des Soviets*, published in 1922.

On April 12, 1918, Sovnarcom (the Council of People's Commissars) decreed that all remaining monuments and other artefacts from the tsarist period not demolished in the upheavals of the Revolution should be replaced by works reflecting the cultural and political aims of the new regime. Soon cubo-futurist sculptures looking vaguely like Beethoven, Dostoevsky, Robert Owen and others began to appear in the streets of Moscow and Petrograd. Unfortunately, gypsum was the material most commonly used by the artists and their work deteriorated rapidly. In September 1918, Lenin wrote in fury to Anatolii Lunacharsky, his Commissar of Enlightenment: "There is no outdoor bust of Marx... I scold you for this criminal negligence." Lunacharsky's response was swift and within two months the first commemorations devoted to the founding father had been put in place.

*Above left:* Alexander Matveyev's "Monument to Karl Marx" photographed moments after its inauguration on the first anniversary of the Revolution, November 7,1918. The plaster statue is standing in front of the Smolny Institute, the Bolsheviks' headquarters in Petrograd, guarded by two Red soldiers.

*Below left:* At the same time in Teatralnaya Square, Moscow, high-ranking Bolsheviks can be seen at the unveiling of S. Mezentsev's plaster sculpture of Marx, this time with Friedrich Engels. Lenin made a speech about "their great world-wide historic service in proving, by scientific analysis, the inevitability of the downfall of capitalism and its transition to communism under which there will be no more exploitation of man by man." The inscription on the plinth reads: "The revolutionary whirlwind thrusts back all those who resist it." Both sculptures suffered from the Russian winter and needed replacement within a few years.

*Right:* A poster of Karl Marx by an unknown artist from Baku, circa1918.

جمله جهان مقراى كلمائى يرداسكا

КАРЛ МАРКС.    قارل مارقس.

حكومت نشرياتى
« آذربايجان مطبوعات مركزى »

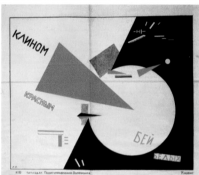

*Top:* Nikolai Kolli's street sculpture of a white block (representing the forces of counter-revolution) fractured by a red wedge (the victorious Red Army) was erected in Revolution Square, Moscow, in 1918 on the first anniversary of the October Revolution. The plywood box structure had a door in the back and was large enough to double up as a store room for the local street cleaners' brooms and shovels. The modernist architect Berthold Lubetkin was studying in Moscow at this time. He recalled that a fellow student, desperately needing accommodation, secretly lived inside the sculpture during the particularly harsh winter of 1918; his own flat in the heart of the city!

Kolli's avant-garde monument predates El Lissitsky's famous "Beat the Whites with the Red Wedge" poster (*above*) by at least one year and there is every reason to suspect that Lissitsky was influenced by it.

*Left:* Xenia Boguslavskaya's suprematist contribution to the decoration of Uritsky Square in Petrograd for the first anniversary parades,1918. She was married to another avant-garde artist, Ivan Puni. They left Russia to live in Paris, where he became known as Jean Pougny.

61

*Top left:* The cover of the first edition of Lenin's *Constitution for the Russian Socialist Federative Soviet Republic*, published on July 19, 1918 in Moscow. The hammer and sickle makes its first official appearance as the emblem of the new Soviet state, having been formally approved nine days earlier at the Fifth All-Russian Congress of Soviets.

The symbol had been seen on a banner in Saratov before the Revolution and was chosen by Anatolii Lunacharsky, who commissioned various designers and artists to use it, including Evgenii Kamzolkin and Sergei Chekhonin.

However, the design of one of the world's greatest symbols was neither original nor Russian. The enlargement (*centre*) of a humble one peso coin from

Chile, showing a hammer and sickle at its base, surrounded by laurel leaves, predates the October Revolution by twenty one years.

The symbol has been used in a million variations.

*Top centre:* Soviet textile design, circa 1930.

*Top right:* Album cover. *Peasants' Gazette*, 1929.

*Far left and left:* Two covers from the early 1930s, one in Russian, the other French.

*Above:* Enjoying a Soviet picnic in 1932.

*Opposite page:* Sergei Chekhonin's beautiful cover design for the Second Congress of the Communist International, 1920. Here both sickle and hammer rest peacefully after the struggles of the Civil War.

*Overleaf:* Leon Trotsky addresses the latest recruits to the newly-formed Red Cavalry, 1918.

"Proletarians of all Lands, Unite. Long Live the International Army of Labour.
Only Commanders from the People will Lead the Red Army to Victory". A poster by Dmitrii Moor for the newly-formed Red Army, 1918.

A rare cubo-futurist portrait of Trotsky (based on the photograph on page 43), circa 1920, artist unknown.
From the late 1920s, possession of anything relating to Trotsky or other so-called "enemies of the people" meant imprisonment, the Gulag, or death.

No sooner had Lenin's new government agreed peace with Germany than civil war broke out across Russia. Numerous rebels, ranging from monarchists to right-wing socialists, but all united in their hostility to the Bolsheviks, were backed by the interventionist forces of many capitalist countries including Britain, France, Germany, the United States, Canada, Japan and Poland.

On February 24, 1918, Trotsky was appointed Commissar for War with the task of transforming the newly-formed Workers' and Peasants' Red Army into a coordinated fighting force. Within two years he had organised an army five million strong, victorious against the combined legions of Admiral Kolchak, Generals Denikin and Yudenich, Baron Wrangel and others.

The Civil War was fought over vast distances; from Murmansk and Archangelsk in the north to Vladivostok in the east, Baku in the Caucasus, Tashkent in Central Asia and across Ukraine, Poland and the Baltic states in the west. Trotsky was able to communicate with the fighting units by radio and telegraph ("For the henchmen of Kolchak and Denikin – lead, steel and fire!") from his legendary "Train of the Chairman of the Revolutionary Military Council of the Republic", known simply as "Trotsky's Train".

He lived on the train, with short breaks, for two and a half years, completing thirty six journeys to the various fronts and travelling over 100,000

kilometres. This mobile command post of fifteen carriages included his secretariat ("Educate, inspire, supply, chastise and reward"), a radio and telegraph station, printshop, library, electricity generator, a mobile garage equipped with cars and trucks for visiting and supplying the fronts at close range and a kitchen and bathroom. The train's crew wore a uniform of black leather. Trotsky thought this gave them "an imposing, heavyweight presence".

*Above:* Trotsky, flanked by Lenin, takes the salute in Red Square, Moscow, on the second anniversary of the Revolution, November 7, 1919.

*Left:* A photomontage of Trotsky's travels by train and ship to the far-flung regions of Russia from the album *Oktyabr*, Petrograd, 1921.

*Opposite page:* Trotsky's train was decorated in 1919 with the Order of the Red Banner for its part in the defence of Petrograd. Trotsky can be seen on the right of the photograph, raising his cap in acceptance of the honour. A wall newspaper of the time headlined "Crush the Counter-Revolution and the War will End," quotes Trotsky: "Soviet Russia is awake. It will not give up Petrograd. Our response to the attack on the first city of the proletarian revolution will be a crusade of death and devastation." Also in the photograph, below Trotsky and holding a cigarette, is the popular poet of the time, Demyan Bedny. He supported Trotsky during the Civil War but later turned against him, often viciously attacking him in print.

"November 7, 1918. Stand up, Working People". An early Civil War poster by G.F. Zeiler.
The lower text reads: "Hold On! The Working People of All the World are Going to Help You!" The red star, hammer and plough were the symbols
of the Workers' and Peasants' Red Army (RKKA) until 1920 when the plough was replaced by the sickle.

"February 23, 1919. The Red Army is the Defence of the Revolution". A poster published in Petrograd
celebrating the first anniversary of Red Army Day. The red star resembles a red flower. The date commemorates the tens of thousands of volunteers who joined
the Red Army on the same day in 1918 in response to Lenin's call, "The Socialist Fatherland is in Danger".

Vladimir Lebedev's poster "RSFSR", published by the Political Department of the Revolutionary Military Soviet of the Baltic, circa1920.
The initials of the new state and its full name were adopted in Lenin's Constitution, July 19, 1918. From the 1930s, the words "socialist" and "soviet" were interchanged.

"Women Workers, Take Up Your Rifles!" An early Civil War poster, artist unknown.
*Overleaf:* Women newly recruited into the Red Army for the defence of Petrograd in the Civil War, 1918.

# ВОЙНА

ВСЕ НА ЗАЩИТУ ПРОЛЕТАРСКОЙ РЕВОЛЮЦИИ

И я иду с братом!

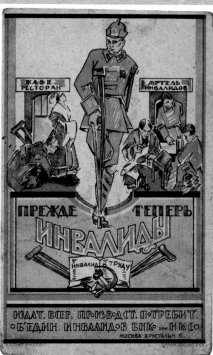

ДЕЗЕРТИРОВ К ПОЗОРНОМУ СТОЛБУ.

*Opposite page:* "War". A highly decorative illustration from *Sovetskii Kalendar* (Soviet Calendar), published by the All-Russian Central Executive Committee in Moscow, 1919. The fanciful style was unusual in Soviet publishing at this time of great strife.

*Above:* "Everyone to the Defence of the Proletarian Revolution", artist unknown. Grave concern is the subject of this Civil War poster as a young man is taken from his family to be conscripted into the Red Army. The lower right caption reads, "I'm going with my brother!"

*Left:* A Bolshevik poster from Odessa during the Civil War. The theme is medieval. The slogan reads, "The Deserter is Put to Shame".

*Far left:* "Invalids to Work". A postcard contrasting the plight of war wounded, shown begging in the streets in tsarist times, with their involvement in the war effort under the Bolsheviks.

77

The "October Revolution" agitational propaganda train arrives at Sorotskinskoe station, near Samara, in 1919. The carriages were decorated with themes of revolution and

the struggle against capitalism. On board, the local population could visit the cinema, bookstore, radio station and printshop. There was even a complaints department.

The Bolsheviks equipped and mobilised agitational propaganda trains during the Civil War, sending them to all parts of Russia to inform the population about the ongoing struggles in defence of the revolution and to help organise lectures, meetings and discussions on the meaning of the new workers' state.

The first train, named after Lenin, went into service on August 13, 1918. Others soon followed, bearing titles such as "October Revolution", "Red East", "Soviet Caucasus" and "Red Cossack". The carriages were famously decorated with paintings, graphic or satirical, on subjects that reflected the names of the trains and the places where they were headed.

There was also an agitprop ship, the "Red Star", which made two summer voyages along the Volga in 1919 and 1920, towing an iron barge with a cinema for over 800 persons.

*Above:* Crowds eagerly surround the entrance to one of the carriages on the "October Revolution" agitprop train. To the left of the door, a hand-lettered poster from the Russian Telegraph Agency ("Rosta") is partly decipherable: "As a result of the battle in the region south of Shipovo station, the enemy has incurred heavy losses." The smaller sign to the right of the door reads, "Paintings carried out by a group under the leadership of Viktor Vinogradov." The "Lenin" and "Red Cossack" agitprop trains were also decorated by Vinogradov.

*Right:* A rare agitprop train poster, circa 1920. The text reads: "From far-away this train has brought us valuable presents. Hurry up, comrades! The train won't be staying long. You must realise that a truthful and intelligent book will light your path in the struggle for a better future."

*Overleaf:* The basic iconography of an agitprop train. Fat capitalists command a blindfolded White soldier to fight against the Bolshevik Enlightenment, symbolised by a trusty print worker protected by a soldier of the Red Army with the world and some heavily-polluting smokestacks in the background.

Из далекаго тыла примчался к нам вагон.
с драгоценным подарком. Спешите товарищи!
ит долго на одном месте. Знайте что разумная
га озарит путь ваш для борьбы за лучшее будущее.

Изд. ПОЛИТУПРАВЛЕНИЯ НАРКОМВОЕН Киев 1919 г

*Opposite page:* Vladimir Lenin making a gramophone recording on March 29, 1919, in a hastily-constructed studio in the Moscow Kremlin. The photograph was taken by L. Leonidov. Lenin made thirteen recordings of his speeches in total, of which eight were made at this time. The new medium was considered, like film, to have great propaganda value. The records were often played in public on wind-up gramophones, as can be seen in the two photographs of agitprop train interiors (*above*). Here is a short excerpt from "What is Soviet Power", recorded at the same time that Leonidov took his photograph: "Soviet power is not a miracle-working talisman. It does not, overnight, heal all the evils of the past – illiteracy, lack of culture, the effects of a barbarous war, the aftermath of predatory capitalism. But it does pave the way to socialism. It gives those who were formerly oppressed the chance to straighten their backs and, to an ever-increasing degree, take the whole government of the country, the whole administration of the economy, the whole management of production, into their own hands."

*Top:* A young agitator, perhaps inspired by Lenin's recordings, declaiming from the roof of the "October Revolution" agitprop train, Tula, 1919.

*Left:* "Third International". The writing is on the wall for this terrified capitalist in Viktor Deni's poster from 1921. Karl Marx founded the First International in London in 1864. Its aim was to coordinate working-class movements worldwide and establish international socialism. It dissolved in the early 1870s in the aftermath of the Paris Commune. The non-revolutionary Second International existed from 1889 until the First World War, when it collapsed. The Third Communist International was formed by Lenin at a congress held in Moscow in 1919 to "see the victory of communism throughout the world".

*Overleaf:* Lenin (seen standing on the left of the bottom step) with comrades at a May Day rally in Red Square, Moscow, 1919. Marx's First International and the Third International are graphically celebrated in the festivities. There is, however, no representation of the Second International, whose leaders Lenin mercilessly lambasted on another gramophone record: "They betrayed the workers, prolonged the slaughter, became enemies of socialism and went over to the side of the capitalists."

*Right:* Dmitrii Moor's poster, "Death to World Imperialism", an allegorical masterpiece from 1919. Moor was the Bolsheviks' foremost political poster artist of the Civil War period. Later, in 1922, he became co-founder of the satirical magazine *Krokodil.* He also became art director/illustrator of *Bezbozhnik* (The Godless), a journal infamous for its virulently anti-religious caricatures. *Opposite page:* Viktor Deni's 1920 poster, "Capitalists of the World, Unite!", attacking the newly-formed League of Nations and subtitled "The Yellow International". The Soviets only changed their minds about the League years later, finally joining it in September 1934 in order to help build the anti-Axis alliance after the departure of Germany, Italy and Japan. Although their work was sometimes almost artistically interchangeable, Moor and Deni were far apart in personality. Moor was a friendly individual, much loved for his sense of humour and looked up to by younger artists. Poor Deni, two years younger than Moor, suffered from hypochondria, was a misanthropic loner, thin and mournful.

Both these posters carry a sinister warning in small print: "Anyone who tears down this poster or covers it up is performing a counter-revolutionary act."

Товарищи Мусульмане! Под зеленым знаменем Пророка шли вы завоевывать ваши степи, ваши аулы. Враги народа отняли у вас родные поля. Ныне под красным знаменем Рабоче-Крестьянской революции под звездой армии всех угнетенных и трудящихся собирайтесь с востока и запада, с севера и юга. В седла товарищи! Все в полки Всевобуч!

ОБРАЩАЙТЕСЬ ЗА СПРАВКАМИ ИНСПЕКЦИЯ
Кавалерийских Формирований Центр. Упр. Всевобуч.
Всеросс. Главн. Штаба.
Москва. Малый Ржевский, 3.

D.MOOP.

Издание Центр. Управл. Всевобуч.

Dmitrii Moor's spectacular Civil War poster from 1919, calling upon Muslims to join up with all oppressed peoples under the red banner. The hammer and sickle is replaced by a crescent and star.
The full slogan: "Comrade Mussulman! Under the green banner of the Prophet you fought for your land and villages. But then the enemies of the people took your land. Now, under the banner of the workers' and peasants' revolution, under the star of the army of all oppressed and working people, join up from the east and west, north and south. Saddle up, comrades! Everyone to the Enlightenment!"
*Opposite page:* Viktor Deni's poster "Capital", his most famous artistic contribution to the class struggle, was published in 100,000 copies in Moscow, 1919.

17-я Государств. типо-лит. (бывш. Кушнерева). Москва.

# КАПИТАЛ.

Да не будут тебе бози инии разве мене.

ВСЯКИЙ, СРЫВАЮЩИЙ ЭТОТ ПЛАКАТ ИЛИ ЗАКЛЕИВАЮЩИЙ ЕГО АФИШЕЙ,— СОВЕРШАЕТ КОНТР-РЕВОЛЮЦИОННОЕ ДЕЛО.

Любуясь дивною картиной,
Рабы, склонитесь предо мной!
Своей стальною паутиной
Опутал я весь шар земной.
Я—воплощенье КАПИТАЛА.
Я—повелитель мировой.
Волшебный блеск и звон металла—
Мой взгляд и голос властный мой.

Тускнеют царские короны,
Когда надену я свою.
Одной рукой ломая троны,
Другой—я троны создаю.
Моя рука чертит законы

И отменяет их она.
Мне все „отечества"—загоны,
Где скот—людские племена.

Хочу—пасу стада в долинах,
Хочу—на бойню их гоню.
Мой взмах—и области в руинах,
И храмы преданы огню.
Средь всех твердынь—моя твердыня
Стоит незыблемой скалой.
Храм биржевой—моя святыня,
Конторский стол—мой аналой.

Мое евангелье—балансы,
Богослуженье—„игра",
Дары священные—финансы,

Жрецы—мои бухгалтера.
Я в этом храме—жрец верховный,
Первосвященник ваш и вождь.
Свершая подвиг мой духовный,
Я золотой сбираю дождь.

Мои сокровища несметны.
Их не отдам я без борьбы.
Да будут вечно ж безответны
Мной усмиренные рабы!
Да будут святы им ступени,
Где жду я жертвы их трудов!
Да склонят все они колени,
Целуя прах моих следов!

№ 47.

*Демьян Бедный.*

„Моя банда"

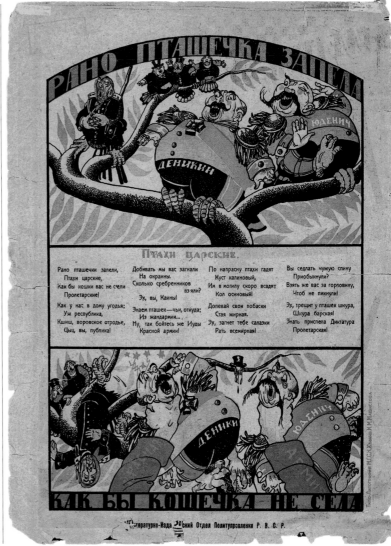

*Opposite page:* "My Gang", a tough and uncompromising Red brigade commanded by Vasilii Blyukher and ready for trouble in the fight against Ataman Dutov, the commander of the Orenburg Cossacks under Admiral Kolchak in the Urals, 1919. After his defeat, Dutov fled to China where he was assassinated by a Chekist agent in 1921.

*Above left:* Dmitrii Moor's famous poster from 1919, "The Birds of the Tsar". The text at the top and bottom reads, "It is too early for the bird to sing – The cat might get it." In the top frame, three unsuspecting White generals, Kolchak, Denikin and Yudenich, twitter away on the branch in close harmony with a capitalist, a priest and a kulak in the background.

In the bottom frame, all hell breaks loose as Denikin and Yudenich are grabbed at the throat by the hands of the "Dictatorship of the Proletariat". Note the fate of the capitalist under the top hat.

*Above right:* A rare version of the poster, redrawn by Moor for a Red Army satirical magazine in 1922. This time the words "Red" and "Army" are printed on the sleeves of the predator and the leaves have turned a shade sickly.

*Right:* Pavel Dybenko (with beard) was a sailor with the Baltic fleet who played a large part in mobilising the Baltic sailors during the October Revolution. He commanded Red partisan units in Ukraine and Crimea during the Civil War and is seen here with Nestor Makhno, the organiser of the largest anarchist movement in Ukraine. Makhno's troops fought both alongside and against the Soviets. When his usefulness to them came to an end in 1921, the Soviets called him a gang leader, bandit and robber. He fled, eventually to Paris, where he died in 1934. He is buried in Père Lachaise cemetery.

Dybenko held many high-ranking military posts in the USSR, but in 1938, during Stalin's Terror, he was arrested and shot.

*Overleaf:* Hundreds of Red Army prisoners of war huddled together in fearful conditions on a prison ship near Kazan on the River Volga in 1919.

They had been captured by the White forces of Admiral Kolchak, who had recently seized a vast quantity of the old tsarist state's gold reserves in a military offensive and proclaimed himself "Supreme Ruler of All the Russias". His time was short. In the autumn of 1919, his army suffered complete collapse at the hands of a Red Army counter-attack and he was shot by leaders of the Irkutsk Soviet on February 7, 1920. It is not known what happened to the captives on Kolchak's death ship, but the admiral's innate brutality would have made their chances of survival slim.

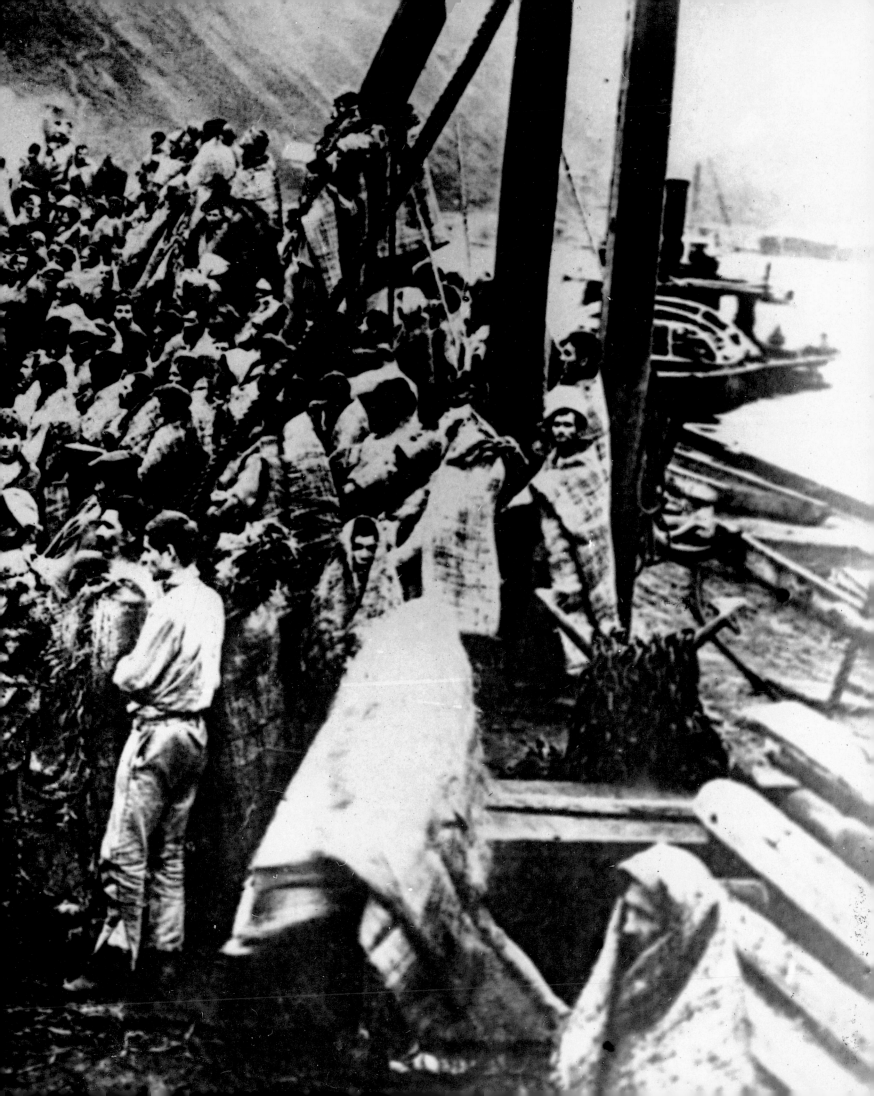

Viktor Deni's poster, "A Pig Trained in Paris", published in 1920 at the time of the Russo-Polish war.
The pig, whose hatband reads "The Poland of the Landlords", is in the arms of its ally "France" and carries a proclamation, "Frontier of 1772",
referring to Poland's desire for the restoration of its historical borders.
*Opposite page:* A horseman in the Red Cavalry reading his unit's newspaper, "To Victory!" The Red Army considered literacy
and education classes for its troops to be of the highest priority.

The Russo-Polish War began on April 25, 1920 when Marshal Pilsudski's Polish army invaded Ukraine and quickly took Kiev. The Red Army recaptured the city on June 12 and soon the Poles were in full retreat.

Trotsky urged that Red troops should stop at the Polish frontier but Lenin believed that a Soviet Poland was in his sights.

Pilsudski was forced back to Warsaw but the Red Army's swift gains left them overstretched and a blistering Polish counter-attack drove them back across the border. Peace talks began at the end of September.

*Top:* "Be On Guard!", Dmitrii Moor's poster, with text by Trotsky, published at the time of the Russo-Polish War. A soldier of the Red Cavalry stamps on the Polish landlords.

*Above:* "Peace and Freedom in Sovdepia". An anti-Semitic White Russian poster depicting Trotsky as the ogre of the Kremlin. "Sovdepia" was a pejorative used by the Whites for the Soviet state.

*Right:* Trotsky in intense discussion with his officers and men during the Civil War.

УКРАИНЦЕВ и РУССКИХ КЛИЧ ОДИН –

РОСТА

ДА НЕ БУДЕТ ПАН НАД РАБОЧИМ ГОСПОДИН!

*Opposite page:* Viktor Deni's gruesome poster, "The Butchers are Tearing Ukraine to Pieces – Death to the Butchers!" A Polish landlord, "Pan", nails "Ukraine" to the stake aided by Petlyura, commander-in-chief of the Ukrainian army and counter-revolutionary in the Civil War. After his defeat by the Red Army, Petlyura fled to Paris where he was assassinated by a Chekist agent in 1926.
*Right:* A mass hanging of revolutionaries in Ekaterinoslav, Ukraine, by troops of the Austro-German army in 1918.

*Above:* "Ukrainians and Russians have a Common War Cry – Pan will not be the Master of the Worker!" Vladimir Mayakovsky's "Rosta" poster of 1920 satirising the landowners of Poland at the time of the Russo-Polish war. Mayakovsky later estimated that he made about 3,000 agitational posters in the Civil War. "Rosta" posters were hand-painted by teams of artists, often using stencils, and displayed in the windows of the offices of the Russian Telegraph Agency throughout the country. "Art must be everywhere – on the streets, in trams, in factories, in workshops, in workers' apartments," Mayakovsky wrote.

ВСТУПАЙТЕ ДО ЧЕРВОНОЇ КІННОТИ!

Червона кіннота знищила Мамонтова, Шкуро, Деникина.
Вона била панів і Петлюру,
зараз потрібно знищити недобитка Врангеля.
**Робітники й селянє—вступайте до лав Червоної Кінноти.**

"Join the Red Cavalry!" A recruitment poster published in Ukrainian from Kiev, 1920. Artist unknown. The text reads: "The Red Cavalry fought against Mamontov, Shkuro, Denikin. They fought against Pans and Petlyura. Now it is Wrangel's turn. Workers and peasants – Join the Red Cavalry."

"To Horse, Workers and Peasants! The Red Cavalry is the Guarantee of our Victory!" Another recruitment poster, this time in Polish. Also from Kiev, 1919. Artist unknown.

*Opposite page:* Isaak Babel at work, photographed in 1933 by Georgii Petrusov. Thirteen years previously, at the age of 26, the distinguished writer and horseman had joined up as a journalist, under the pseudonym Kiril Lyutov, to write about Semyon Budenny's First Red Cavalry who were fighting against the Poles in Ukraine. Babel (who as a Jewish child born in Odessa had witnessed first hand the pogroms of 1905) kept his notes of the 1920 campaign in diary form; detailed vignettes and personal impressions, reminders of the horrors of everything he had witnessed. Here is an entry, dated August 28, 1920, from the small town of Komarow:

"... Rumour of atrocities. I walk into town. Indescribable terror and despair. They tell me about it. Privately, indoors, they're afraid the Poles may come back. Captain Yakovlev's Cossacks were here yesterday. A pogrom. The family of David Zys, in people's homes, a naked, barely breathing prophet of an old man, an old woman butchered, a child with fingers chopped off, many people still breathing, stench of blood, everything turned upside down, chaos, a mother sitting over her sabred son, an old woman lying twisted up like a pretzel, four people in a hovel, filth, blood under a black beard, just lying there in their blood. The Jews on the square, an agonised Jew showing it all to me, a tall Jew takes over from him. The rabbi hid, his whole house was taken apart, he waited till evening to creep out of his hole. Fifteen people killed, the Hasid Itska Galer, aged 70, David Zys, the synagogue caretaker, 45, his wife, his daughter, aged 15, David Trost and his wife – the ritual slaughterer...

"At night, a walk around the town. Moonlight, their life at night, behind closed doors. Wailing beyond those walls. They'll clean it all up. The fear and horror of the inhabitants. The worst of it is – our men nonchalantly walk around looting wherever possible, stripping mangled corpses. The hatred is the same, the Cossacks just the same, the cruelty the same, it's nonsense to think one army is different from another. The life of these little towns. There's no salvation. Everyone destroys them – the Poles gave them no refuge. The girls and women, all of them, can scarcely walk. In the evening – a talkative Jew with a little beard, used to keep a shop, daughter threw herself out of a second-storey window to escape a Cossack, broke her arms, one of many. What a mighty and marvellous life of a nation existed here. The fate of Jewry. At our place in the evening, supper, tea, I sit and drink in the words of the Jew with the little beard, wistfully asking me whether it will be possible to trade. An oppressive, uneasy night."

Babel used his 1920 diary as the starting point for his masterpiece of semi-documentary short stories, *Red Cavalry.*

The book was to receive overwhelming praise on its publication in Moscow in 1926 and Babel was catapulted to fame, but one lone voice of antagonism turned out to be Field Marshal Budenny's. Stalin's long-term comrade furiously denounced the author as a "literary degenerate", calling the book "a slander" which relied on "the gossip of old women". Six years later, in 1932, Stalin himself started grumbling: "... our feverish Babel who always writes about that which he knows nothing. Like, for example *Red Cavalry.*"

As the Stalinist doctrine of Socialist Realism started to strangle cultural life in Russia from the early 1930s onwards, Babel's own creative output receded. In 1934, speaking at the first Union of Soviet Writers Conference, he announced: "I have invented a new genre, the genre of silence."

But as late as 1937, at the height of Stalin's Great Terror when many of his fellow writers found themselves in deep trouble, Babel was still being officially admired and respected, even lauded for his "great mastery" of story telling in the new *Small Soviet Encyclopedia.*

Babel was protected from arrest during this period by Evgenia Khayutina, the wife of the vicious NKVD boss, Nikolai Yezhov. In 1927, before she met her husband, Evgenia had an affair with Babel in Berlin. While Yezhov was in power, she could put in a good word for her old lover, but when it came time for Yezhov himself to be arrested and tortured, things turned bad; the ex-secret police chief testified against Babel in an act of jealousy and revenge. Isaak Babel was arrested, tortured and eventually shot on January 27, 1940.

*Top:* Semyon Budenny saluting from his staff car during the campaign against the Poles in Ukraine, 1920. Mikhail Kalinin (the Russian Head of State) looks on, clapping his hands. On the far right of the picture, Babel smiles and salutes.

*Centre:* Red Cossacks posing for the camera during the Civil War in 1920. Some of their number have been hacked out of the print (probably because they had gone over to the Whites). Babel once remarked, "Cossacks, however, don't always behave well."

*Below left: Konarmiya* – the first Russian edition of *Red Cavalry,* published in Moscow in 1926. Reprints and many foreign language editions followed rapidly. The blue crayon cross in the top left-hand corner of the cover is the mark of the Stalinist censor, signifying that the book had been banned following Babel's arrest on May 15, 1939.

*Below right:* A rare picture, taken in 1932, of Babel with Mikhail, his son from an affair with the actress Tamara Ivanova. Mikhail, who became an artist, hardly ever saw his father again.

*Overleaf:* Budenny (with large moustache, fifth from the right in the first row of seats) with officers and men of the First Red Cavalry, circa 1920.

По воздушному мчася пути,
Красный летчик в Ягу луч пустил:
„Эй, Яга,
Костяная нога!

Чай уж косточки старые ноют?
В отставке твоя ступа,
В отставку сама ступай,—
Не угнаться, старуха, за мною!"
Гл. 5833.

Змея Горыныча
Побит рекорд нынче,
(Нос драл, под облака взлетая,
Ишь—невидаль какая)!

Летчика кровь горячая:
Сердце не знает страху—
Мечем рубанет с плеча,
Отрубит все головы смаху.
Гл. 5831.

The Workers' and Peasants' Military Air Fleet was established in May 1918 but its operations in the Civil War were limited to six aeroplanes making in total fewer than two hundred sorties.
Approximately eleven hundred aircraft should have been available but over half of them were not serviceable (163 had no engines at all). There was also a permanent shortage of fuel.
Alongside military work, aeroplanes were usefully employed in anti-religious campaigns to "discredit superstition" among the peasants. Agitators would take frightened village folk on daring flights above the clouds to prove that neither gods nor angels resided there.

*Top, left and right:* Two postcards published at the time illustrating the Red airman's Herculean superiority over both witch and Hydra.
*Far left:* The First Red Cavalry's air squadron lined up for action, Ukraine, 1919.
*Left:* The haphazard nature of flying in its early days is depicted in this print published during the Civil War and long before air traffic control.
*Above:* Members of the Red Cavalry's air crew survey the result of a fatal crash landing.
*Opposite page:* A pilot of the First Red Cavalry's air squadron poses for the camera in the Civil War.

*Above:* Two Ukrainian revolutionary posters by I. Padalka, Kiev, 1919. The flags read "Unity is Strength" (*left*) and "Unity is Beauty".
*Opposite page:* "The Pans Destroy – The Proletariat Creates". A poster design from 1920 by Anatolii Petritsky, also from Kiev.
All three works are reproduced from the printer's proofs, with many tipped-in colour plates, of a projected album entitled *The Ukrainian Revolutionary Poster.* It was edited by A. Berezinsky, Vasil Khmurii and V. Sedlyara of the publishing house "RUK" (meaning "Hand" but also the initials for "Revolutionary Ukrainian

Artists"). Photographs of a rare series of constructivist compositions by the Kharkov-born artist Vasilii Ermilov commemorating Lenin's death were also included alongside works by O. Khvostov, Adolf Strakhov and O. Marenkov. Publication was set for 1932 to coincide with the fifteenth anniversary of the October Revolution but no trace can be found of the finished volume ever appearing. Perhaps it became an early victim of Stalinist censorship, its contents considered either too revolutionary by this time or not conforming sufficiently to the dictator's burgeoning appetite for Socialist Realism.

The Civil War ended in November 1920 with the defeat of the White armies under Baron Wrangel in the Crimea. The old tsarist cavalryman had launched an attack, in support of the Poles, against the Red Army in Ukraine. Having regrouped after the retreat from Poland, however, the Red Army got its revenge, driving back Wrangel's stricken forces into an unseemly evacuation by boat from Sevastopol to Turkey.

*Above:* Viktor Deni's 1919 illustration of Trotsky slaying the counter-revolutionary dragon.

*Left:* Trotsky, in victorious mood, with Jules Humbert-Droz at a demonstration in Red Square, Moscow, 1920. Born in Switzerland, Humbert-Droz trained as a pastor before becoming a communist. He was elected Secretary of the Executive Committee of the Third International and was for many years the Comintern's chief emissary in the West, known as "The Eye of Moscow". Between them, out of focus, can be seen Alexei Rykov who took over as Chairman of the Council of People's Commissars after Lenin's death in 1924. He was arrested by Stalin in 1937 and shot after the third Moscow Show Trial of 1938.

Two and a half years of Civil War had the most catastrophic effects on Soviet Russia; the loss of life, the brutalisation of many of those who had survived, the resulting famine of 1920–21 and the increasing influence of the political police. Lenin and Trotsky's hopes for a world revolution were all but obliterated; potential revolutions in Germany and Hungary had been swept aside.

In March 1921, sailors from the naval base at Kronstadt who had played such an heroic part in the October Revolution rebelled against Lenin's government under the slogan "Soviets without Communists". Their demands included free elections, freedom of speech, the liberation of socialist political prisoners, economic reforms and an end to Bolshevik political domination. Fifty thousand Red Army soldiers under the command of Mikhail Tukhachevsky, supported by heavy artillery, crossed the ice on March 17 and crushed the uprising. Hundreds of rebel sailors were rounded up and shot by the Cheka.

*Overleaf:* The Workers' and Peasants' Red Army celebrating victory over Baron Wrangel in the Crimea, 1920.

*Opposite page:*
"Proletarian Youth from the Countryside and Town, Unite!", a poster from Odessa, Ukraine, 1920. Artist unknown.
*Left:* A poster from Belorussia, circa 1920. "Workers! A Few More Blows will Finally Eliminate the Capitalists and the Proletariat will Get Everything it Wants". "Socialism" is imprinted on the sun in the top left-hand corner. Belorussia had been occupied by the Germans in the First World War and had suffered fearfully from both conflict and famine.

After October 1917, power and land rapidly changed hands between Belorussian nationalists, Bolsheviks, Germans, Poles and Lithuanians. The Belorussian Soviet Socialist Republic was formed in late 1918 but it was not until July 1920 that the Red Army finally captured Minsk from the Poles.

Chaos and economic hardship fuelled a series of peasant uprisings which were ruthlessly suppressed by the Bolshevik secret police. Lenin's New Economic Policy considerably eased the strain on the country from 1921.

*Overleaf:* Viktor Bulla's photograph, intensified by multiple exposure, documents the attention given by the audience to the full force of Lenin's opening speech at the Second Congress of the Third International in the Uritsky Palace, Petrograd, July 19, 1920. The picture came from an album of 120 original photographs celebrating the Congress that was presented to one of the visiting foreign delegates.

**КУЗНИЦА**

„Пролетарии всех стран, соединяйтесь!"

*Opposite page:* Boris Kustodiev's cover for the Bolsheviks' polemical journal, *Communist International*, edited by Grigorii Zinoviev and published from the Smolny Institute, Petrograd, in Russian, English, French and German. The journal first appeared on May Day, 1919 and Kustodiev's famous illustration was repeatedly used on the cover for most of the 1920s.
*Left:* Nikolai Kochergin's cover for *Kuznitsa* (The Forge), a periodical of proletarian writers published by the People's Commissariat of Enlightenment in 1921. Kochergin, like Kustodiev, illustrates the conclusion to Marx's *Communist Manifesto* for his cover, but in a much more colourful way. Kochergin also painted camouflage for the Red Army and decorated agitprop trains during the Civil War.
*Overleaf:* Red stars in Petrograd. Celebrating the dawn of a new age at the Second Congress of the Third International in Petrograd, 1920.

In 1920, the offices of the Bolshevik delegation in London were situated at 128 New Bond Street. The Soviet ambassador to England at the time was Leonid Krassin, who worked there with other high-ranking diplomats including Maxim Litvinov and Lev Kamenev. It was still a year before the Anglo-Soviet trade agreement would effectively recognise the new Russian state and the comings and goings of the Bolsheviks in Bond Street were watched with both interest and alarm by the British secret service. One rather unlikely newcomer who appeared at the Reds' offices in September was Clare Sheridan, a remarkable woman from a wealthy background and a cousin of Winston Churchill. Having lost her husband in the First World War and with two young children to support, Sheridan had taken up sculpture, mainly portraiture, somewhat in the manner of Epstein. She was invited to make busts of both Krassin ("sphinx-like") and Kamenev ("even when his mouth is severe, his eyes laugh") and they both sat for her at her studio in Queen's Terrace, St John's Wood. Kamenev, particularly, loved his portrait and a whirlwind friendship developed between them, taking in dinner at Claridges and the Cafe Royal, visits to Hampton Court and the Tate Gallery (where Kamenev stood for a long time in front of Burne-Jones', "King Cophetua and the Beggar-maid") and a few days on the Isle of Wight. Kamenev proposed to Clare that she should return with him to Moscow and make portraits of the Bolsheviks, including Lenin and Trotsky.

The Civil War was drawing to a close but the capitalist's blockade was still in force and Western propaganda cast the Bolsheviks as murderous and bloody-minded proletarians who had even nationalised women. "I was insatiably interested," she said, "I loved Slavs, Slav music, Slav literature, Slav art and decoration and had always, since childhood, been drawn to Russia." Clare left her children with her parents and, together with Kamenev, made the arduous journey by train and ship across Europe to Moscow.

Kamenev had often told Clare how well she would get on with his wife Olga, who also happened to be Trotsky's sister. As the train pulled into the Moscow station, Olga was there on the platform. She greeted Kamenev with a terrible tirade against the "bourgeois" artist: "I won't have that woman under my roof." Kamenev crumbled in the face of his wife's onslaught. Clare thought that he "cut a poor figure". She had no idea that "a Bolshevik could be so easily terrorised" but she stood her own ground, casting Olga as a "thin-lipped, hard-eyed bitchovitch".

After a spell adjusting to the austerity of everyday life in Moscow – spartan accommodation, no heating or hot water, inedible food – Sheridan set to

work. Kamenev arranged a freezing cold studio space for her in the Kremlin and over the next two months (with help from Kamenev and others as she could speak no Russian), Grigorii Zinoviev, Felix Dzerzhinsky, Lenin and Trotsky all sat for her.

Zinoviev, she found arrogant; he was restless and impatient, he sighed and groaned. She described him: "His face was thick, his neck short, his chest pulpy, his hair curly, his lips petulant, his eyelids heavy. The effect was of a shrewd, fat, middle-aged woman."

Dzerzhinsky, the boss of the Cheka (Lenin's secret police), was next on Sheridan's list. He was reclusive and sick, a small man whose "eyes seemed to be swimming in tears." She wrote movingly that he had spent a quarter of his life in tsarist prisons, that he hated his current position as boss of the "Red Terror" and only did it "for the sake of the cause."

Sheridan believed that being the object of vilification in the minds of so many millions had influenced Dzerzhinsky's health to such a degree that he was doomed, "dying, choking, suffocating, from thought-waves of hatred."

Lenin greeted Sheridan in his well-lit room in the Kremlin, telling her amicably that he knew nothing about art and that it didn't interest him. Almost at once, however, he started to express strong opinions about "bourgeois art", how it always aimed at beauty and adding contemptuously that beauty was nothing more than an abstract ideal. The long sittings passed in silence but when Clare ventured to ask him if her cousin, Churchill, was the most hated man in Russia, Lenin replied, "He is our greatest enemy because all the forces of capitalism are behind him, as well as the court and the military."

Sheridan felt Lenin to be at once severe,

thoughtful and humorous, with an expression at times so piercing it could penetrate your brain.

Trotsky was the final Bolshevik to sit for her. The work took place at night in his palatial office at the War Ministry. Clare and he got on well. Trotsky: "You shall make this your permanent studio. I like you working here. As soon as you have finished the bust we will destroy it and begin again!" Thus spoke the theorist of the permanent revolution. Sheridan noted her subject's eyes "flashing like electric sparks." His mood swings could disconcert her: "Much as I admire you as a woman, I assure you that if I knew you were an enemy, or a danger to our revolutionary cause I would not hesitate to shoot you down with my own hand." Sheridan admitted that she found this ruthlessness "most attractive." She was pleased with the finished result of the bust of Trotsky and returned to England with his words ringing in her ears: "It is easy enough here to be blinded by the squalor and suffering, and to see no further, but people forget there is no birth without pain and Russia is in the throes of a great birth."

Clare Sheridan was greeted with much excitement by the press on her return to London and the *Times* ran a column, "Mrs Sheridan's Diary". But familial animosity unsettled her greatly. Her father had expressed the wish that her throat might be cut in Moscow as vindication of the family's honour. Her mother wrote, "I forgive you, darling, as I would even if you had committed a murder." Former friends avoided her, referring to her as "The Bolshevik". Churchill never spoke to her again. It was time to leave. She set sail for New York. Once there, she had a successful exhibition of her Bolshevik busts at Knoedler's art gallery on Fifth Avenue. On average there were two hundred visitors every day.

Clare Sheridan continued to live a full and eventful life as a sculptor, novelist, journalist and traveller until her death on May 31, 1970, aged 84. She was buried at Brede Place, Sussex.

*Top left:* Kamenev, in white shirt, at the funeral of John Reed, Moscow, 1920.
*Top right:* Olga Kameneva in her apartment in the Kremlin.
*Centre:* Clare Sheridan in New York, working on the finishing touches to her bust of Lenin before the exhibition.
*Above left:* Sheridan's bust of Lenin on display in the Lenin Museum in Moscow, 1937.
*Above right:* Sheridan's bust of Trotsky at his house in Coyoacán, Mexico City, where he was assassinated in 1940.
*Opposite page:* A portrait of Clare with one of her busts of Trotsky, taken at the time of her New York exhibition. Photograph by Brugière.
*Overleaf:* Trotsky salutes the crowds as he leads a group of high-ranking Red Army officers across Red Square, Moscow, in the chill mid-winter of 1920.

Dmitrii Melnikov's poster, "Down with Capital, Long Live the Dictatorship of the Proletariat", celebrates the third anniversary of the October Revolution. Moscow, 1920. Melnikov also worked with Viktor Vinogradov on the decoration of agitprop trains.

Ivan Simakov's poster, "Long Live the Proletarian Holiday – May 1st". Petrograd, 1921.
Simakov's portrayal of life under the silver birches for peasant and worker was sadly misplaced; the bleak reality for millions of Russians at this time was famine.

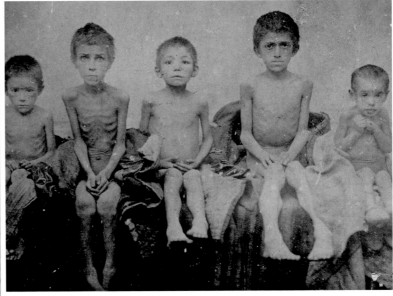

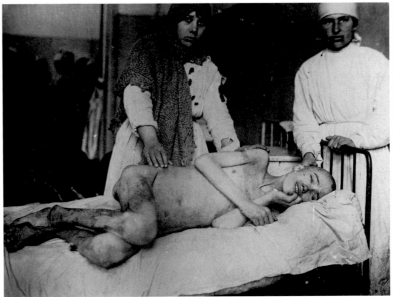

In 1918 the Bolsheviks called for the forced requisition of surplus grain from the peasants in the countryside to feed the urban population and the Red Army during the Civil War. In defiance, the majority of peasants reduced their crop yields to the minimum rather than have their stockpiles confiscated by the hated Bolsheviks. No safety margin therefore existed between a bad harvest and hunger.

Drought hit the Volga Black Earth region in 1920 and again in 1921. A catastrophe ensued comparable only to the Black Death. Countless millions were to die. The scorching sun cracked the soil, making it unworkable, while locust and vermin devoured the last traces of vegetation and food. On June 26, 1921 *Pravda* announced that 25,000,000 people in Russia and parts of Ukraine were starving. The majority of them were the rural poor and many fell victim to typhus, cholera or typhoid fever. There were corpses everywhere and there was cannibalism.

In July, the writer Maxim Gorky appealed to Herbert Hoover, who had established the American Relief Administration to provide food and medicines to Europe in the aftermath of the First World War, to help alleviate the disastrous situation. Hoover, a future President of the United States and no friend of the Bolsheviks, agreed to send aid out of humanitarian considerations. At its height, American Relief was feeding 14,000,000 starving people every day, clothing them and providing medicines to combat the epidemics.

By the summer of 1922 the famine had been defeated and because the Americans also provided farming tools and huge quantities of seed, there were bumper harvests for the next two years. The Americans altogether spent over 60,000,000 dollars on the relief work. There was help from other sources as well – the Red Cross shipped in 90,000 tonnes of food – but the League of Nations sent nothing. Maxim Gorky was full of praise for Hoover and the efforts of the Americans but Lenin, unfortunately, could only bring himself to accuse them of spying.

*Left:* Refugees from the famine in one of the camps set up by the Americans.
*Top:* Orphaned and starving children taken into care, 1921.
*Above:* Severe stomach illness caused by food substitutes in Alexandrovsk, Ukraine.

*Top:* A curiously romanticised view of the plight of a gang of "bezprizornye", homeless waifs who had been either orphaned or abandoned as a result of the chronic social breakdown caused by the Civil War and famine. By 1922, some seven million children had taken to the streets in the towns and villages of Russia, living in abject squalor, their existence depending on mindless violence, theft, begging and child prostitution.

The Soviet authorities tried to combat this terrible state of affairs by re-educating as many of them as they could in special institutions, often unsuccessfully. Thousands wound up in prisons or labour camps. Large numbers were also conscripted into the Red Army. Their lack of squeamishness, due to the terrible scenes they had witnessed or been a part of in their short lives, turned them into tough soldiers once they had been taught army discipline and received a basic education. The photograph was taken by Moisei Nappelbaum.

*Above left:* "Help the Starving in the Volga Region", a porcelain dish by the artist Rudolf Vilde, 1921. Many Soviet artists and designers made plates and dishes to be sold for famine relief.

*Above right:* Cannibalism in Ukraine during the famine, 1921.

*Right:* Sleeping conditions in a hostel for the homeless, destitute and those recently released from prison. Petrograd, 1920.

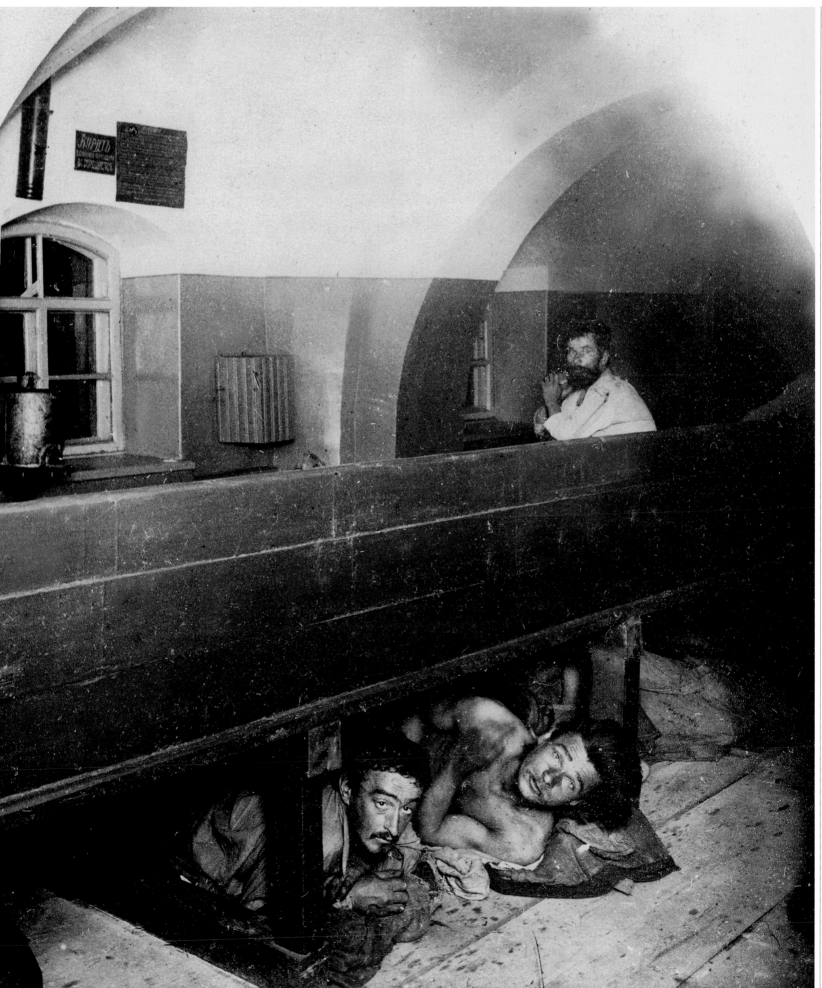

Lenin's secret police, the Cheka (the acronym stands for "Extraordinary Commission to Fight Counter-revolution and Sabotage") was formed in December 1917 with the chivalrous but ruthless Felix Dzerzhinsky as its boss. He packed the Cheka's ranks with non-Russians, especially Latvians, who were considered disciplined, tough and not at all squeamish.

On August 30, 1918, Lenin addressed a meeting of workers at an industrial plant across the Moskva river: "Slavery and bondage... Imperialist slaughter... Besieged fortress... Victory or Death!" As he left the factory he was shot twice by an assassin's bullets in the left arm and neck. Lenin survived a serious haemorrhage and recovered in a matter of weeks. Meanwhile Dzerzhinsky unleashed the Red Terror throughout the land in brutal retribution, cutting down all real or perceived opposition. *Krasnaya Gazeta* (Red Gazette) screamed: "For the blood of Lenin... let there be floods of the blood of the bourgeoisie – more blood, as much blood as possible!"

*Above:* Two postcards from Odessa distributed in 1921 by the All-Ukrainian State Publishing House demanding vigilance against anti-Soviet saboteurs. The card on the left reads: "The Bandit is the Enemy of the Peasant. Peasants! Eliminate the Bandits!" The right-hand card reads: "Death to the Bandits who are Destroying the Railroads!"

*Left:* A group of Chekists on parade in Rostov-on-Don, May Day, 1920. Their banner reads: "In the Struggle Against Economic Wreckers, We Know of No Hesitation on the Time of the Workers."

*Opposite page:* "To Comrade Sergei Shumolov on the 15th anniversary of the Cheka – OGPU. For active work in the liquidation of the anti-Soviet movement in Central Asia and the successful struggle against banditry. From the OGPU". Above the solid brass profile of Dzerzhinsky on this commemorative plaque is engraved one of his quotations: "I am proud that the people love me and the enemy hates me." The Cheka was reorganised into the GPU in 1922, became the OGPU in late 1923, the NKVD in 1934 and eventually the KGB.

134

"Я буржуа любовью
народа и ненавистью врагов"

Тов. Шумилову С.Г.
В день 15-летия ВЧК-ОГПУ
За активное участие
по ликвидации басмачества
и успешную борьбу с бандитизмом
от ПП.ОГПУ.СКК.

*Left:* Anatolii Lunacharsky with his second wife, the silent film star Natalya Rozenel, in the mid-1920s. Lunacharsky came from a well-educated, radical background and his great powers of oratory thrust him into the centre of the Revolution. He once reminisced, "I became a revolutionary so early in life that I do not remember when I was not one." The late historian Isaac Deutscher described Lunacharsky's outstanding role in the events of 1917: "... with the air of the absent-minded professor, [he] surprised and astonished all who saw him by his indomitable militancy and energy. He was the great orator of Red Petrograd, second only to Trotsky, addressing every day, or even several times a day, huge, hungry and angry crowds of workers, soldiers and sailors, and breaking down almost effortlessly, by his sheer sincerity and sensitivity, all barriers of social origin and education that might have separated him from them. The crowds were spellbound by him and loved him." Lenin appointed Lunacharsky as the first Commissar of Education and Enlightenment in November 1917, reasoning that, "in matters of culture, nothing is as harmful and pernicious as hate, arrogance and fanaticism. In these matters great care and tolerance must be exercised."

Lunacharsky's first task was to wage war on one of the worst legacies of the old regime: widespread illiteracy. The new Commissariat reformed the educational system, modernised teaching methods and encouraged the mass of the people to enjoy and take part in music, drama, literature and the visual arts. By the time Lunacharsky left office in 1929, virtually the whole country was literate and numerate and a good Soviet education was something of which to be very proud. Lunacharsky often had to defend himself (as well as legions of avant-garde Soviet artists and writers) against the Bolshevik's wrath on the cultural front. Trotsky was in agreement with Lunacharsky's tolerant attitude towards all forms of creative work, but Lenin could never quite live up to his own philosophy, quoted above. For example, after reading Mayakovsky's poem "150,000,000", Lenin raged: "Nonsense! Foolish! Double-dyed folly and pretentiousness... and Lunacharsky should be flogged for his futurism!" Had it been some years later, he almost certainly would have been but a severe heart condition caused him to die in 1933 on a train at Menton in France on his way to becoming the new Soviet ambassador to Spain. Lunacharsky rather brilliantly once described himself: "I am an intellectual among Bolsheviks, but a Bolshevik among intellectuals."

*Above: Krasnii Petrograd* (Red Petrograd), a journal from 1919, welcomes the Bolshevik Enlightenment.

"We Defeated the Enemy with Weapons – With Hard Work We Will Get Our Bread.
Everyone to Work, Comrades". Nikolai Kogout's inspiring 1920 poster for post-Civil War reconstruction.

БЕСПЛАТНОЕ ПРИЛОЖЕНИЕ К КУБАНСКО-ЧЕРНОМОРСКОМУ НАСТОЛЬНОМУ КАЛЕНДАРЮ на 1922 г.

Р.С.Ф.С.Р.

ГОСУДАРСТВЕННОЕ ИЗДАТЕЛЬСТВО КУБАНСКО-ЧЕРНОМОРСКОЕ УПРАВЛЕНИЕ.

The same message of constructive labour is conveyed more quietly
in this neoclassical-influenced cover for a calendar published in the Kuban-Black Sea region in 1922, artist unknown.

"Comrade Workers! Write to the Newspaper!" An anonymous poster from Kazan, 1921, urging those who had benefited from the Soviets' literacy campaign to make use of their new skills. Lenin's New Economic Policy of 1921 sought to reverse urban depopulation and strikes by disgruntled workers who were sick to death of shortages of food, clothing and almost everything else. Small-scale privately-run industries and services, as well as peasant markets selling surplus foodstuffs, helped revive the economy to pre-war levels by the mid-1920s.

*Opposite page:* Alexander Zelensky's poster, "To Have More, You Must Produce More – To Produce More, You Must Know More", published in Petrograd, 1920.

With its depiction of the sickle and a bookmark of wheat, Zelensky's poster forcefully lays down the benefits of hard work and literacy to the peasants.

Liubov Popova's cover design for *Muzikalnaya Nov,* a journal of the musical arts
published in Moscow and Petrograd in 1923. *Opposite page:* An impromptu performance, 1920s.

Alexander Lebedev's poster for the All-Russian Agricultural and Industrial Crafts Exhibition held in Moscow, August–September 1923. The exhibition was an important propaganda success, showing thousands of foreign visitors how rapidly Soviet agriculture had developed in the two years since the famine.

It also happened to be the destination of Lenin's last outing. Against the wishes of his doctors, who were trying to nurse him through a long convalescence, he demanded to be taken on a round trip to visit the exhibition, although when he got there he was too ill to leave his car.

*Opposite page:* "Red Moscow – The Heart of the World Revolution", a bilingual poster published in 1921 by the Higher State Artistic and Technical Studios in Moscow, known as "Vkhutemas". Lunacharsky had proposed in 1919 that Soviet artistic training should "give production more importance than fine art." Vkhutemas was founded the following year to train socialist "artist-constructors" to combine art and design in a wide range of subjects. The list of leading avant-garde artists, designers, architects and cineastes who taught there at various times in the 1920s included El Lissitsky, Liubov Popova, Alexander Rodchenko, Varvara Stepanova, Vladimir Tatlin and Alexander Vesnin. By the end of the decade, the work of these great experimental artists and designers was being treated with increasing hostility by the flag-wavers of Socialist Realism. In 1930 Vkhutemas was shut down and replaced by the conservative Moscow Art Institute.

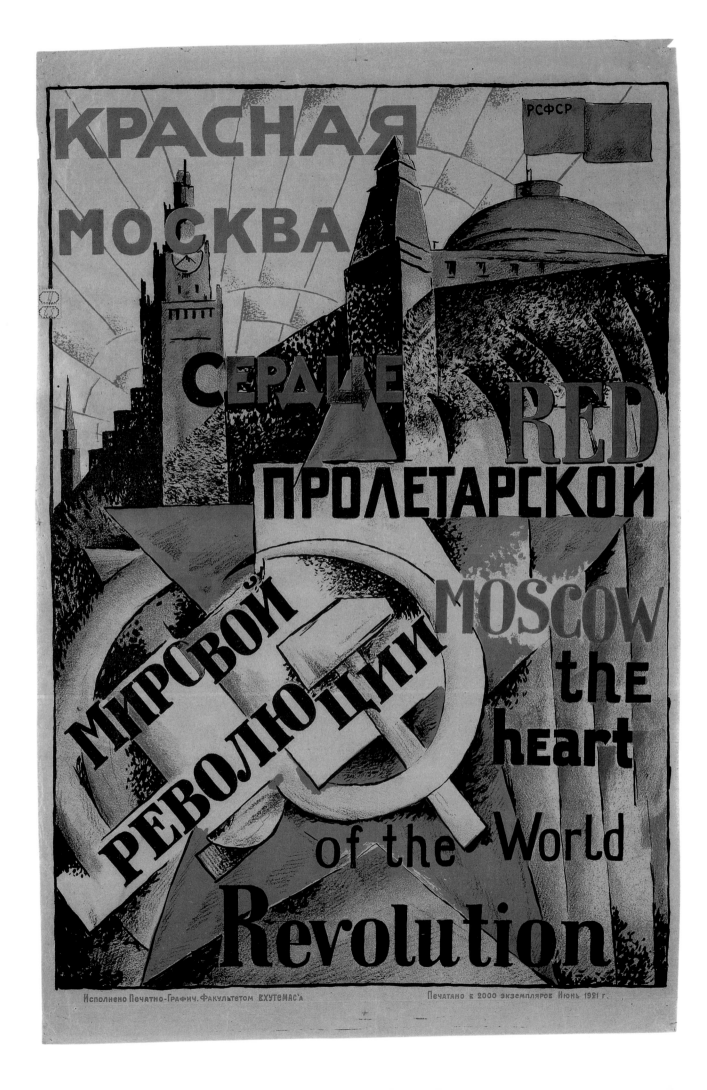

Pyotr Galadzhev's multi-language cover design for the first issue of the journal, *Art Workers' Herald*, Moscow, 1924.

Another cover by Pyotr Galadzhev, for *Kino Zhurnal*, a periodical published by the Association of Revolutionary Cinematographers, Moscow, 1925.

*Above:* A gouache and montage artwork promoting one of the "Blue Blouse" political theatre groups in the early 1920s. "Blue Blouse" groups took their agitational productions straight to the workers in the factories and the fields. Their name and costumes derived from the blue overalls of "the unclean" in the Vsevolod Meyerhold production of Mayakovsky's play, "Mystery-Bouffe" in 1921.

*Right:* Two photographs from a "Blue Blouse" play featuring the Third International's victory over a very sinister capitalist.

*Opposite page:* The front cover of *Contemporary West*, a journal of literature, science and art, published in Leningrad, 1924. Designer unknown.

*Above:* Natan Altman's logotype for the Moscow Kamerny Theatre, 1923. The Kamerny presented classical theatre in avant-garde settings. It was founded by the director Alexander Tairov and his leading actor and wife, Alicia Koonen. Altman's logotype was based on Alexander Vesnin's costume design for Koonen in her hit role in Racine's "Phèdre".

СОВРЕМЕННЫЙ

ЗАПАД

№ 1

+5+

ЛЕНИНГРАД.

1924

At 6pm on January 21, 1924, Lenin's temperature rose sharply. He suffered a series of violent convulsions and sank into a coma. He was pronounced dead at 6.30pm, aged 54. Since suffering his first stroke in May 1922, Lenin had spent most of his time at Gorki, the country estate near Moscow. His wife Nadezhda Krupskaya (*above*), his sister Maria and numerous secretaries, doctors, nurses and maids were always in close attendance. The Politburo needed someone to take overall responsibility for him; they chose the recently appointed General Secretary, Stalin. Two more strokes were to follow. The last one, on March 9, 1923, left him in a very poor condition (*top*), wheelchair-bound and with little speech. The artist Yuri Annenkov, who visited Gorki the following December to draw Lenin for a portfolio of Bolshevik leaders, was shaken: "Wrapped in a blanket and looking past us with the helpless, twisted, babyish smile of a man in his second infancy, Lenin could serve only as an illustration of his illness, and not as a model for a portrait."

After his death, Lenin's body was brought to Moscow where it lay in state in the Hall of Columns. In one of the coldest midwinters that Muscovites had ever known, thousands of mourners, their streaming tears turning swiftly to ice as they rolled down their cheeks, waited patiently in line to glimpse their leader in the open coffin. *Right:* Lenin's death mask by the sculptor, Sergei Merkurov.

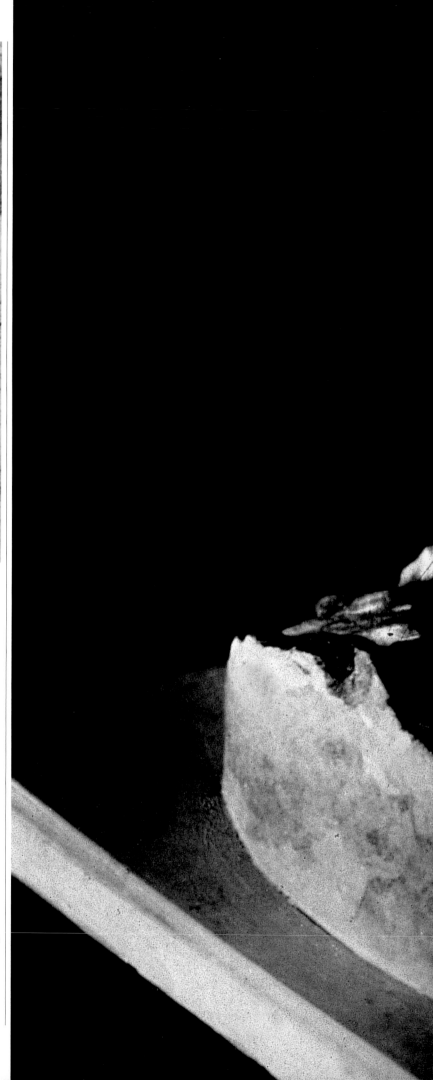

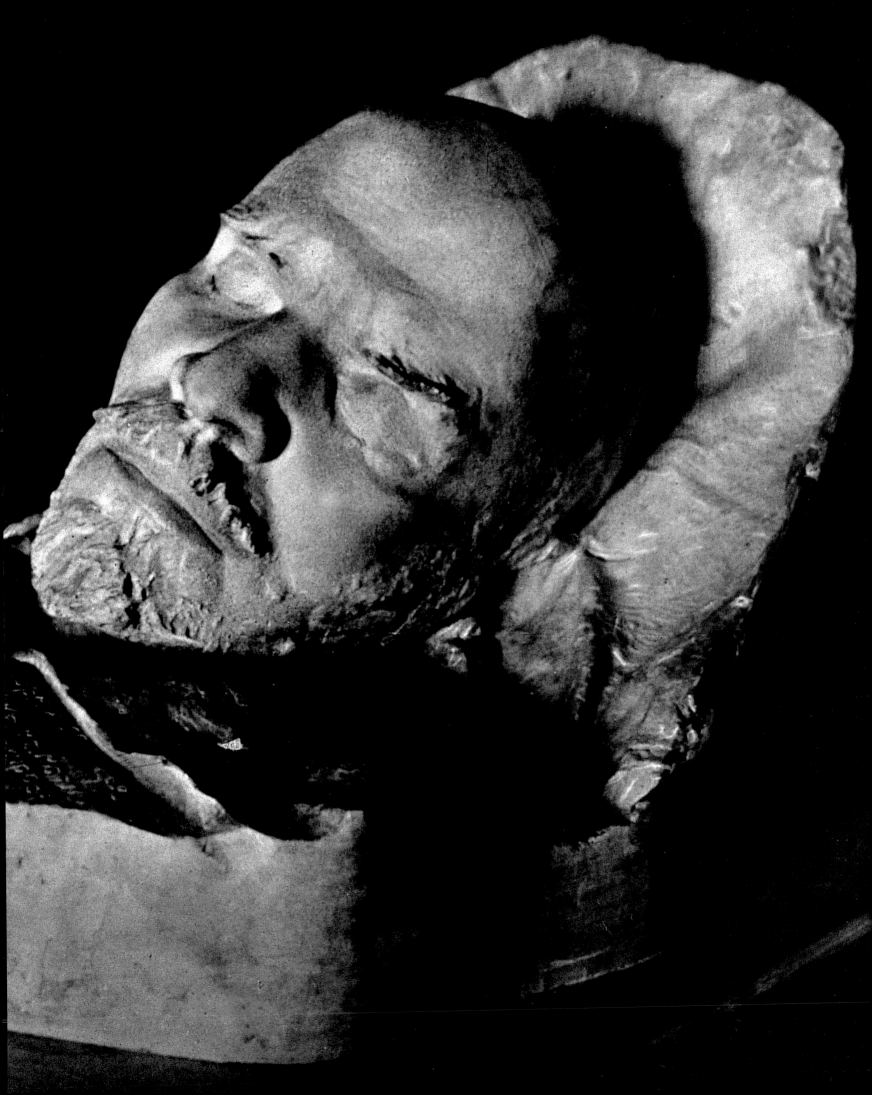

*Above and opposite page:* Twelve photographs of different stages in the construction of the second Lenin Mausoleum in Red Square, Moscow, spring 1924. Alexei Shchusev's design in oak made exemplary use of the fine skills of traditional Russian craftsmen.

*Right:* Lenin lying in state in the Hall of Columns. From there his body was transferred to its first resting place in Red Square, a temporary box-like structure (*second right*), with a huge sign on the front which simply read "LENIN". While the harsh winter temperatures remained, the body stayed frozen.

As spring approached and the ice melted, Lenin's body started to show signs of decomposition. It was secretly taken to a laboratory where two professors, Vorobiev and Zbarsky, embalmed it after a hurried Central Committee decision proposed by Stalin. Krupskaya shared her late husband's abhorrence of the cult of personality and had requested for him to have a decent burial but she was overruled.
*Left: Ilyich.* The first book of photographs about Lenin, published in 1924, and the start of a huge industry. *Second left:* Shchusev's 1930 Lenin mausoleum, made of granite and still in Red Square.

153

Trotsky's intermittent ill health throughout the 1920s and his unwillingness to engage with someone he regarded as his political inferior allowed Stalin, step by step, to slander, exile and eventually extinguish him. Beyond the borders of the Soviet Union, however, the Marxist revolutionary and hero remained as relevant to historians and Sovietologists as he did to those fighting for socialism.

In his book, *The Life of Lenin*, the distinguished political writer, the late Louis Fischer, had this to say:

"Leon Trotsky had biological magnetism which excited those who came within the field, and excitement is the prerequisite of revolutionary action. He was a genius of the stinging word and sweeping argument. Trained in the aim-to-kill school of revolutionary polemics (object: to demolish rather than convince) he could whiplash enemies with his tongue and pen...

"Some said Trotsky had a Mephistophelian face. Actually he had the dark, pale face of a Russian Jewish intellectual: high brow, full lips, dense, curly hair, thick moustache, small pointed goatee, and weak, shortsighted eyes behind pince-nez. It was the fire within that gave him the visage of an angry fighter. He loved combat. Perhaps he invited it by his unharnessed individuality. The trodden path did not lure him. Challenged to choose one of two roads he chose a third. Before the Revolution he accepted Lenin and opposed Lenin, supported Bolshevism and rejected Bolshevism, adopted Menshevism, and finally remained aloof... until the prospect of decisive action in the Russia of 1917 drew him into the Bolshevik Party...

"Trotsky was many-faceted. Steeped in politics, he loved literature... he read new fiction and poetry and wrote beautiful prose... While making history he wrote history."

*Right:* A conté drawing of Trotsky made in 1923 by Sergei Pichugin. Following Trotsky's downfall, the portrait had to be hidden from view. The artist glued a sheet of white card over it and the forbidden likeness was only rediscovered by the artist's family seventy five years later.

*Left:* The cover of Stalin's book, *On Lenin and Leninism,* published in Moscow in 1924 after the author had organised his subject's body to be safely sealed in the sarcophagus. Whilst Lenin was alive, Stalin slavishly followed his every word. In 1917 his master rewarded him with the post of Commissar of Nationalities. Later the Central Committee made him boss of "Rabkrin" (the Workers' and Peasants' Inspectorate), a gigantic bureaucracy that severely hampered economic growth after the Civil War. Stalin filled it with toadies who were answerable only to their boss – Stalin. In 1922 Stalin also became General Secretary of the Central Committee of the Communist Party (another bureaucratic post). With each quiet step Stalin acquired a little more power and a lot more ruthlessness. By the time Lenin started to get seriously worried about the "wonderful Georgian" (as he had called him back in 1903), it was too late. Lenin's high blood pressure, migraines, his nervous fits and, after each stroke, his increasing loss of speech made it impossible for him to carry out his plan to have "rude" Stalin removed from office. After Lenin's death the real political battle, the outcome of which was to destroy all hope of building a decent socialist society in Soviet Russia, began in earnest. Stalin's vendetta against Trotsky was motivated by intense personal jealousy. Stalin was no theoretician. He was a poor orator, his speeches turgid in both form and content. Trotsky described him as the "most distinguished mediocrity in our Party". Stalin created a network of opportunistic political alliances to make the Party his own. He packed it with hundreds of thousands of new members, political illiterates who shared little with the "Old Bolsheviks". Stalin was nothing more than a bureaucrat, but one who would later murder millions.

*Top:* A formidable Nadezhda Krupskaya, Lenin's widow, portrayed by I. Rabichev, in *Krasnaya Niva* (Red Field) magazine celebrating International Women's Day, March 8, 1925.

*Above:* A confident Stalin, General Secretary of the Central Committee of the Russian Communist Party, also portrayed by Rabichev in *Prozhektor* magazine, June 20, 1924.

Krupskaya hated Stalin for his extreme rudeness. Stalin had viciously threatened and cursed Krupskaya when Lenin was very ill, accusing her (ridiculously) of neglecting her husband's health. Lenin responded to this by adding the famous postscript to his last will and testament, demanding Stalin's removal from the post of General Secretary ("Stalin is too rude... "). Stalin had it suppressed.

Krupskaya later joined the Leningrad Opposition in trying to stop Stalin from seizing power.

*Right:* The full force of Lenin's fury is depicted by the Ukrainian artist Adolf Strakhov on the cover of *The Life of Lenin is the Story of the RKP* (Russian Communist Party), Ukraine, November 1924.

Красная Газета

*Opposite page:* "The Eternal Leader of October – Lenin – Has Shown Us the Path to Victory. Long Live Leninism". A poster published in 1924 in Moscow on the seventh anniversary of the October Revolution. Artist unknown.

*Left:* Lenin seems intent on leaving the planet in Nikolai Kochergin's front page drawing for the broadsheet newspaper *Krasnaya Gazeta* (Red Gazette), published in Leningrad, 1927.

In real life Lenin was a modest and hard-working man who hated anything to do with the personality cult. John Reed described his appearance at the time of the October Revolution: "A short, stocky figure, with a big head set down in his shoulders, bald and bulging. Little eyes, a snubbish nose, wide, generous mouth, and heavy chin... Dressed in shabby clothes, his trousers much too long for him." Lenin sometimes was appalled when he read about himself in the Soviet press: "It is shameful to read... All our lives we have waged an ideological struggle against the glorification of the personality... and suddenly here again is a glorification of the individual!" (He also raged with fury when the *Communist International* ran an article in which a French comrade described him as "a guillotine who thinks"). Whilst he was alive most of the adulation Lenin received, whether he liked it or not, was from the grass roots and probably well meant. The real Lenin cult began immediately after his death and it was orchestrated by Stalin. Towns and factories were renamed. Museums full of paintings and sculpture devoted to the earthly life of "Lenin the Immortal" sprang up all over the land. The Lenin poster, the badge, the Lenin pictorial album (sometimes almost too heavy to lift), the "Lenin Corner" (after the devotional icon corner of the peasants), huge Lenin monuments...
All this was part of Stalin's plan; the Lenin cult laid the foundations for the Stalin cult that was to supercede it. In the 1930s, Stalin would stand where Lenin had once stood and become known as "The Lenin of Today".

The front and back cover design by Gustav Klutsis for the large-format album, *In Memory of our Fallen Leaders*, published in Moscow, 1927. Among the contributors, Bukharin and Stalin remember Lenin; Yakov Peters, a particularly sadistic Chekist, warms to Felix Dzerzhinsky, his one-time boss; and Nadezhda Krupskaya writes about the life of Inessa Armand, including her friendship with Lenin.

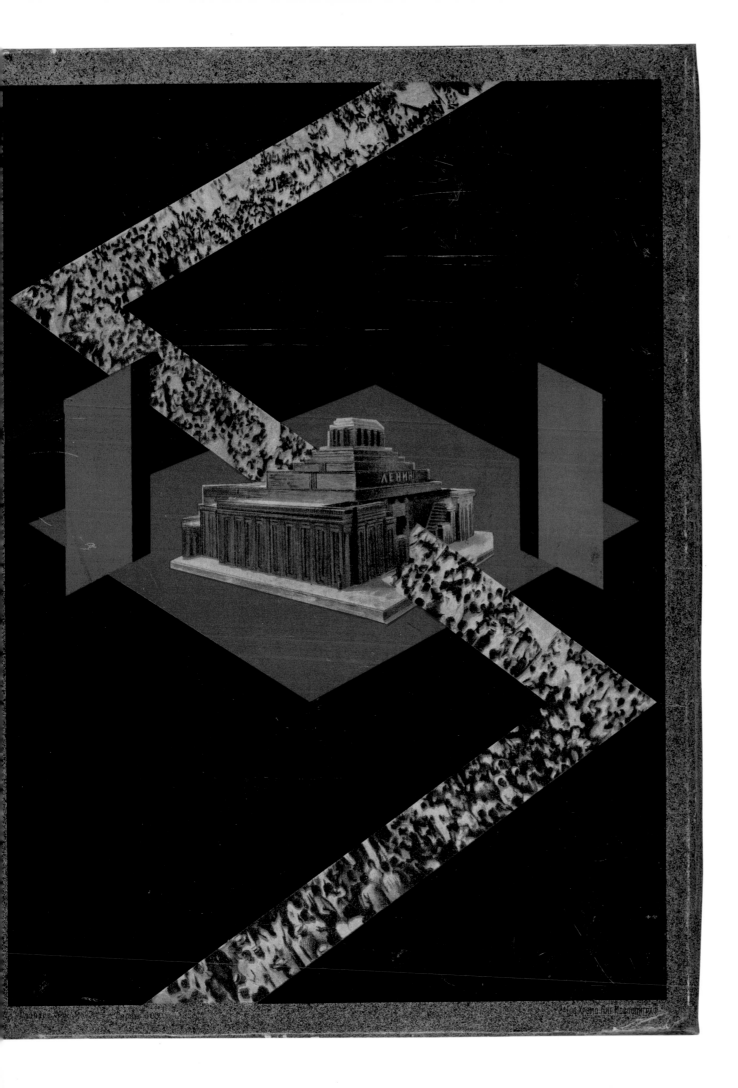

161

*Opposite page: Krokodil* magazine ridicules Zinoviev, Trotsky and Kamenev, leaders of the Left Opposition against Stalin, in November 1927. Trotsky is the organ-grinder, Kamenev the parrot and Zinoviev the chanteuse: "We play and play but nobody listens!" Caricature by K.Eliseyev.

Trotsky and Zinoviev were expelled from the Communist Party on November 14, 1927. Zinoviev soon recanted and, with Kamenev, deserted the Opposition; Trotsky, his wife Natalya and elder son Leon Sedov faced exile, first to Alma Ata in Central Asia and later, in February 1929, from Soviet territory altogether.

*Top left:* Trotsky, Kamenev and Zinoviev with Oppositionists in happier times.

*Top right:* Trotsky, dressed in white, sitting next to Joseph Gothon-Lunion, a young lawyer and leader of the Communist Party of Guadeloupe. Next to him, smoking a cigarette, is Nguyen Ai Quoc, later known worldwide as Ho Chi Minh, leader of the Vietnamese people's victorious war of liberation. This very rare photograph was taken at the Fifth Congress of the Comintern in Moscow, 1924. It was Ho's first visit to the Soviet Union. He found the Soviets' attitude to the class struggle in Vietnam a disappointment. The Vietnamese masses were criticised for being "politically inert" and lacking any coherent leadership. The Soviets were also far more preoccupied with the power struggle for Lenin's successor. Ho wrote an exposé for *Prozhektor* magazine entitled "Lynching in the USA" while he was in Moscow.

*Above:* "Lenin and Art". A double-page spread in *Krasnaya Niva* magazine from January 1925, documenting the latest contributions by Soviet sculptors to the Lenin cult on the first anniversary of his death.

"The Emancipated Woman is Building Socialism". A poster by Adolf Strakhov. Kharkov, 1926.
Strakhov portrays the politicised woman factory worker as an integral part of the class struggle. Soviet communist policy,
overwhelmingly decided by men, opposed the idea of an independent women's liberation movement.

"Cooperatives are the Path to Socialism". A calendar for 1927. Artist unknown.
The contrast between this hallucination of a lovingly-protected land of peace and plenty and Strakhov's
powerful "rabotnitsa" on the opposite page could not be more pronounced.

*Above:* A double-page illustration by Dmitrii Moor, published in the satirical anti-religious journal *Bezbozhnik u Stanka* (Godless at the Workbench), Moscow, 1923. The text underneath the drawing helps to explain the scene: "This is what happens in the backyard of our landlord, God the father, creator of heaven and earth, of all that is visible and invisible."

*Bezbozhnik u Stanka* was edited by Maria Kostelevskaya, an activist in the Moscow Communist Party whose confrontational style became known by her detractors as "clergy eating". Dmitrii Moor, the great poster artist of the Civil War period, art directed the magazine from its beginning in 1923 and, with the help of his many comrades in caricature, was able to keep up a never-ending visual assault in full colour against the enemies of atheism.

Kostelevskaya was wholly dedicated to the "establishment of an anti-religious proletarian dictatorship of the atheistic city over the countryside" but her past friendship with Trotsky led to conflict with the pro-Stalinist Soviet Anti-religious Commission and in 1931 the journal was closed down.

*Top left:* A full-page illustration by Mikhail Cheremnykh entitled "The Holy Ghost bestowing precious gifts on the apostles", published in *Bezbozhnik u Stanka* in 1923.

*Top centre:* Two Muscovites enjoying another anti-religious propaganda journal in 1929.

*Top right:* A 1930 poster version of Cheremnyk's "apostles" caricature. Now a slovenly group of religious personages are seen grovelling for the cash.

*Opposite page:* The destruction of the Saint Simonov Monastery in Moscow, 1927. Lenin had once described religion as "a sort of spiritual booze in which the slaves of capital could drown their human image."

167

The Bolsheviks realised that in parallel with their planned destruction of religion, new forms of ceremony would have to be introduced that appealed to the mystical and ritualistic needs of large sections of the Russian population. Baptism, for example, was replaced in the 1920s by "Oktyabrina" (literally Octobering), where young children were "consecrated into the cause of communism".
In one such ceremony (*top left*), a Moscow family pose for the camera with a local

Party official who has just enrolled their newly-born "into the ranks of our international proletarian army". The banner replaces the icon.
*Above left:* A Russian Orthodox church is used as a grain store, 1927.
Creches (*top*) and education for all children (*centre*) up to the age of fourteen allowed the time for workers to attend study groups at their local clubs (*above*).
*Opposite page:* The Young Communist leader of a shock workers' brigade, 1924.

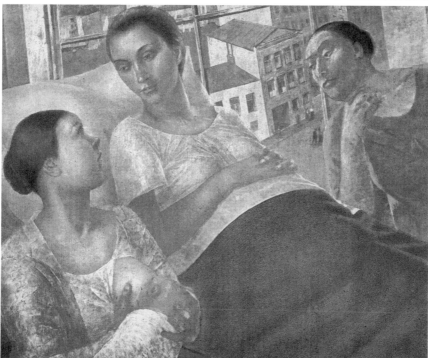

*Krasnaya Niva* (Red Field) was a mass circulation weekly journal of literature and art started in Petrograd in 1923. The editor-in-chief was Anatolii Lunacharsky, the Commissar of Education and Enlightenment. He was joined on the editorial board by Vyacheslav Polonsky who had been very influential in organising and publishing the work of the great Bolshevik political poster artists during the Civil War.

Lunacharsky's aim as Commissar was to educate and encourage Soviet workers and peasants to enjoy and participate in the rich new cultural life of the 1920s.

To help this the magazine regularly printed large-format reproductions in colour of paintings and graphics by Russian and foreign artists. Lunacharsky and Polonsky presided over this successful mass education project, radical for its time, until 1930, when Stalin's grip on cultural matters began to tighten.

*Opposite page:* Cover of the 1927 New Year's edition of *Krasnaya Niva* by Rudolf Frentz.

*Above:* Vasilii Rozhdestvensky's painting, "The Harvest" reproduced in *Krasnaya Niva*, October 9, 1927.

*Left:* Kuzma Petrov-Vodkin's painting, "Maternity", from *Krasnaya Niva*, May Day, 1927.

As well as works by Soviet artists, reproductions of paintings by Renoir, Cezanne, Gauguin and others were also published, and the magazine commissioned some covers from Diego Rivera, the left-wing Mexican painter and muralist.

171

*Above:* "Peasant Women Bleaching Linen". Zinaida Serebryakova's painting reproduced in *Krasnaya Niva*, April 10, 1927.
*Right:* "Young Communists", a painting by Sergei Bogdanov, from *Krasnaya Niva*, March 4, 1928.

*Left:* Konstantin Yuon's painting, "In the Fields", reproduced on the cover of *Krasnaya Niva*, August 21, 1927.
*Opposite page:* "In Adzharia", a painting by Fyodor Antonov for the cover of *Krasnaya Niva*, November 30, 1930.

«В. Аджарии» рисунок худ. Ф. Антонова.          Издание «Известия ЦИК СССР и ВЦИК», 1930 г.

Martiros Saryan's painting, "In Armenia" on the cover of *Krasnaya Niva*, September 15, 1929. *Opposite page:* Another Saryan cover for the August 22, 1926 issue.

Martiros Saryan, an Armenian, lived in Erevan. He established its Museum of Archeology and Ethnography, the School of Art and the Union of Armenian Painters.

تاتار خاتون - قزلارى!

روسيه شورالار حاكيمييتنده بولغان اوز
كوچى بلن كون كوروچى بار خاتون - قزلار صافينا
تزلورگ اومتلوكز!
روس خاتون - قزلارى بلن برگلاب سز
اوزكركزنڭ آقتى چلبرلاركزنى يمرارسز.

Женщина-татарка! Вступай в ряды всех тру-
жениц Советской России.
Об руку с русскими пролетарками ты разобьёшь
последние оковы.

Р. В. Ц.—Казань.   Кз. Отд. Госуд. Изд.   Напечатано   1000 эк.   Лит. 2-й Гос. типографии Казань.

*Left:* "The Nightmare of Future Wars – Workers of the World, Unite!" A poster from Azerbaijan, possibly for the cinema, 1920s. The text is in Tatar. Artist unknown.
*Top:* "Tatar Women! Join the Ranks of the Women Workers of Russia. Arm-in-arm with the Proletarian Women of Russia, You will Finally Break Off the Last Shackles". Text in Tatar and Russian. Kazan, 1920s, artist unknown.
*Above:* "Burning the Yashmak". A gravure from a cycle of prints entitled "Women in the Past and Present" by Alexei Kravchenko and published in 1928.

177

*Top:* "Long Live the Brotherhood of All the Peoples of the Caucasus", a lithograph by the artist Nikolai Kochergin, 1921.

*Above:* "Soviet Power is the Inviolable Pledge of the Union of Peasant and Worker". A poster by Kochergin also from 1921 with text in Georgian and Russian, published in Tbilisi. Menshevik revolutionaries had proclaimed a republic in Georgia in 1917 but in early 1921 the Red Army, under Sergo Ordzhonikidze and with Stalin's support, marched into Tbilisi. Stalin was fiercely opposed to the principle of self-determination for the nationalities of a future Soviet Union, preferring gross Russification. His repressive measures against the Georgian Communist Party boiled over when the physically powerful Ordzhonikidze punched Mdivani, the Georgian Communist champion of independence, in an argument about autonomy.

When Lenin heard the news about Ordzhonikidze's reckless behaviour towards a comrade his furious reaction contributed further to his already serious ill health.

*Right:* "Send Your Sons to the Red Army – The Best and Foremost". A poster by an unknown artist, signed "V.Ch.K", 1920s. Text in Turkmen.

*Left:* A tribal Turkman getting to grips with the difficulties of the Russian language, helped by his secular teacher.

The Turkmen Soviet Socialist Republic was formed in 1924–25 alongside the other new republics of Soviet Central Asia.

Within a few years, the Turkmen were feeling the effects of Stalin's policies and being encouraged by their comrades in Moscow to reject religion, dress in western-style clothes and exchange the Arabic script they had used for centuries for, initially, the Latin alphabet and then Cyrillic. Understandably they were often slow to acquiesce.

*Top:* "Women! Take Part in the Elections to the Soviets!" An Uzbek poster published in Tashkent in the 1920s. Artist unknown. Looking from left to right at this extraordinary poster, we see the gradual appearance of a woman's face from behind the veil, a ghostly response to the efforts of the imploring Uzbek communist in the foreground.

*Above left:* A poster by the artist Nikolai Kochergin, published in Moscow in 1921 in the Tatar language. Militant Soviet women workers are shown on the point of coming together with their Muslim sisters in a great sunburst of unity.

*Right:* Making banners at a Comintern Congress of Eastern Peoples in Baku, Azerbaijan, 1920. Moscow firmly rejected the arguments of their Muslim comrades who had suggested that the Muslim world had a different class structure and that their revolution could be led by petit-bourgeois nationalists.

*Left:* A poster designed by Iosif Gerasimovich for "The Mullah's Third Wife", a silent feature film directed by Vyacheslav Viskovsky in Leningrad for Sovkino in 1928.

A bitter criticism of the lack of freedom for women in the East, the film has since been lost but a short synopsis remains. The story is set in the first year of Soviet power. After the death of his wife, Ganyev (an old mullah), decides to marry her sister, the young and beautiful Aisha, in spite of the fact that Aisha is in love with Shakir, a student and member of the Komsomol (Communist League of Youth).

Aisha is forced to go through with the marriage to Ganyev but on the wedding night she runs away. Homeless, tired and exhausted from her ordeal, she is then raped by a rich merchant, Abdullah. She becomes pregnant. Aisha appeals for help to the Women's Section of the Communist Party which arranges for her to become a primary school teacher and later to have her child attend the local kindergarten. Ganyev and Abdullah hear about all this and conspire to get Aisha the sack. In desperate straits, Aisha writes a letter to Shakir who has now returned home having finished his studies at Saratov University. He marries his beloved Aisha and becomes the stepfather of her child.

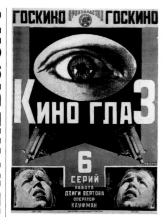

*Above:* Three cinema posters advertising the work of the innovative documentary film director, Dziga Vertov. From the top, Alexander Rodchenko's 1924 design for "Kino Glaz" (Cinema Eye); "Enthusiasm: Symphony of the Donbass", 1930, designer unknown; and spiralling out of control, "The Man with a Movie Camera" by the Stenberg Brothers, 1929.

*Right:* A multiple-image photograph taken at night in Moscow, May Day, 1928. The bright lights are calling: "Under the Rule of the Communist Party and its Central Committee, Forward to New Victories! Proletarians of all the World, Brothers in Class, Stand up under the Banner of the Leninist Comintern! Everyone Rise to the Defence of the Soviet Union".

In 1923, Sergei Eisenstein (*left*), published his first manifesto, entitled "The Montage of Attractions" in Mayakovsky's journal *LEF* (acronym for Left Front of the Arts). His theory stated that two opposing images could be put together to create a new, third image independent and more powerful than its sources. Montage used in this way has sometimes been seen as a graphic equivalent of Hegel's philosophy concerning thesis, antithesis and synthesis, beloved of Marxist dialecticians. Eisenstein's theory led to some of the most exciting counterpoints in cinematic history – a series of explosions on film, he called them. Close-up and longshot, cross-cutting image, sound, tempo, texture, mood, colour and tone; Eisenstein's ideas have influenced film directors, artists, designers and photographers ever since. He finished six films, all of them brilliant.

*Top:* A local cinema poster from Moscow in 1927 advertising "Oktyabr" (October), Eisenstein's film based on John Reed's book, *Ten Days That Shook the World*. It is thought that up to one third of the finished work was cut on Stalin's orders to eliminate the actors playing the parts of Trotsky and other revolutionaries in the film. Even a speech by Lenin was cut: "Lenin's liberalism is no longer valid," Stalin decreed.

*Above:* Another local cinema poster, also from Moscow, for Eisenstein's masterpiece, "Battleship Potemkin" (1925).

*Opposite page:* "Bella Donna", Alexander Naumov's glamorous cinema poster, Moscow, 1927. Starring Pola Negri, Adolphe Menjou and Conway Tearle, the film was directed by George Fitzmaurice in the USA. Foreign films, especially American, were hugely popular with Soviet audiences and brought in much needed revenue for the Soviet's own rapidly expanding film industry.
*Left:* "An Everyday Occurrence", a cinema poster designed by Georgii and Vladimir Stenberg, Moscow, 1927. The film tells the story of the merciless exploitation of a poor young peasant couple. A rich landowner attempts to rape the peasant's wife, then falsely denounces her as being a prostitute in an attempt to cover up his crime. Anna Sten starred as the peasant's wife and the film was directed by Fyodor Otsep.
*Above:* Two film stills showing Alexandra Exter's futuristic costumes and sets for "Aelita", a science fiction epic directed by Yakov Protazanov, Moscow, 1924. Otsep also worked on this film, writing the screenplay about two cosmonauts landing on Mars and starting a revolution.

*Above and continuing to page 193:*
Lazar "El" Lissitsky's unstoppable photomontage from the catalogue of the Soviet pavilion at "Pressa", the international press exhibition held in Cologne, Germany in 1928.

The original artwork was put together using installation photographs from Lissitsky's exhibition design. The photomontage is reproduced here over eight pages at about 85% of its final printed dimensions.

Huge rolling conveyor belts, revolving spirals and illuminated flashing spheres were constructed for the exhibit to give a powerful impression of how the Soviet press spoke to the newly-literate workers and peasants of the USSR.

El Lissitsky fought a long and heroic battle for most of his working life against tuberculosis. In spite of this he was probably the most prolific and certainly the greatest avant-garde designer, painter and three-dimensional artist ever to work in the Soviet Union.

Also continuing to page 193, below Lissitsky's photomontage, are other examples of graphic design from this intensively creative period.

*Below: Elephants in the Komsomol.*
Poems by Vladimir Mayakovsky, Moscow 1931.
Cover design by El Lissitsky.

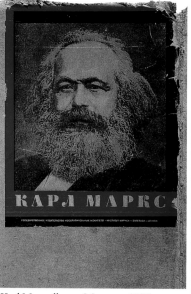

*Karl Marx* album, Moscow, 1933.
Cover designed by El Lissitsky.

*Russland* (Russia) by El Lissitsky, Vienna, 1930. Lissitsky's illustrated book on the reconstruction of architecture in the Soviet Union, for which he also designed the cover.

*Proletarian Students*, No.2, 1923.
Cover by Gustav Klutsis, Moscow.

*Student Revolution*, No. 7, 1925.
Journal published in Kharkov, Ukraine.
Cover designed by Adolf Strakhov.

*Below:* Back and front cover of the
journal *Rost*, No.21. Moscow, 1932.
Designer unknown.

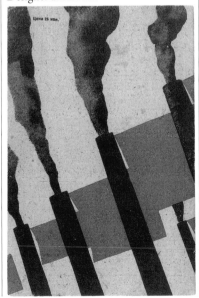

*Painting and Photography* by Moholy-Nagy. Moscow, 1929.
Russian edition of Moholy-Nagy's famed *Bauhaus Book* No.8,
first published in Munich in 1925.

*Lef Propaganda*, Moscow, 1925. Poetry
by Mayakovsky, Aseyev and Tretyakov.
Agit-notes by Alexei Kruchenykh.
Cover by Valentina Kulagina-Klutsis.

*Below:* Back and front cover of the
journal *Revolutionary East*, No.2, 1927.
Published in Moscow by the University
of the Working People's of the East in
the name of I.V. Stalin.
Cover designer/illustrator unknown.

*Below:* Back and front cover of *Cinema and Revolution* by Willi Munzenburg, Moscow, 1925.
Cover designed by V. Trivas. Munzenberg was the founder of the German Communist Party and was famous throughout the 1920s and 30s for his leading role in the fight against fascism. He fell out of favour with Stalin in 1938 and died in mysterious circumstances – his body found hanging in a forest – in 1940.

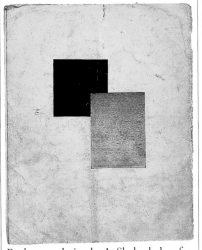

Back cover design by A. Shcherbakov for *The Krassin in the Ice* by Yem Mindlin, Moscow, 1930.

Alexander Rodchenko's cover design for the catalogue of the Soviet pavilion at the International Exhibition of Decorative Arts held in Paris in 1925.

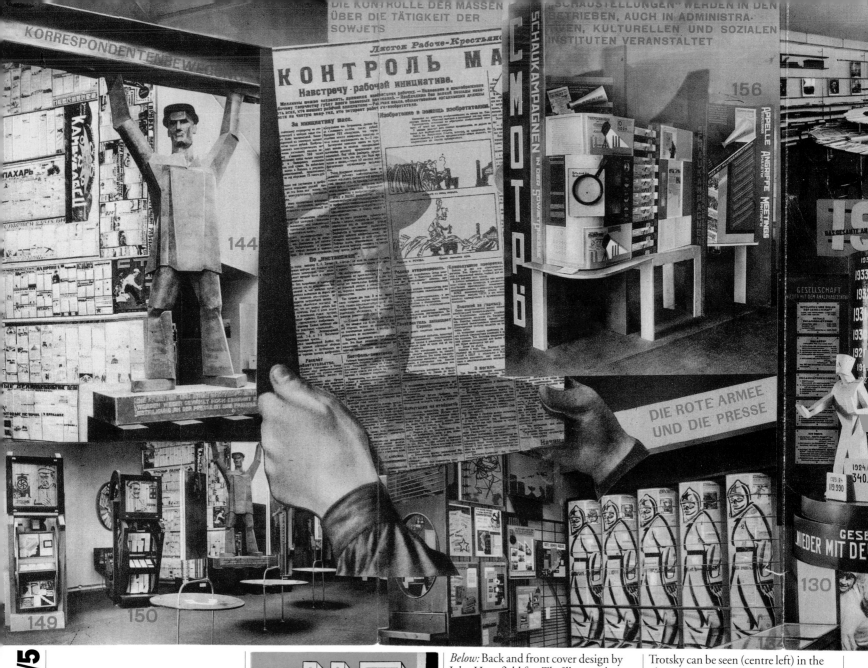

Baggage label for the Evropeiskii Hotel, Leningrad, 1920s. Designer unknown.

*Not a Fellow Traveller* by Osip Brik, 1923. Published by LEF, Moscow/Petrograd. Cover design by Anton Lavinsky.

*Below:* Back and front cover design by John Heartfield for *The Illustrated History of the Russian Revolution*, published as a weekly partwork series in 1927 by Willi Munzenberg at Neue Deutscher Verlag, Berlin.
The quote from Lenin on the back cover reads: "Revolution is the locomotive of world history." A picture of Leon Trotsky can be seen (centre left) in the photomontage on the back cover. His downfall was taking place at the same time as the publication of the first few issues of the partwork, and the back cover was soon replaced by a bland advertisement.

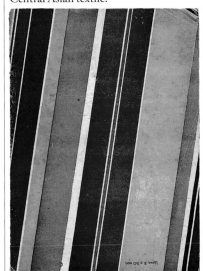

*Below:* "Uzbekistan, Turkmenistan, Tadjikistan 1924–1934".
Back and front cover of a special issue of *Ogonyek* magazine. N. Zhukov and S. Melnikov's design is based on a Central Asian textile.

*Above:* El Lissitsky's poster for the Russian Exhibition held in Zurich in 1929. The somewhat unnerving image of the fused heads in the poster is taken from the original photograph next to it

of two "young Leninists" at a rally in Moscow. Lissitsky has reversed the picture left to right and dissolved the two faces together using montage and the airbrush.

VÖLKERSCHAFTEN
IN DER UdSSR

DAS BUCH DEN MASSEN

227

PRODUKTION DES STAATS

85 ZEITSCHRIFTEN REDAKTIONST

225

226

DIE ERZIEHUNG DER MASSEN
IST DIE HAUPTAUFGABE DER
PRESSE IN DER ÜBERGANGSZEIT
VOM KAPITALISMUS ZUM
KOMMUNISMUS

115

*Below:* Young photographer, 1931. Photographer unknown.

*Below:* "Rabotnitsa" (Woman Worker) by Liubov Mileyeva. A postcard from Leningrad, 1927.

О. МАНДЕЛЬШТАМ

КАМЕНЬ

ГОСИЗДАТ

*Above:* Kamen (Stone) by Osip Mandelstam. Poetry written between 1908–15. Published by "Gosizdat", the State Publishing House, in 1923.

*Below:* "The Wandering Musicians". Self portrait by Alexander Rodchenko with his wife, the artist and designer Varvara Stepanova. Moscow, 1922.

192

UNION DER
SOZIALISTISCHEN
SOWJETREPUBLIKEN
PRESSA
KÖLN

*Below: From Cezanne to Suprematism* by Kazimir Malevich. Published by the People's Commissariat of the Enlightenment (Narkompros) in 1923.

*Below:* Front and back cover of Ilya Ehrenburg's novel, *The Loves of Jeanne Ney,* published in Moscow in 1924 by Rossiya. Designer unknown.

*Above: Rabis,* No.3, 1933. A theatrical journal published in Moscow. The issue is devoted to the memory of Karl Marx on the 50th anniversary of his death. The photomontage shows Marx, Lenin and Stalin in descending order.

193

VIVE LA COOPÉRATION OUVRIÈRE !

ES LEBE DIE ARBEITER-KONSUMGENOSSENSCHAFT-BEWEGUNG!

МЕЖДУНАРОДНЫЙ ДЕНЬ КООПЕРАЦИИ

КООПЕРАЦИЯ СССР

В МЕЖДУНАРОДНЫЙ ДЕНЬ КООПЕРАЦИИ
УКРЕПИМ СВЯЗЬ СОВЕТСКОЙ КООПЕРАЦИИ
С РАБОЧЕЙ КООПЕРАЦИЕЙ ВО ВСЕМ МИРЕ

"International Cooperation Day: Let us strengthen the link between Soviet cooperatives and workers' cooperatives all over the world". A poster from Moscow, 1929. Artist unknown. Most producer cooperatives had been nationalised in 1918 but under NEP they were allowed to resume operating independently. Tight government controls were imposed once more in 1929.

"Bread to the Factories – They produce hundreds of thousands of harvesters,
seeders, ploughs, tractors, harrows and tonnes of fertilizer – Peasants Strengthen the Power of our Factories".
Poster by Nikolai Kogout, Moscow, 1929.

Lenin's great plan for the electrification of Russia was ratified by the Eighth Congress of Soviets held in Moscow at the Bolshoi Theatre in December 1920, at a time when the country was in a state of chaos and ruin caused by the Civil War and resulting famine. The GOELRO plan (State Commission for the Electrification of Russia) envisaged major advances in industry based on new technology, electrification to link the towns with the countryside so as to end their cultural division, and the complete eradication of ignorance, poverty, disease and barbarism. It was accomplished in about twelve years.

Lenin's famous slogan, "Communism is Soviet Power Plus the Electrification of the Whole Country" became, with a number of variations, a powerful inspiration for many Soviet poster designers, film makers, composers, writers and artists.

*Opposite page:* A poster from 1924 by Alexander Samokhvalov portrays Lenin as the master of ceremonies of hydroelectricity. The message reads, "Soviets and Electrification – This is the Foundation of the New World."

*Top left:* Manufacturing non-conducting porcelain parts for Soviet pylons, 1920s.

*Top right:* "Volkhovstroi Gives Current!" A 1925 poster celebrating the opening of the first of thirty new power plants.

*Above:* The electrification of Lenin. A contribution in neon to the Lenin cult, 1936.

*Overleaf:* El Lissitsky's dynamic photomontage illustration on the GOELRO theme published in the photographic album, *The USSR is Building Socialism*, Moscow, 1933.

КОММУНИЗМ—Э
ПЛЮС ЭЛЕКТРИ

КАРТА
СТРОИТЕЛЬСТВА
ПО ПЛАНУ
ГОЭЛРО

СССР

*Above:* Six front covers from *Stroim* (Building), a large format journal devoted to Soviet industry. Its layout, a weekly bombardment of constructivist typography combined with photographs, montage and duotone printing, was a great example of late avant-garde graphic design dovetailing perfectly with its heavyweight subject matter. The paper was art directed in its early years by Vladimir Stranich and published from the time of the First Five-Year Plan until the late-1930s. The First Five-Year Plan (1928–1932) was the beginning of Stalin's attempt to put his distinctly un-Marxist theory of "Socialism in One Country" into practice. Regarding the world proletarian revolution with suspicion and as something that should, at best, be totally subservient to Moscow, Stalin turned his back on the struggles of working people throughout the world. His aim instead was to concentrate on transforming the economically backward Soviet Union into a gigantic industrial power capable of overtaking the mighty outputs of the major capitalist countries. The Five-Year Plans were to continue (except during the war years) until the demise of the Soviet Union itself. Inevitably the Soviet statisticians' hopes were far too optimistic, yet the plans' results were invariably greeted with great enthusiasm.

*Opposite page: Stroim*'s addition to the theme of the electrification of Lenin can be seen in this montage celebrating the twelfth anniversary of the October Revolution. In Soviet Russia the light bulb was widely known as "Ilyich's Lamp" and Lenin's head here suffers a claustrophobic mummification.

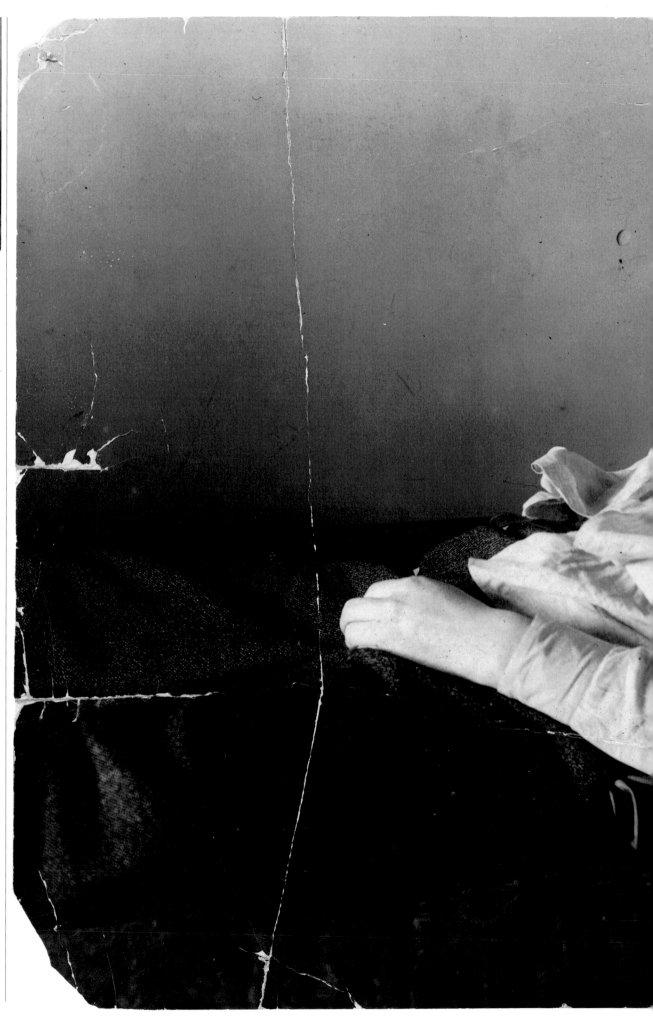

The hand writing in pencil on the back of the photograph (*right*) simply gives the date and time: "14/IV-30... 10h 15m."

"Never blame him. Things were beyond his control," grieved more than one of his lovers. An old Futurist friend murmured that, as with the Russian aristocracy, he had been presented with a pistol and a shoe box. It meant death or humiliation; commit suicide or lose your good name.

Another lover and close friend tried to rationalise it: "The idea of suicide was like a chronic disease inside him... and it worsened under circumstances that, for him, were undesirable."

He had put on a clean, light blue shirt just an hour or so before. Now his body lay stiff, eyes shut, mouth wide open, on the print-covered ottoman, his head flat back on an antique rug. His trademark bow tie lay on his thick neck, disconsolate. Sitting uneasily around the body in the room were friends and associates; uneasy because they rarely associated with one another, only him. Shoulders shaking. Silent sobbing.

Thinking back: "A handsome young man with a gloomy expression... overflowing with lethal and incessant cleverness."

Poet, Futurist, propagandist – Vladimir Mayakovsky had shot himself through the heart: "If you like, I'll be furious flesh elemental, Or changing to tones that the sunset arouses, If you like, I'll be extremely gentle, not a man, but a cloud in trousers."

*Top:* The Futurist in 1914, at the age of 21.

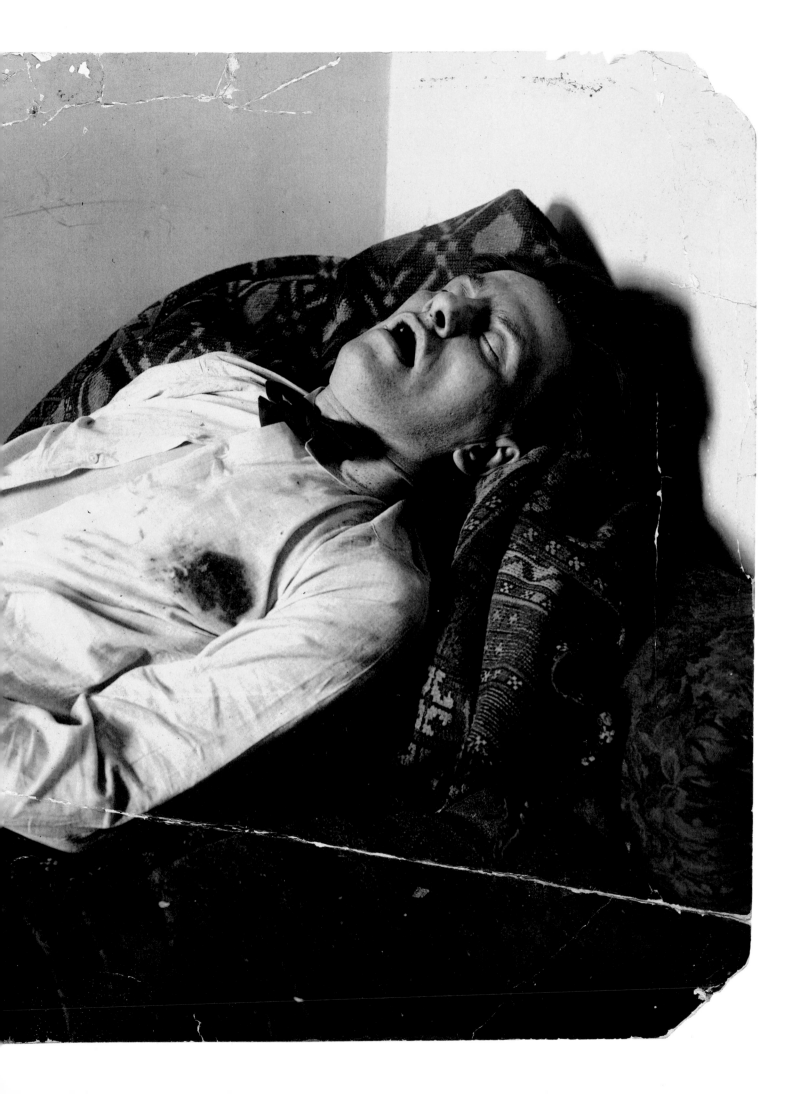

Stalin threw down the photographs on the floor: "Moisei Solomonovich," he growled in fury, "My tunic has come out too creased! Why didn't you remove the creases? I look anything but military!" This was in 1930. The tall, distinguished 61-year-old photographer (*above*) had portrayed every high-ranking Bolshevik and Stalinist from Lenin downwards. Moisei Nappelbaum was now down on his knees grovelling on the carpet, hands shaking, trying to retrieve his prints. One of them can be seen on the *opposite page*; for once Stalin might have had a point. It was also a bad idea to show the "Leader and Teacher" reading with his index finger when the campaign for literacy was in full swing.

Away from the Kremlin, Nappelbaum photographed Russia's intelligentsia. Chaliapin, Blok, Akhmatova, Tatlin, Meyerhold, Esenin, David Oistrakh and countless others all sat for him.

So did Boris Pasternak, who Nappelbaum photographed from the poet's early days (*shown right*) until his death.

Nappelbaum longed for an album of his work to be published. The Soviet authorities found this problematical. So many people he had portrayed over the years had become "enemies of the people" and the list was always lengthening.

In 1958, five years after Stalin's death, Nappelbaum finally got his wish but sadly he died, aged 89, before *From Craft into Art* was printed.

For months afterwards the complete print run of the book lay undisturbed in the printer's warehouse. The reason? The authorities shouted one name – Pasternak! His novel, *Doctor Zhivago*, frowned on by the regime but published to great acclaim in the West, had just won the Nobel Prize. He was forced to renounce it and was expelled from the Writers' Union in a public campaign of vilification ("Pig under an oak tree", "Foreigner and traitor").

After Pasternak's portrait had been torn out of all 20,000 copies, Nappelbaum's book was published. Placed in each copy of the book was this statement: "Correction. Technical difficulties in the publication of this edition of the album caused an error in the sequential order of the page numbers."

"Under the Banner of Lenin for Socialist Construction". Photomontage poster designed by Gustav Klutsis, 1930.
Stalin's shadowy face looms menacingly behind an unsuspecting Lenin.
Klutsis' photomontage perfectly illustrates the moment of metamorphosis from the Lenin cult to the Stalin cult.

Gustav Klutsis' 1931 poster depicts the Politburo heading a column of the world's workers. The montage follows the shape of the Dniepr Dam.
Front row, left to right: Voroshilov, Molotov, Stalin, Kaganovich, Ordzhonikidze. Second row: Kalinin, Kuibyshev, Rudzutak, Kossior, Kirov. Third row, centre: Andreyev.
Before the end of the decade, Kirov had been assassinated, Rudzutak and Kossior shot, and Ordzhonikidze had committed suicide.

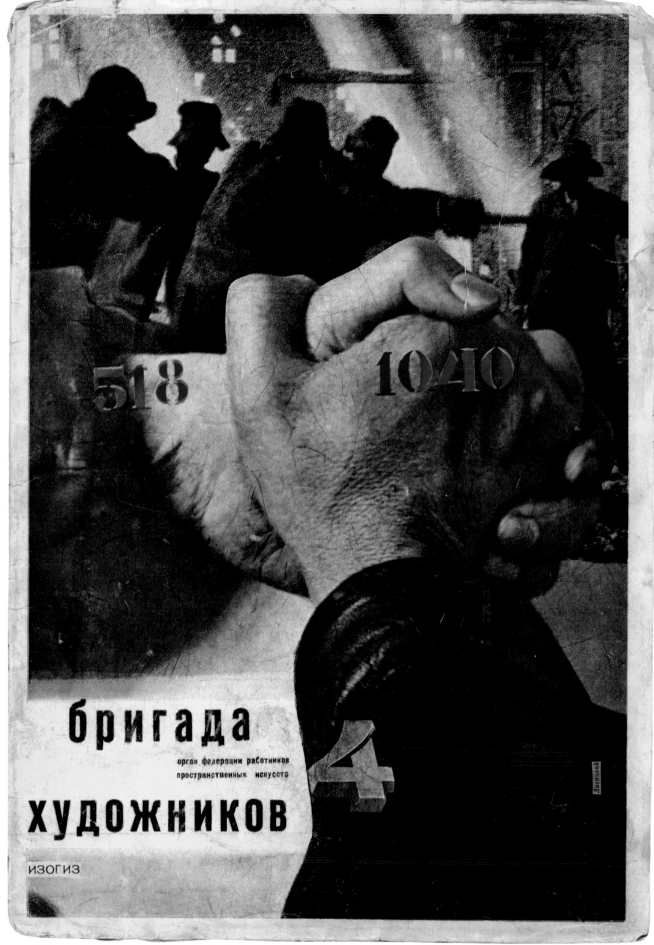

El Lissitsky's photomontage cover design for *Brigade of Artists*, No.4, 1931, the journal of the "Federated Workers of Spatial Arts".
*Brigade of Artists* only lasted for seven issues. It published informative articles
on subjects relating to agitational propaganda and monographs on the artists and designers involved.

Gustav Klutsis' back cover for *Brigade of Artists*, No.1, 1931. A rougher, more exciting version of his famous photomontage poster.
The slogan reads, "Workers and Women Workers – Everyone for the Re-election of the Soviets".
"Comrade Klutsis" is praised by the editors: "We note artistic force and political conviction. The best poster of the election campaign."

*Above:* "Industrialisation is the Path to Socialism". A poster by Adolf Strakhov from 1928.

*Top:* "Fulfill the Five-Year Industrial–Financial Plan in Four Years". A poster by Yakov Guminer from 1931.

*Right:* Designers working for the "Dinamo" forge and cast iron foundry painting banners for a "5 in 4" mass demonstration in Moscow, circa 1930. With the First Five-Year Plan came a new direction in visual propaganda. Gone was the depiction of the revolutionary worker, soldier and peasant slaying the fat capitalist in the posters of the Civil War period, and going was the productivist graphic and typographic design of the 1920s. The new approach was to show, often in montage and photomontage, images of skilled workers in the vanguard of Soviet agriculture and industry, their labour scrutinised from on high by an increasingly authoritarian leadership always demanding the Plan be finished a year ahead of time.

ПРОЛЕТАРИИ ВСЕХ СТРАН, СОЕДИНЯЙТЕСЬ!

НАЧАТОЕ СОВЕТСКОЙ ВЛАСТЬЮ ДЕЛО МОЖЕТ БЫТЬ ЗАКОНЧЕНО ТОЛЬКО ТОГДА, КОГДА В НЕМ ПРИМУТ УЧАСТИЕ МИЛЛИОНЫ И МИЛЛИОНЫ РАБОТНИЦ И КРЕСТЬЯНОК.

ДОРОГОЙ ИЛЬИЧ! МЫ ПОМНИМ ТВОИ ЗАВЕТЫ.

DAS NEUE RUSS LAND

ZEITSCHRIFT FÜR KULTUR WIRTSCHAFT UND LITERATUR

HEFT 1 / 5. JAHRG. / 1928
PREIS: 0.80 MARK

ПУСТЬ ГОСПОДСТВУЮЩИЕ КЛАССЫ СОДРО- ГАЮТСЯ ПРЕД КОММУНИСТИЧЕСКОЙ РЕВОЛЮЦИЕЙ

1917   1922

ГЛАВНЫЙ ДОКЛАДНИК ПЯТИЛЕТИЯ   4го КОНГРЕССА О РЕВОЛЮЦИИ

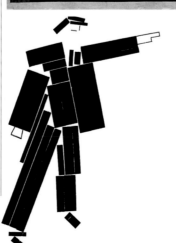

1870-1924

*Opposite page:* "From NEP Russia will come Socialist Russia (Lenin)". Gustav Klutsis' photomontage poster from 1930 shows a gigantic Lenin purposefully striding forward against a background of the Dniepr Dam in construction. Klutsis' depiction of the late leader was based, like the other images shown here, on a photograph (*top left*) taken by Pyotr Otsup on October 16, 1918 in the grounds of the Kremlin. It was the first time Lenin had been photographed since the attempt on his life seven weeks earlier. Lenin looks a bit frail; two bullets were still lodged in his upper body. No photographs were taken of him raising his arm that day – he left that to the artists...

*Above left:* Anatolii Sokolov's illustration on the front page of a Baku newspaper celebrating the fifth anniversary of the Revolution, 1922.

*Top centre:* An unsigned poster from Moscow, 1924, shows "Ilyich" in roughly the same avuncular pose and mobbed by adoring women. The sun rises dramatically over the smokestacks behind him.

*Above centre:* Adolf Strakhov's famous poster (also from 1924) presents Lenin in a much more determined manner at the forefront of the October Revolution.

*Top right:* A touching contribution from *Das Neue Russland*, a journal published in Weimar Germany until Hitler came to power. Lenin has lost his cap. Cover by John Heartfield.

*Above right:* Sergei Merkurov's maquette for a giant Lenin monument, 1930s. Made after the Klutsis poster, at the height of Socialist Realism, and numbingly stylised.

*Left:* Lev Kovalev's contribution of genius to the Lenin Cult, made in metal from the printer's tray, Kiev, 1924.

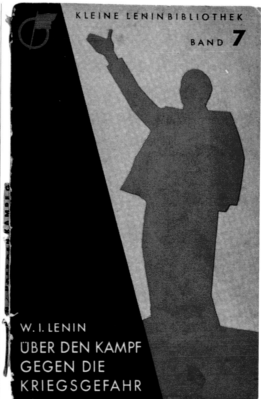

*Above centre:* Lenin making a speech on May Day, 1919, from Lobnoye Mesto, a round stone dias in Red Square, Moscow, used as a place of execution in the sixteenth and seventeenth centuries. Lenin was unveiling a monument to Stepan Razin, leader of the greatest peasant rebellion of the seventeenth century, put to death there in 1671. The photograph was taken by G.P. Goldshtein.

During the speech, Lenin looked forward to the final victory of Soviet power all over the world: "The majority of those here today are no older than 30 to 35 years of age. They will live to see the full bloom of communism, from which we are still remote. Our grandchildren will examine the documents and other relics of the epoch of the capitalist system with

amazement. It will be difficult for them to picture how the trade in articles of primary necessity could remain in private hands, how factories could belong to individuals, how some men could exploit others, how those who did not work could continue to exist."
On the subject of freedom Lenin concluded: "The best of the proletarians and peasants – the freedom fighters – perished, but they did not do so in the fight for the sort of freedom that capital offers; freedom in which the banks, private factories and profiteering are retained. Down with such freedom! What we need is real freedom and that is possible only when society consists entirely of working people. To achieve such freedom much labour and many sacrifices will be required. We shall do everything possible to achieve

that great aim, to build socialism." (Stormy applause). Goldshtein's photograph also became a rallying point – for artists and designers. The image has been used in a thousand ways, six of which are shown here.
*Top left: Young Guard.* A 1924 cover by Gustav Klutsis.
*Top centre:* Lenin in silhouette on a German pamphlet.
*Top right:* A poster for the New York release of Mikhail Romm's Mosfilm production, "Lenin in October".
*Above left:* Goldshtein's image is reversed left to right for the cover of *Krasnaya Sibiryachka* (Red Siberian) magazine, November 1932.
*Above right:* Lenin in Samarkand, late 1920s.
*Opposite page:* "We are Building a Fleet of Airships in the Name of Lenin". A poster by Georgii Kibardin from 1931 with text in old-style Azerbaijanian.

"He's been silent for three days now. He speaks to no one. He is a particularly difficult person." Towards the end of her marriage Nadezhda Alliluyeva, Stalin's wife, had to endure her husband's terrible mood swings. Sullenness would turn to rage; those who witnessed them were shocked at the obscenities he yelled at her. When she wasn't at the mercy of catastrophic and undiagnosed headaches she could fight back: "You're a butcher! You torture your own son, torment your wife, and you have tortured the whole of your nation to death!"

*Right:* The last photograph ever taken of Nadezhda Alliluyeva. "Citizen, you should not do that," she told the newsman. She is seen leaving the Industrial Academy in Moscow where she had enrolled as a student in textile manufacturing to escape her depressing marriage and the claustrophobic world of motherhood to Svetlana and Vasilii in the Kremlin.

Nobody heard the shot on the night of November 8, 1932. There had been a dinner party in their good friend Voroshilov's Kremlin apartment. Stalin, with his moods, his deformed hand, his yellowed teeth, his pockmarked skin and his foul manners had recently embarked upon a series of casual affairs. Tonight he was flirting with a glamorous actress. Feeling humiliated, Nadezhda hit the roof. Reacting to his insults she threw down her glass and left. The next morning she was found dead in her room with a gun next to her and, it is rumoured, a suicide note attacking her husband, both personally and politically. Stalin's ashen response? "I was a bad husband. I did not have time to take her to the movies."

*Top:* Stalin and Nadezhda put on a show for the camera with the Voroshilovs and a guard on a summer's day. Georgia, 1930.

*Opposite page:* "The butcher" in contemplation, unretouched.

217

The atmosphere of fear and persecution felt in political circles opposed to Stalin as he tightened his grip on power in the late 1920s, engulfed a much wider audience by the turn of the decade. In a new world of rapid industrialisation and the forced collectivisation of agriculture, many ordinary workers and peasants (*top*), often politically illiterate, found themselves taking the blame (along with middle management) when the reality of Stalin's Plan refused to match the forecasts. The trials of "wreckers" in industry that ensued, like the Shakhty trial of 1928, or the "unmasking of conspirators" at the Promparty (Industrial Party) trial in 1930, were also dress rehearsals for what Stalin later had in mind. In the countryside, a war of attrition was started against the kulaks (so-called rich peasants) who were seen as a major threat to collectivisation. At least one million were brutally forced off their land and left to starve in the winter of 1929–30.

*Above left:* Workers demonstrate on a collective farm in 1929. Their banner reads, "Liquidate the Kulaks as a Class".
*Above right:* "Bash the Kulak off the Kolkhoz". A poster from 1930.
*Opposite page:* Hard labour in Soviet Central Asia. Uzbekistan, 1930.

*Left:* In 1931 Stalin gave his secret police, the OGPU, led by the sinister Genrikh Yagoda, the task of organising the construction of the Stalin-Belomor Canal linking the Baltic to the White Sea. Using slave labour, the project became a blueprint for the Gulag empire that was to follow. Tens of thousands of workers died building the canal, but on completion it was rarely used. It was too shallow for the ships and its wooden structure constantly needed repair. The canal's construction was glorified in a large-format book entitled *Kanal Imeni Stalina* (Canal in the name of Stalin), published in 1934. Its joint editorship was led by Maxim Gorky, Leopold Averbakh (a militant Socialist Realist theorist who Stalin later liquidated) and Semyon Firin, who was the OGPU's onsite commander. Many photographs in the book show prisoners working in extreme sub-zero conditions. Soon after publication the censors decided the book should be banned.

*Top:* "Ten Years of Komi". A poster by V. Malakhov from 1931 celebrating the Komi Autonomous Region, a vast territory in north east Russia rich in oil, coal and wood. In the 1930s many infamous Gulags of the Stalin era were located here including Ukhtapechorlag, Sevlag and Vorkuta.

*Above:* The famine in Ukraine. The body count of Stalin's victims rose by millions in 1932–3. Forced collectivisation was followed by drought and bad harvests, and the secret police took mercilous retribution against peasants who hid their meagre stocks of grain from punitive expropriation. The resulting death by hunger ("holodomor" in Ukrainian), has often been described as genocide.

221

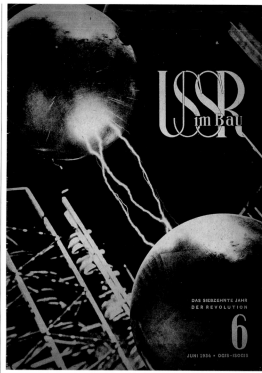

*USSR in Construction*, the legendary propaganda magazine, was published monthly in Moscow from January 1930 until May 1941. It was printed in four languages (Russian, English, French and German) and, for a short time, Spanish.

Stars of Soviet design and photography including El Lissitsky and Alexander Rodchenko contributed ground-breaking photo-graphics to promote the infinite virtues of the Stalinist state and its leader.

*Right:* George Bernard Shaw, the Irish playwright, settles down with a new issue at his London home.

*Opposite page:* "Builders of Socialism, Get the Latest News on the Great Project! USSR in Construction for 1931". A poster by Nikolai Troshin, resident art director of the magazine, who designed many marvellous issues.

Six covers of the magazine are shown above:

*Top left:* "The Maxim Gorky Agitational Propaganda

Squadron", 1935, No.1. Design by Nikolai Troshin.

*Top centre:* "The Workers' and Peasants' Red Army", 1933, No.2. Design by El Lissitsky.

*Top right:* "Soviet Science", 1934, No.6. Design by Es and El Lissitsky.

*Above left:* "The Ferghana Canal", 1940, No.1. Photographs by Max Alpert.

*Above centre:* "Soviet Childhood", 1940, No.6. Design by Valentina Khodasevich.

*Above right:* "The Soviet North", 1941, No.5. Design by Solomon Telingater. The final issue, published only in Russian, before the Nazi invasion.

A further issue on the Moscow State Circus designed and photographed by Alexander Rodchenko only reached the maquette stage.

*USSR in Construction* returned for a year in 1949, a pale shadow of its former self. It became *Soviet Union* magazine in 1950.

Медникова изучила укладку парашюта. Здесь ты каждой сборкой, каждой складкой, каждым стропом отвечаешь за жизнь человека. Малейшая неточность, незаметная морщинка на шелке, захлестнувшемся за строп, и... тебе уже не разгладить потом морщин горя у десятков людей...

## ПРЫЖОК
### к о м с о м о л к и
## КАТИ МЕДНИКОВОЙ
### б ы л  н а з н а ч е н
## на 4 ОКТЯБРЯ

Уложенный, упакованный в ранец парашют, заряженный на вытяжную шпильку, ждал Катю Медникову на старте.

— Ну, как? —спросил у Медниковой инструктор - комсомолец летчик Балашов.

— Все в порядке, — сказала Катя.

Балашов одел на Катю парашютные ранцы, один сзади, другой на всякий случай спереди, застегнул лямки.

— Ты чего это смеешься? — спросил он.

— А что ж мне плакать...

— Ну, раз смеешься, значит дело пойдет, — сказал Балашов. — садись, заезу.

Подошел врач. Катя отмахнулась. Но врач поймал ее руку и стал считать пульс.

— Пульс немножко учащенный, ровный, хорошего наполнения, — сказал врач.

Катя полезла в самолет. Балашов занял свое место впереди.

...Что-то выхлестнулось за спиной, ее с силой здернуло кверху, начало, все в мире стало ясным, сразу встало на свое место — и земля, и небо, и аэродром внизу. Распахнувшийся большой напряженный зонт закрыл полнеба. И Катя Медникова, смеясь от радости, переполнившей ее, стала спускаться.

ПОТОМ — ЗЕМЛЯ!

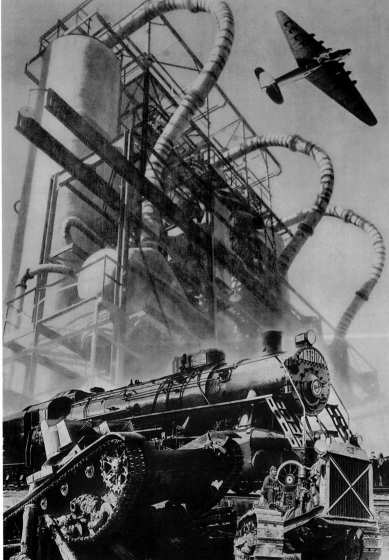

*USSR in Construction* was printed in duotone gravure in various colours. The format was large for a magazine: 420x300mm, and the use of enormous gatefolds (sometimes six pages across) enabled the designers to use gigantic photographs and photomontages. There was absolutely nothing being produced in the West to match its graphic brilliance; the overall effect was cinemascopic.

Four more examples are shown here:

*Top:* A four-page gatefold designed by Nikolai Troshin photomontaging Stalin, Maxim Gorky, the ANT-20 eight-engined aeroplane (which subsequently crashed killing all on board) and a column of jubilant demonstrators in 1935.

*Above left:* "Heavy Industry". A full page photomontage by El Lissitsky, 1935.

*Above right:* "Bolsheviki". Another full page photomontage by El Lissitsky from an issue on electrification, 1932. The banner reads: "There are no citadels that the Bolsheviks cannot storm." That was certainly true of their graphic designers.

*Opposite page:* A paper parachute blossoms like a flower when the gatefold is opened in this limited edition album of *USSR in Construction*, designed by Alexander Rodchenko and printed specially for Stalin's Central Committee in 1935.

Back and front cover of the May Day, 1932 issue of *Smena* (Change), a magazine of literature, art and politics for proletarian youth. Artist unknown.

Milkmaids patiently waiting in line to fill their buckets on the collective farm, early 1930s.

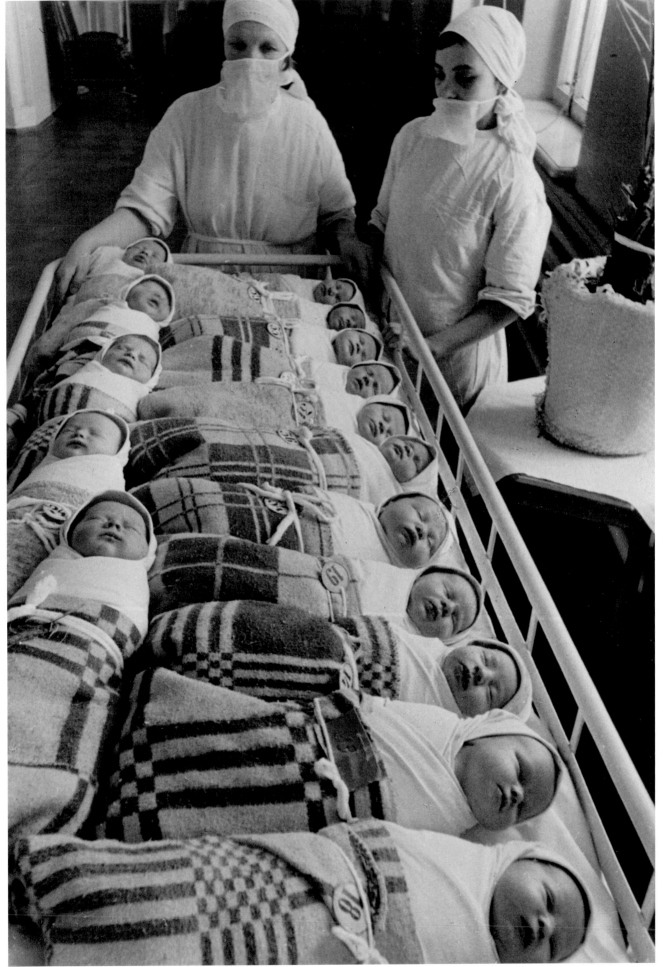

Newborn babies peacefully sleeping under the nurses' watchful gaze in the maternity ward of Moscow State University Clinic No. 1 in 1936.

Soviet women activists set about organising much-needed support networks in factories and collective farms during the First Five-Year Plan. They established creches and kindergartens, children's camps and sanatoria, literacy clubs and libraries, public baths and cafeterias to improve life generally and give working mothers the time and help they needed to cope with their often tiring and difficult jobs.

*Top:* Wet nurses at a collecting station for the distribution of mothers' milk to industrial areas.

*Above left:* Off to work on the collective farm.

*Right:* Lunchtime for the "children of the working masses" on the collective.

*Above right:* A "traktoristka" (woman tractor driver), free of the burden of childcare, leading a huge motorised column ploughing the fields.

*Opposite page:* The orphans of Stalin. Mugshots of the children of "Traitors to the Motherland" from an OGPU children's home in the 1930s. Their teachers encouraged them to denounce their parents, living or dead.

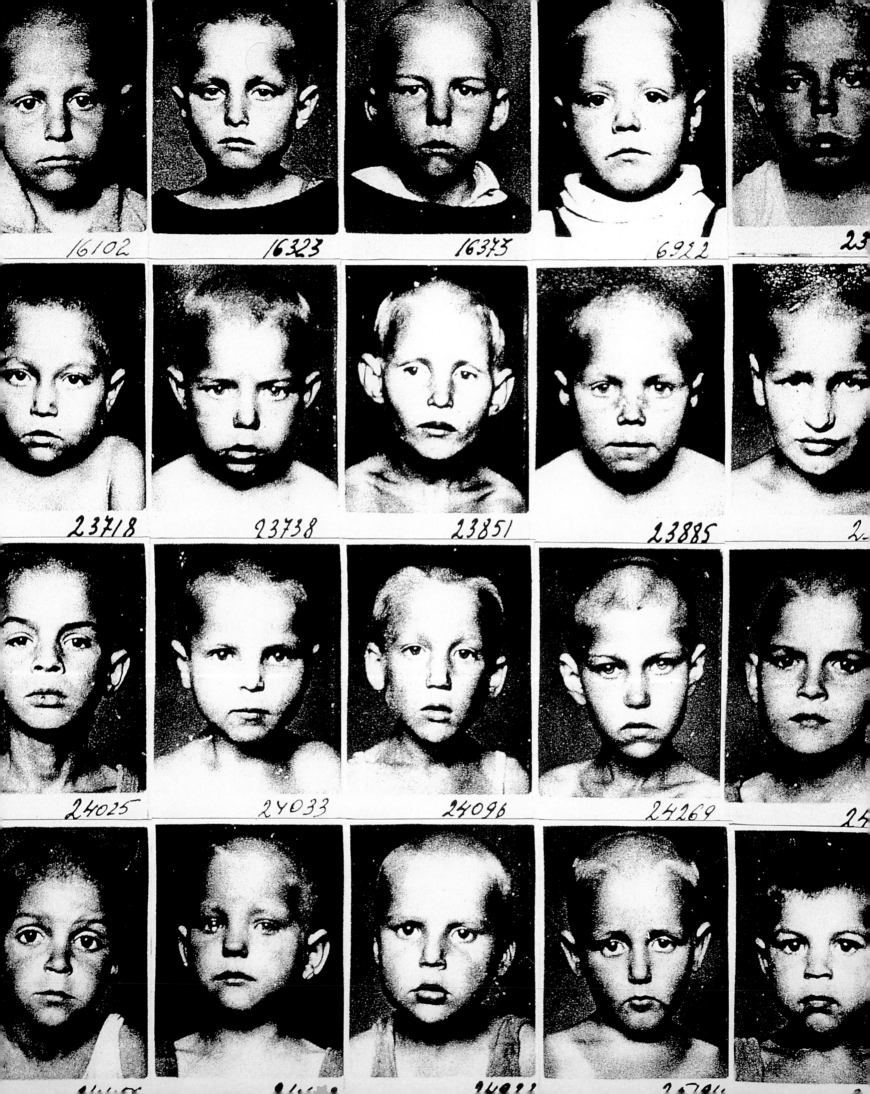

ОЧИСТИМ ПАРТИЮ ОТ КЛАССОВО-Ч
ПЕРЕРОЖДЕНЦЕВ, ОППОРТУНИСТО
ШКУРНИКОВ, БЮРОКРАТОВ И МО

*Above:* "Cleanse the Party of Class Aliens and Hostile Elements, Degenerates,
Opportunists, Double-Dealers, Careerists, Self-Seekers, Bureaucrats and Morally-Decayed Persons".
A poster from Moscow, 1933. Typographer unknown.
*Below:* "For the Builders of a Socialistic Industry – Culturally Socialist Cities". A poster by Daniil Cherkes, Moscow, 1932.

КДЫХ И ВРАЖДЕБНЫХ ЭЛЕМЕНТОВ,
ДВУРУШНИКОВ, КАРЬЕРИСТОВ,
ЛЬНО РАЗЛОЖИВШИХСЯ ЛЮДЕЙ.

ЕЛЯМ СОЦИАЛИСТИЧЕСКОЙ ИНДУСТРИИ —
УРНЫЕ СОЦИАЛИСТИЧЕСКИЕ ГОРОДА.

РЕАЛЬНОСТЬ НАШЕГО ПРОИЗВОДСТВЕННОГО ПЛАНА — ЭТО МИЛЛИОНЫ ТРУДЯЩИХСЯ, ТВОРЯЩИЕ НОВУЮ ЖИЗНЬ. (И. СТАЛИН)

*Left:* Uralmashstroi, early 1933. A satellite city newly constructed in the Urals for workers at the Soviet machine-building plant of the same name. The white apartment blocks in the photograph would have been reserved for foreign specialists helping to design and build the factory, as well as for the factory's management and high-ranking Party officials. Ordinary workers had to make do with far less, including tents. The Uralmashstroi plant was born as a result of the first Five-Year Plan's directive to free the Soviet Union from economic dependence on foreign countries for heavy machinery. Along with its sister plant, Krammashstroi, the gigantic production output included blast furnaces, open-hearth furnaces, rolling machines, blooming machines, gas generators, gas blasting machines, equipment for coloured metal foundries and the mining industry, turning lathes, power hoists, industrial presses and heavy forged drums and rotors.
*Above:* "The Reality of Our Plan of Production – Millions of Workers Creating a New Life. (Stalin)". A typographical poster from 1933.

*Top:* Alexander Bezymensky (far right) with members of his circle, circa 1930. Bezymensky, the "Komsomol's poet" was heralded by communist youth in the early 1930s as the mouthpiece of his generation. His poem, "The Party Card", was received with much acclaim. Its subject was how the enemy had killed a communist with a bullet that had pierced through the Party card he naturally kept in his breast pocket close to his heart: "Just one small, one card lost but in the body of the Party – a gaping hole." Bezymensky quickly went out of fashion when the members of the literary high command described him as a "lightweight".

*Above and far left:* Two photographs of Fizkult (physical culture) demonstrations in Red Square, Moscow, mid 1930s.
*Left:* A Fizkult women's group pose for the camera with their (male) trainer on International Women's Day, March 8, 1933.
*Opposite page:* The dedication on this photograph reads: "In loving memory of the commander of our squadron, Comrade Kalmykov, from your physical culture students, M.Borisyuk, E.Uspensky, T.Dzugayev and R.Usupov, 1934."

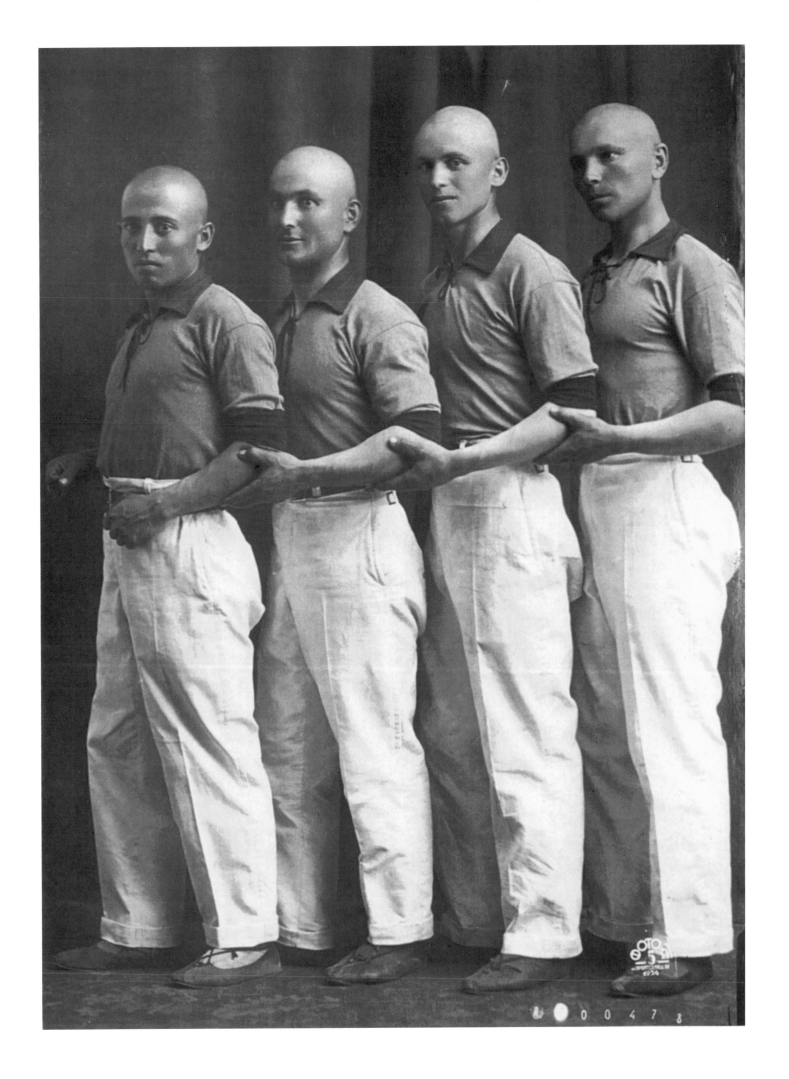

„Со знаменем Ленина победили мы в боях за Октябрьскую революцию".

„Со знаменем Ленина добились мы решающих успехов в борьбе за победу социалистического строительства. С этим знаменем победим в пролетарской революции во всем мире Да здравствует Ленинизм". (Сталин).

„История показала, что пятилетка является не частным делом Советского Союза, а делом всего международного пролетариата". (Сталин).

„Успехи пятилетки мобилизуют революционные силы рабочего класса всех стран против капитализма — таков неоспоримый факт". (Сталин, Из доклада на объединенном Ярославском пленуме ЦК и ЦКК ВКП(б)).

„В странах напитала катастрофическое падение производства, массовое свертывание и остановка фабрик и заводов, неслыханное разрушение производительных сил". (Из резолюций XVII конференции ВКП(б)).

Four posters from a series of twenty designed by a group called Artists' Brigade and published in Moscow in 1933. The posters visualised in powerful photomontage graphics and slogans the major achievements and objectives of Stalin's plans for the rapid expansion of industry, the forced collectivisation of agriculture, and propaganda on the political, educational and cultural fronts.
*Left:* "The USSR is the Centre of International Socialism".
*Top:* "Communism is Soviet Power Plus the Electrification of the Whole Country". The poster features the Dniepr Dam.
*Centre:* "The All-Union Communist Party – Bolsheviks – The Assault Army of Socialism". The theme of this poster is the forthcoming Seventeenth Party Congress in late January 1934. Out of the 1,961 delegates who attended the congress, no fewer than 1,108 had been liquidated by the end of the decade. The congress became known in Stalinist circles as "The Congress of Victors".
*Above:* "The working classes struggle for education because they need it for victory. (Lenin)".

די רעאַלקייט פון אונדזערע פּלעֶנער־דאָס זײַנען מיר מיט אײַך

ВЫШЕ ЗНАМЯ МАРКСА ЭНГЕЛЬСА ЛЕНИНА и СТАЛИНА!

*Top:* "We are the Realisation of the Plan". A poster in Yiddish with Hebrew script illustrated by Adolf Strakhov in 1933–4. Stalin is flanked by Maxim Gorky (behind him to the left) and some idealistic participants of the second Five-Year Plan.
*Above:* "Under the Banner of Marx, Engels, Lenin and Stalin". A poster by Gustav Klutsis from 1933 published to

commemorate the fiftieth anniversary of Karl Marx's death.
*Opposite page:* "Everybody Sign Up as a Shockworker". The rectangles of colour in V.D.Gushchin's poster from 1932 are for workers to fill in their names and contact addresses to apply for the toughest and most urgent jobs in Soviet industry. Different teams of "udarniki" (shockworkers) were often mobilised in

"socialist competition" against each other to increase production.
The cult of the shockworker reached a new level in the mid-1930s with the arrival in the Donbass of a young miner called Alexei Stakhanov. In August 1935 he mined 102 tonnes of coal in 5 hours and 45 minutes. The following month he set a new record, mining a staggering 227 tonnes of coal in a single shift. It was

later rumoured that he might have had a bit of help, but even so he became famous throughout the world and from then on the shockworkers were known as "Stakhanovites".

*Above, left and overleaf:* These textile designs, published for the first time, come from an exceptional portfolio of original artwork by a little known textile designer called Nikolai Prakhov. He graduated in art at the Kiev Academy of Literature and Fine Arts in 1903 and went on to study at the Museum of Industrial Design in Naples until 1909. The works shown here are initialled and dated, but whether the designs were used and what became of him is unclear.

*Top:* Original gouache signed "NP" in Cyrillic, dated 1903.
*Above:* Original gouache signed "NP" in Cyrillic, dated 1920.
*Left:* Original gouache signed "NP" in Cyrillic, dated 20/X/1927–1935.
*Overleaf left:* Original gouache signed "NP" in Cyrillic, dated 1930.
*Overleaf right:* Original gouache signed "NP" in Cyrillic, dated 1933.

1930. H.
45 X 52

„В ГРОМАДНОМ РОСТЕ НАЦИОНАЛЬНЫХ КУЛЬТУР НА СОЦИАЛИСТИЧЕСКОЙ ОСНОВЕ НАЙДЕТ СВОЕ ВЫРАЖЕНИЕ ПОБЕДОНОСНЫЙ РОСТ СОЦИАЛИЗМА В СССР". (МОЛОТОВ)

*Opposite page:* "Lenin, Stalin". A poster by M.Glik from 1934, with a quotation from Vyacheslav Molotov: "The victorious development of socialism in the USSR will find its expression in the colossal development of national cultures on a socialistic foundation."
As Chairman of the Council of People's Commissars (Premier of the Soviet Union) from 1930–41 and then Foreign Minister, Molotov was Stalin's most trusted and faithful aide.
He never protested, not even against the arrest, imprisonment and torture of his Jewish wife, Polina Zhemchuzhina during the post-war anti-Semitic campaign that started in 1949. (After Stalin's death she was released by Beria, who called her a "true communist").
*Top:* Boris Kudoyarov's photograph of Uzbek women attending a literacy class during their work break at the Stalin Textile Kombinat in Tashkent, 1935. Lenin looks on.
*Above left:* A Russian teacher in Kazakhstan with her factory-worker students in the early 1930s.
*Above right:* A deceptively avuncular Stalin, puffing on his pipe at a conference of Central Asian Peoples in the Kremlin in 1935.
Less than two years later, a campaign of extreme repression would sweep through every republic in the Soviet Union. Hundreds of Communist Party leaders in Uzbekistan were liquidated and in Kazakhstan the whole of the Party's Central Committee would be arrested and shot.

On December 1, 1934, Sergei Kirov, the Party boss in Leningrad, was gunned down in a corridor outside his office at the Smolny Institute by a student named Nikolayev under very suspicious circumstances.
Officially the assassination was blamed, rather predictably, on fascists but it is more likely to have been engineered by Stalin. It was widely known at the time that Stalin was jealous of Kirov's immense popularity in the Party and that the charismatic and recently elected Politburo member might one day challenge him for the leadership.
Kirov had already voiced criticism of Stalin's aggressive handling of the collectivisation of agriculture. The assassination was certainly in Stalin's interest; as a way of eliminating a rival and as an excuse for opening the floodgates to the unprecedented tidal wave of blood that followed.
The secret police rounded up in retribution thousands of so-called "assassins of Kirov" in the beginning of what was to become known as the "Great Terror".
*Right:* Kirov (left) in happier times with Sergo Ordzhonikidze, 1924.
*Second right:* Kirov lying in state.

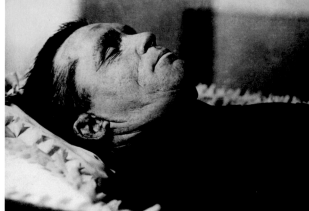

*Above:* Stalin and friends waiting to receive delegates from Tadzhikistan and Turkmenistan in the Kremlin, 1935. Seated, left to right: Anastas Mikoyan, Vyacheslav Molotov, Mikhail Kalinin, Stalin (instructing an aide), Kliment Voroshilov and Sergo Ordzhonikidze, the heavy industry boss who committed suicide in 1937 over Stalin's murderous policies. The obliterated head behind Molotov probably belonged to Yan Rudzutak, who voiced doubts about the Plan and was arrested and shot in 1937. Many of the Tadzhiks and Turkmens at the conference would later be tortured and shot by the secret police as counter-revolutionaries.

*Left:* A suspect enters the Lubyanka prison by a side door to undergo interrogation.

*Second left:* Stalin making notes.

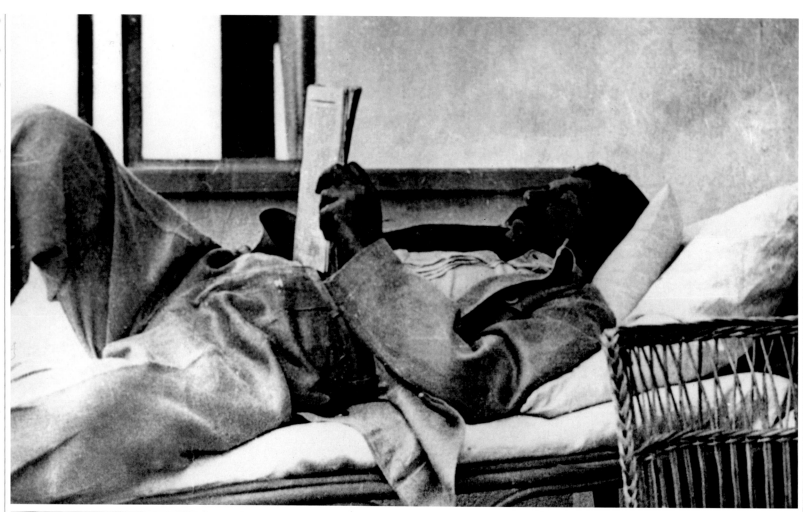

*Above:* Ekaterina Dzhugashvili, Stalin's mother, in Tbilisi in 1930.
In an interview that day she reminisced about her son's childhood: "Soso was always a good boy. I never had to punish him... Soso was my fourth son. All the others died before he was born. Of course I treasured him. Above everything in the world... You know, we had other things planned for Soso. His father, Vissarion, said he would make a good cobbler out of Soso. But his father died when Soso was eleven... and then, you see, I didn't want him to be a cobbler. I

didn't want him to be anything but a priest..."
Soso (the Georgian diminutive for Joseph) hardly saw his poor old peasant mother after 1903. She travelled on two occasions to visit her son in Moscow but preferred Georgia. She died in 1937.
The other photographs shown above and opposite were taken by one of Stalin's bodyguards, Lieutenant General Nikolai Vlasik. Known to all in the Kremlin as "Stalin's faithful dog", Vlasik acted as Stalin's personal secret agent, wielding great power in running his

everyday life. After Nadezhda's suicide, he was given day-to-day responsibility for her children. Their daughter Svetlana found him "incredibly stupid, illiterate and uncouth" but he never went anywhere without his Leica until 1952 when he was arrested, badly beaten and sent to the Gulag.
Vlasik's off-the-record photographs of the dictator caused a sensation in the early 1960s when an enterprising Soviet journalist spirited a number of them out to the West, selling them to newspapers and magazines all over the world.

*Top:* Stalin doing some holiday reading at his dacha in the Caucasus, circa 1932.
*Centre:* The dictator catches up on some paperwork while in the foreground, understandably uncomfortable, his daughter sits on the lap of "Uncle" Lavrentii Beria, his repulsive secret police boss.
*Right:* Svetlana gets a kiss from Papa.
*Opposite page:* Stalin portrayed by Vlasik, who has never been rehabilitated.
*Overleaf:* May Day in Red Square, 1936. Photograph by S. Loskutov.

МОЛОДЕЖЬ – НА САМОЛЕТЫ

*Right:* Beginner-pilot Shura Kuvshinova (at the controls), a metal lathe machinist at the Aviopribor aeroplane instruments factory in Moscow, shares her excitement before take-off with instructor-pilot Tonya Kamenskaya, a specialist mechanic at Moscow airport. Thousands of young women from factories and offices in the Soviet Union learned to fly in their spare time in the 1930s, some of them later becoming air aces in the Red Air Force in the Great Patriotic War. The photograph was taken by Mark Markov-Grinberg in May 1936.
*Above:* Gustav Klutsis' poster, "Young People – To the Aeroplanes", 1934.

*Right:* "Long Live Our Happy Socialist Land! Long Live Our Beloved Leader, the Great Stalin!" Gustav Klutsis' wild adulation and mind-bending perspective takes his poster from 1935 into the parallel universe of Soviet socialist surrealism. The aeroplanes over Red Square are named "Vladimir Lenin", "Joseph Stalin", "Maxim Gorky", "Mikhail Kalinin", "Vyacheslav Molotov", etc., and the formation in the distance on the right spells out "STALIN".

*Opposite page:* Shura Kuvshinova (see previous page) became the glamorous face of a Soviet advertising campaign for "Sanit" toothpaste, launched in 1938 by Polina Zhemchuzhina, People's Commissar of the Food Industry USSR Perfume Directorate.

The "Sanit" poster was painted and designed by the Moscow artist, Izrael Bograd. He was arrested as an English spy and shot in June 1938, one month before his poster hit the hoardings.

ДА ЗДРАВСТВУЕТ НАША СЧАСТЛИВАЯ СОЦИАЛИСТИЧЕСКАЯ РОДИНА.
ДА ЗДРАВСТВУЕТ НАШ ЛЮБИМЫЙ ВЕЛИКИЙ СТАЛИН!

*Right:* Underneath a portrait of himself, Stalin lays down the law on collectivisation to his seemingly hypnotised comrades in Moscow on December 4, 1935. Four of the participants in the group were later crossed out of the photograph after they had been arrested and purged. Surviving in the picture can be seen, left to right: Kaganovich, Molotov, Voroshilov, Shaduntz (Party boss of Tadjikistan), Mikoyan, Andreyev and Shkiryatov.

Those who were deleted, also from left to right: Boris Tal, Nikolai Yezhov, Mikhail Chernov and Yakov Yakovlev.

Tal worked for Stalin's censorship apparatus. He was shot in 1938.

Yezhov was head of the NKVD from 1936 to 1938. His reign of terror brought pain and death on an unprecedented scale. He was arrested and tortured in 1939, shot in 1940.

Mikhail Chernov was removed from his post as Commissar of Agriculture towards the end of 1937. He was sentenced to death and shot along with Nikolai Bukharin and others at the Moscow Show Trial of 1938.

Yakov Yakovlev was also a boss of agriculture and a major force in planning collectivisation. Accused of being a "Rightist", his name appeared on an infamous list on which was scribbled "Shoot all 138", signed by Stalin and Molotov on July 28, 1938. Of the survivors, it should be noted that Shkiryatov, who was Yezhov's chief assistant throughout the Great Terror, only died in 1954 and was buried with full honours.

*Overleaf:* The entrance to Svirlag labour camp in the Leningrad region. The photograph was taken in 1936 on the nineteenth anniversary of the October Revolution. It was entirely forbidden and very dangerous to take pictures of a Gulag. The vertical lettering reads "NKVD" (People's Commissariat for Internal Affairs).

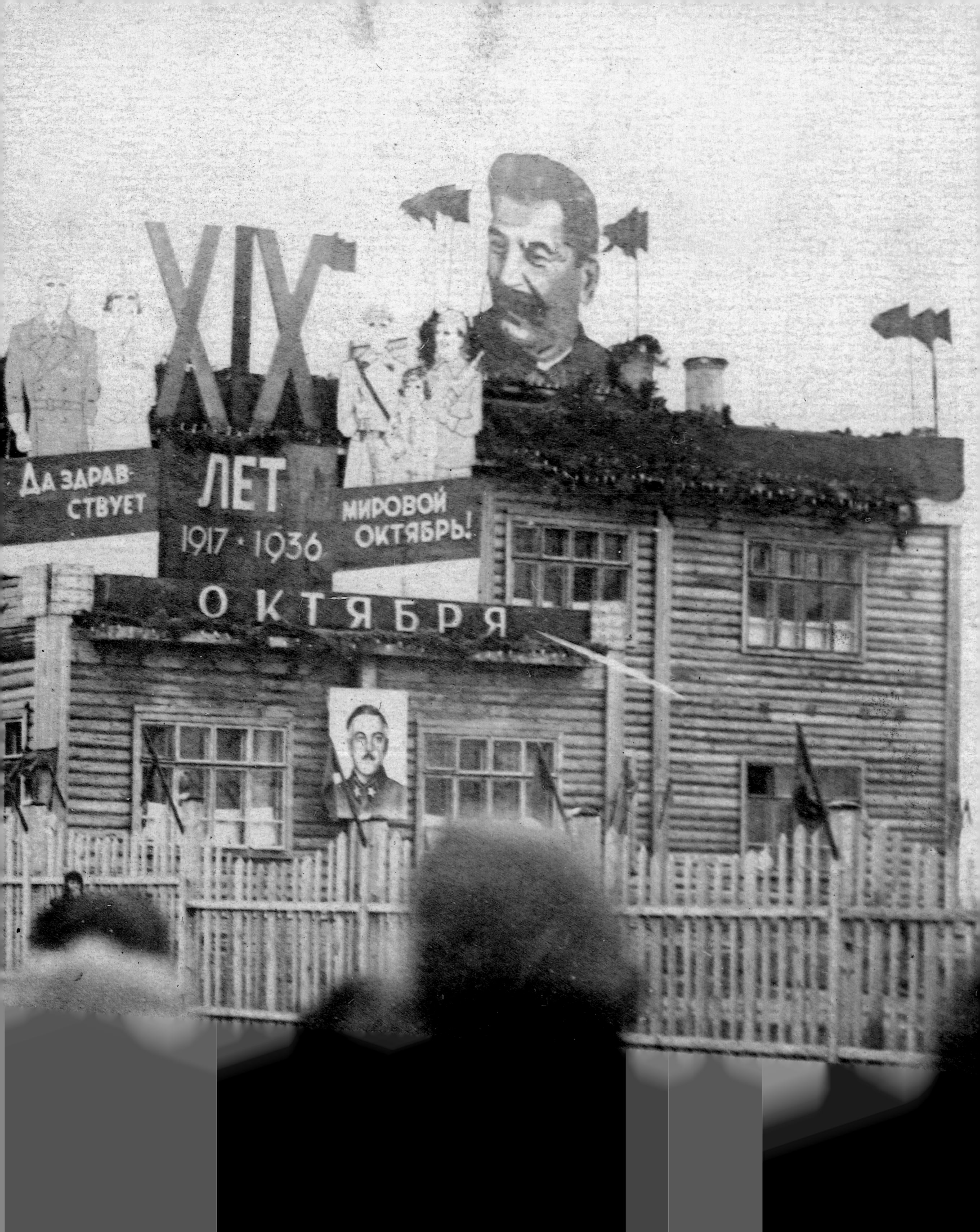
XIX
Да здравствует
ЛЕТ
1917 - 1936
мировой Октябрь!
ОКТЯБРЯ

*Left:* Leon Trotsky with his wife Natalya Sedova and their son Leon Sedov, exiled on the Islands of Prinkipo in the Sea of Marmara, off the coast of Constantinople. In February 1929 they had been forcibly banished from Soviet territory by Stalin's secret police. Trotsky and Natalya lived on the island until 1933. During this period he wrote feverishly. He started a journal, *The Bulletin of the Opposition*, which for a time was smuggled into Russia; he completed his major theoretical work, *The Permanent Revolution*; and published the first volume of his three-part *History of the Russian Revolution*.

The news from the Soviet Union was invariably bad. Trotsky's former associates were being killed, banished to the Gulag or forced into grovelling capitulation by Stalin's secret police.

A parallel campaign was under way to obliterate from Soviet life all mention either in word or image of Trotsky and his comrades, and to falsify history by enlarging Stalin's minor role in the Revolution into something approaching operatic fantasy. Trotsky also heard tragic news about his own family. His first wife, Alexandra, a leader of the Leningrad Opposition, died in exile in Siberia. Their younger daughter Nina succumbed to tuberculosis one month after her husband had been arrested; and in January 1933, their elder daughter, Zinaida, committed suicide in Berlin.

Trotsky now realised that Stalin's murderous grip on power meant that reform from within the Soviet Union was no longer an option. Trotsky and Natalya left Turkey for France in July 1933 before being granted asylum in Norway in 1935, where he completed his devastating critique of Stalin's regime, *The Revolution Betrayed*. In 1937 the artists Diego Rivera and Frida Kahlo arranged for him to move with Natalya to Mexico. He spent the rest of his life there exposing Stalin's crimes. But Stalin's criminals were moving ever closer to him. His younger son, Sergei, who had remained in Russia, died in the Gulag in 1937 and Leon Sedov was murdered in Paris by Stalin's agents in 1938.

*Top right:* "We are Eradicating the Spies and Saboteurs, the Trotskyist–Bukharinist Agents of Fascism!" A poster by Sergei Igmunov for the NKVD, 1937.

*Right:* Another secret police poster, "Twenty Years of the NKVD Border Guards", also from 1937, published in Moscow.

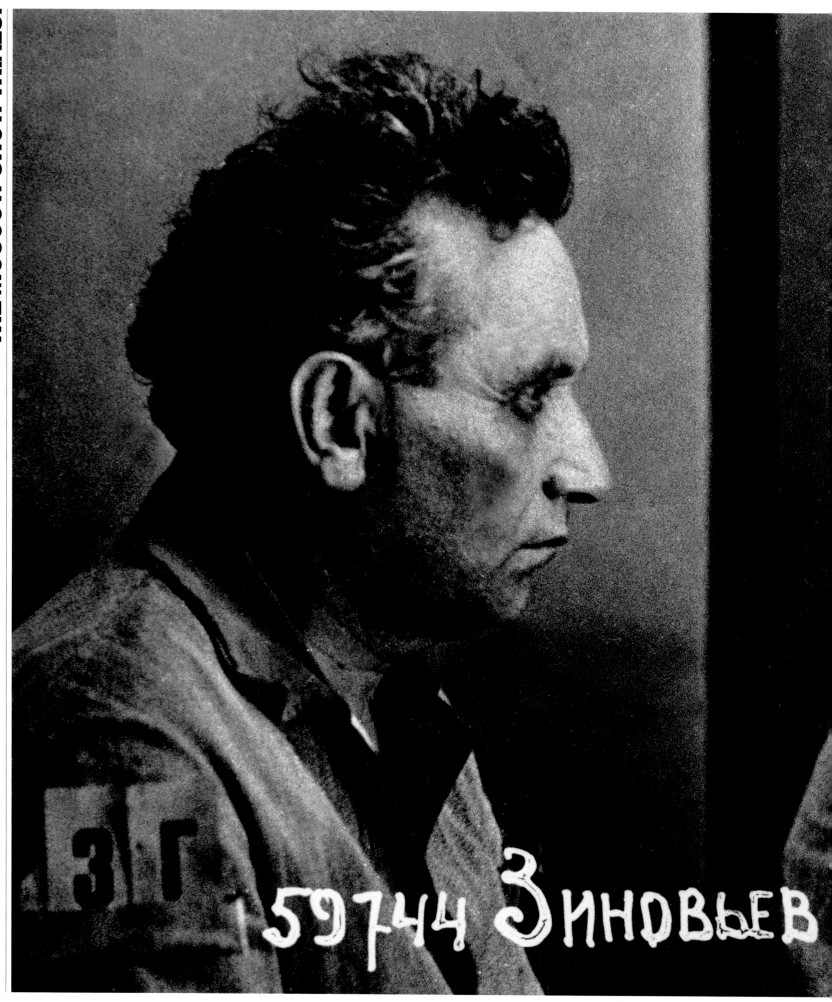

ЗГ · 59744 ЗИНОВЬЕВ

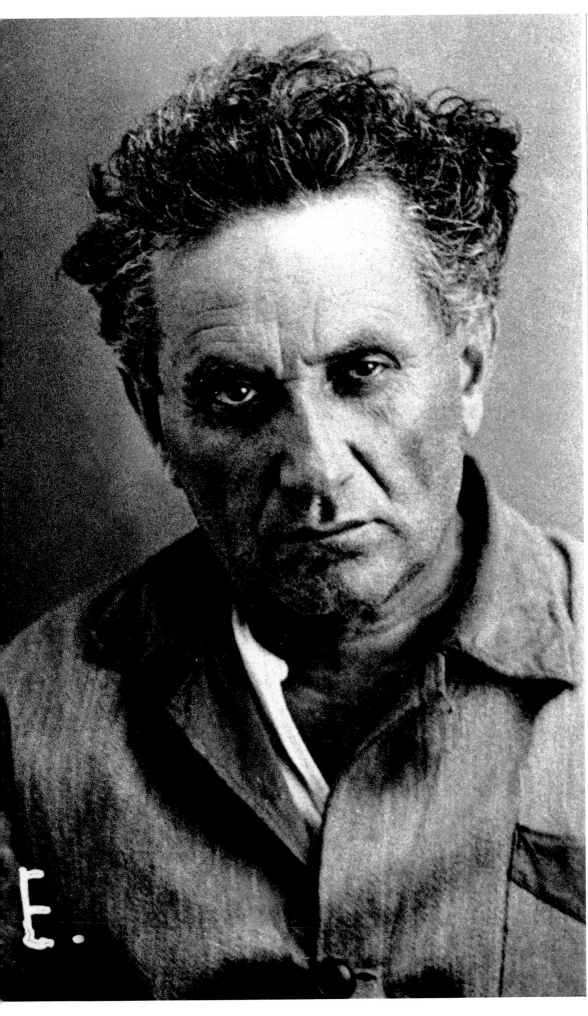

The photographs reproduced here and on the following ten pages are the secret police mugshots of the defendants who took part in the notorious Moscow Show Trials of 1936, 1937 and 1938. This is the first publication for almost all of these alarming portraits.

The majority of Stalin's victims were shot or sent to the Gulag without any trial at all. Such trials as there were, were held in secret. But the three Show Trials took place in open court, the last two being held before an invited audience at the House of Trade Unions, near the Bolshoi Theatre.

The public trials were at the epicentre of the Great Terror and represent Stalin's fanatical determination to destroy the last of the Old Bolsheviks and defenders of Marxism who had fought in the Revolution and of whom he was so jealous. Some dubious defendants were included in the trials to make the Old Bolsheviks seem guilty by association.

The defendants were severely beaten between hearings if their confessions, carefully prepared in advance by their interrogators, did not match up to the insane fabrications hurled at them by the play-acting prosecution.

Every defendant's mugshot from the first and second trial is shown here. Most of the mugshots from the third trial have long since been lost without trace or, in some cases, may never have been taken.

The photographs have been kept for decades in an archive in Siberia now under the direction of the FSB (Federal Security Service of the Russian Federation). Their safekeeping is considered so important that the originals were transported to and from Moscow by special train in order to make these special photographic prints.

All the major trials of the Stalinist era were recorded on film for propaganda purposes but no footage of the defendants at the three Show Trials has ever been found. The historical significance of these photographs, therefore, cannot be overstated. They are the last portraits of the victims of a charade that Trotsky called "the greatest frame-up in history."

*Left:* Grigorii Zinoviev. Chief defendant at the first Show Trial (known as the Trial of the Trotskyist-Zinovievist Terrorist Centre) in August 1936. Party member since 1901. Bolshevik. One of Lenin's closest friends. Comintern and Petrograd/Leningrad Party boss, 1919–26. Expelled thereafter several times by Stalin as an oppositionist. Arrested and put on trial twice in 1935. Sentenced to death and shot on August 24, 1936.

*Top:* Secret police chief Nikolai Yezhov conspiring with his boss, Joseph Stalin, in 1937.

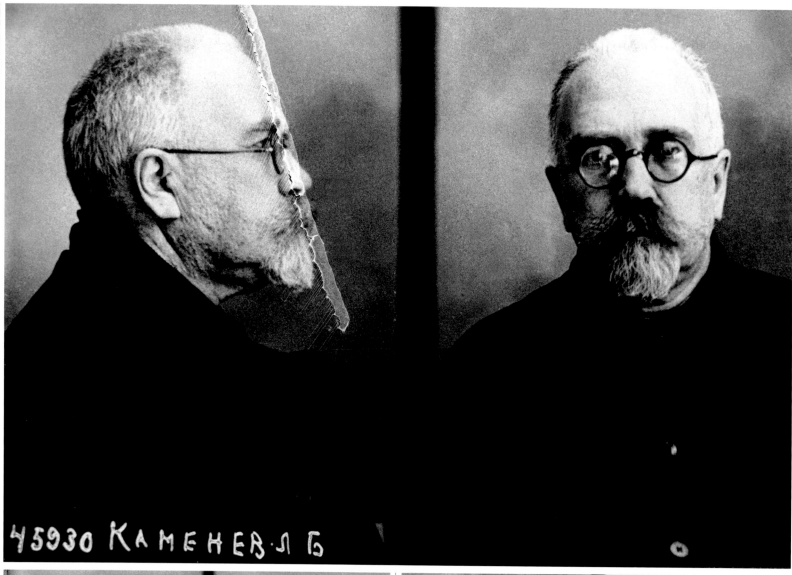

45930 КАМЕНЕВ·Л·Б

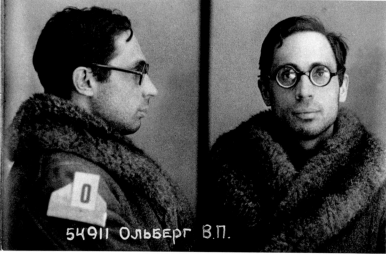

54911 Ольберг В.П.

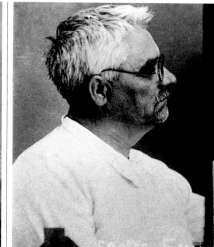

*Top:* Lev Kamenev. Born 1883. Party member since 1901. Close friend of Lenin. Organised Bolshevik Party abroad when in exile with Lenin and Zinoviev. Led Bolsheviks in Petrograd until Lenin's return from Switzerland, April 1917. Supported Zinoviev against Lenin's plans for seizure of power in October 1917. Married Trotsky's sister, Olga. Leader of Moscow Soviet and Party organization in 1920s. After Lenin's death, supported Zinoviev and

Stalin against Trotsky, then Trotsky against Stalin, then Zinoviev against Stalin. From 1927 expelled several times from Party, later reinstated. First arrested in 1935. Sentenced to five years in jail then ten years, accused with his brother (Rosenfeld) of plotting terrorism. Sentenced to death and shot on August 24, 1936. After the trial, Olga was arrested and imprisoned. Both her sons (with Kamenev) were executed and she was shot in prison on September 11,

1941 together with Christian Rakovsky, Maria Spiridonova and 160 others.
*Above left:* Valentin Olberg. German Communist Party member until 1932. Former agent of NKVD Foreign Department, working as secret informer against Trotskyists in Berlin. Attempted, unsuccessfully, to become Trotsky's secretary in 1930. Arrested in 1936 as link to Trotskyists in plot to kill Stalin by Komsomol students. NKVD told him to confess; it was part of an assignment

and he would be freed. He wasn't. Sentenced to death and shot on August 24, 1936.
*Above right:* Ivan Smirnov. Born 1899. Bolshevik and supporter of Trotsky. Political commissar in Civil War, known as "The Lenin of Siberia". Expelled from Party in 1927. Hated Stalin, wanted him removed as General Secretary as Lenin had wished. Stalin hated him. Arrested and imprisoned in 1933. Sentenced to death and shot on August 24, 1936.

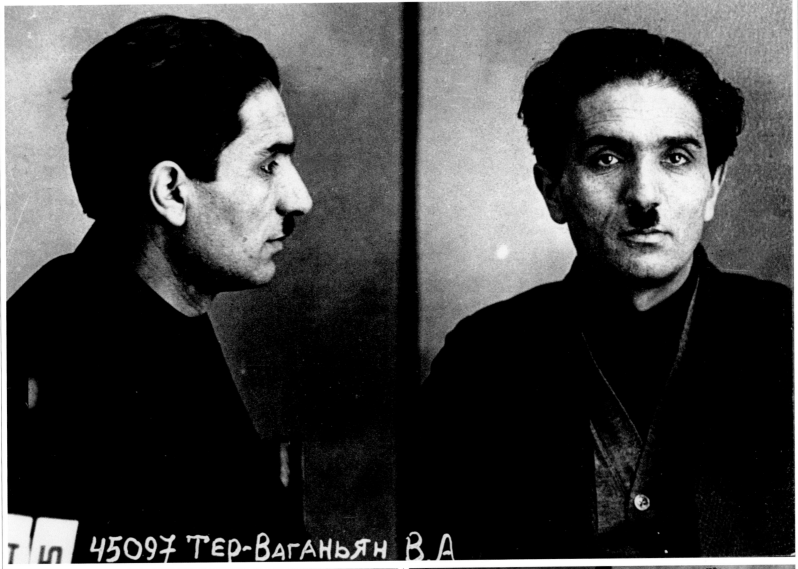

45097 ТЕР-ВАГАНЬЯН В.А.

58728 Гольцман Е.С.

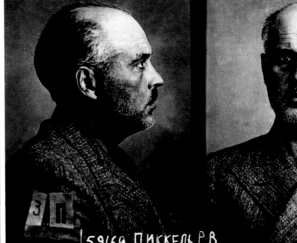

59169 ПИККЕЛЬ Р.В.

*Top:* Vagarshak Ter-Vaganian. Born in 1893. Armenian. Member of the Bolshevik Party since 1912. Marxist theoretician and talented journalist. First Secretary of Moscow City Soviet in 1917. Edited *Under the Banner of Marxism,* a heavily dogmatic monthly journal. Follower of Zinoviev and Kamenev. In 1927 privately published a book exposing much of the official biographies of Stalin and Rykhov as falsifications. Stalin hated him for this.

Expelled from Party in 1927 as a member of the Left Opposition. Exiled to Kazakhstan in 1935, then arrested. Sentenced to death and shot on August 24, 1936.
*Above left:* Eduard Goltzman. Bolshevik Party member since 1903. Engineer. After 1917 worked in the People's Commissariat of Foreign Trade, spending much time abroad secretly working for the Comintern. A former Trotskyist and personal friend of Ivan

Smirnov, he was expelled from the Party after his arrest in 1936. Sentenced to death and shot on August 24, 1936.
*Above right:* Richard Pikkel. Bolshevik Party member since 1917. Active in Belorussia during Civil War. In 1920s, chief of Zinoviev's secretariat in the Comintern. Like Zinoviev, expelled from Party in 1927. Journalist and writer until his arrest in 1936. Pikkel stood up to interrogation for three weeks. Then he was transferred to the

central NKVD where high-ranking officials who had some years previously been his friends offered him his life in return for a (false) confession. It did him no good. In his final plea at the Show Trials he spoke of himself as "the dregs of the land." He was sentenced to death and shot on August 24, 1936.

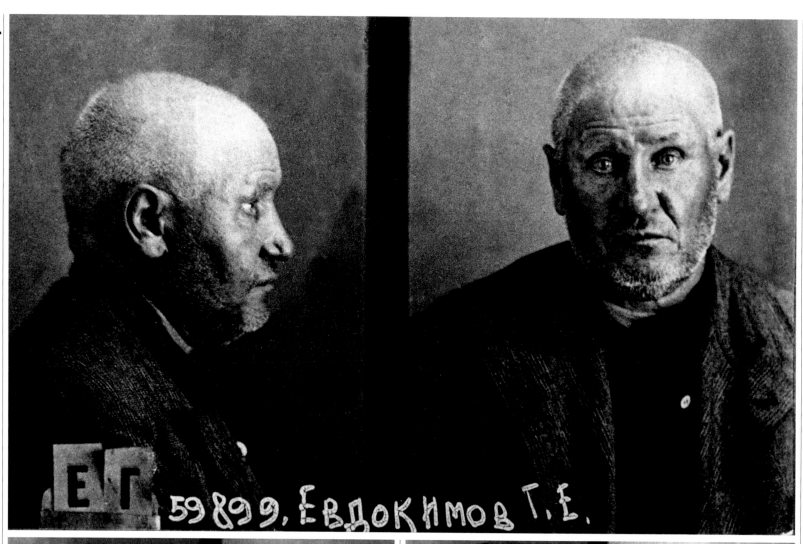

Every defendant at the first Show Trial would be liquidated, but Stalin was even dissatisfied at this outcome. He wrote a memo to *Pravda* furiously complaining at the way the trial had been reported; that far greater emphasis should have been put on a giant conspiracy to overthrow Soviet power rather than report the isolated actions of a few individuals.

*Top:* Grigorii Yevdokimov. Bolshevik Party member since 1903. Worker. Activist in Petrograd Party organisation. Political commissar in Civil War. Head of Petrograd Union of Trade Unions in 1922. Deputy Chairman of Petrograd Soviet, 1923–25. Close friend of Zinoviev. A leader of the Leningrad Opposition from 1925. Secretary of the Central Committee of the Communist Party. Expelled 1927. Reinstated in 1928 after "capitulation". Expelled again in 1934 and arrested in 1935. Sentenced to eight years in prison but brought back for the Show Trials. Treated with extreme brutality in order to extract confession. Sentenced to death and shot on August 24, 1936.

*Above left:* Moisei Lurye. Member of the German Communist Party since 1922. Former Trotskyist. Lived in USSR from 1932. Editor in Foreign Languages Publishing House. Professor of Science at Moscow State University from 1933. Considered by some of his fellow defendants at the Show Trials to be an agent provocateur. Sentenced to death and shot on August 24, 1936.

*Above right:* Nathan Lurye. Born 1901. Member of the German Communist Party since 1925. Left Berlin to live in USSR, 1932. Former Trotskyist. Doctor at Chelyabinsk tractor factory. Accomplice (but no relation) of Moisei Lurye, also thought to have been an agent provocateur at the Show Trials. Sentenced to death and shot on August 24, 1936. On hearing the judgement in court, he jumped up and shouted hysterically, "Long live the cause of Marx, Engels, Lenin and Stalin!"

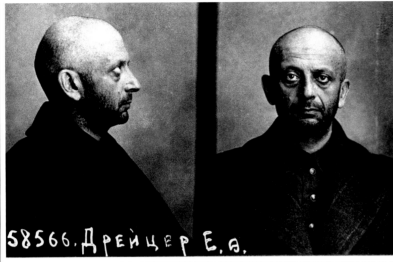

58566. ДРЕЙЦЕР Е.А.

58724 РЕЙНГОЛЬД И.И.

59017 БАКАЕВ. И.П.

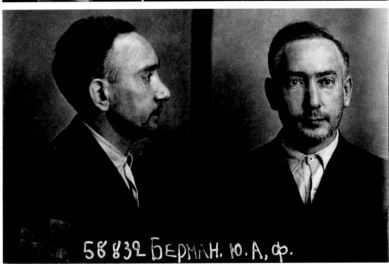

58832 БЕРМАН. Ю.А.Ф.

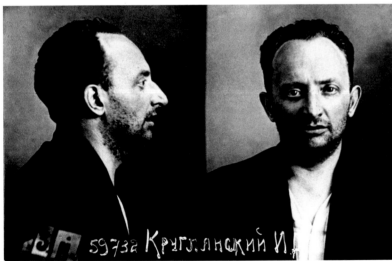

59732 КРУГЛЯНСКИЙ И.

59743 МРАЧКОВСКИЙ С.В.

*Top left:* Yefim Dreitzer. Bolshevik Party member since 1919. Commissar in Civil War, very close to Trotsky, and head of his bodyguard. Received two Orders of the Red Banner for bravery. Expelled from Party in 1928. Capitulated in 1929. Sent to Chelyabinsk Magnesit factory as deputy director. Arrested in 1936 as a "wrecker". Sentenced to death and shot on August 24, 1936.

*Top right:* Isaak Reingold. Born 1898. Bolshevik since 1917. Previously member of Jewish Labour Bund. From 1918 People's Commissar of Finance in Lithuania and Belorussia. Expelled from Party in 1927 as oppositionist. Reinstated in 1929 to become Deputy Commissar of Agriculture of USSR. Expelled from Party again after Kirov assassination and arrested. Interrogated for three weeks, often for forty-eight hours non-stop without food or drink. Sentenced to death and shot on August 24, 1936.

*Centre left:* Ivan Bakayev. Bolshevik Party member since 1906. Active in Petrograd Party organisation. Follower of Zinoviev. Head of GPU in Leningrad and member of the Party's Control Commission. Expelled from Party in 1927. Arrested after Kirov assassination. Sentenced to death and shot on August 24, 1936.

*Centre right:* Konon Berman-Yurin. Member of Lithuanian Communist Party, 1921–23. German Communist Party member living in Berlin until 1933, then USSR. Journalist. Gave detailed testimony (coached by the NKVD) that Trotsky had personally ordered him to kill Stalin at a plenum of the Comintern but he couldn't get a ticket. Sentenced to death and shot on August 24, 1936.

*Above left:* Fritz David (real name: Ilya Krugliansky). Member of German Communist Party. NKVD agent in Comintern. Agent provocateur during the Show Trials who testified that he too had failed to carry out Trotsky's orders and kill Stalin. Sentenced to death and shot on August 24, 1936.

*Above right:* Sergei Mrachkovsky. Old Bolshevik. Hero of Civil War. Chief of military districts in Urals and later Western Siberia in 1920s. Expelled from Party in 1927. Director of Baikal-Amur (BAM) railroad project, 1928–1933. Expelled and arrested. Sentenced to death and shot on August 24, 1936.

269

63954 СЕРЕБРЯКОВ.Л.П.

The second Moscow Show Trial (known as the Trial of the Anti-Soviet Trotskyist Centre) took place at the House of the Trade Unions in January 1937.
*Above:* Bundles of case files arriving at the entrance of a secret police building in Moscow.
*Top:* Leonid Serebryakov. Born 1888. Bolshevik Party member since 1905. Organised political department in Red Army during Civil War to watch over ex-tsarist officer corps. Friend of Trotsky. Secretary of Central Committee of Bolshevik Party, 1920. Tried (and failed) to reach compromise between Stalin and Trotsky in 1925. Arrested in 1927 for setting up an illegal printshop for Trotskyist–Zinovievist Opposition

literature. Capitulated in 1930 to become deputy head of Railroads and Highways. Arrested again in 1936. Accused of being a "wrecker" – organising sabotage groups. Refused to sign (false) confession statements for many weeks in spite of worsening health. Then the investigators told him they had arranged an "appointment" at the Lubyanka for his beloved daughter, Zoya. To save her from the unthinkable, he signed immediately. Sentenced to death and shot on February 1, 1937. The chief prosecutor at the trials, Vyshinsky, then moved into his dacha.
*Above, second left:* Grigorii Sokolnikov. Born 1888. Bolshevik since 1905. Returned to Petrograd with Lenin, 1917.

Responsible for nationalising banks after Revolution. Head of Soviet delegation at Brest-Litovsk, signed the peace treaty with Germany. Political commissar in Civil War. Follower of Zinoviev and Kamenev in 1920s. People's Commissar of Finance and deputy head of Gosplan (the State Planning Committee). Soviet ambassador to Britain, 1929–32. Implicated by defendants at first Show Trial. Stalin promised him that his life would be saved. Sokolnikov confessed to save his young wife (who was previously married to Serebryakov) and son. Sentenced to ten years imprisonment. Either murdered in prison by criminals (or the NKVD), or shot.
*Above, third from left:* Mikhail Stroilov.

Non-Party member. Engineer in Novosibirsk. Arrested as a "wrecker", in contact with German and Japanese intelligence. Sentenced at the second Show Trial to eight years imprisonment. He was shot in 1941.
*Above right:* Gavriil Pushin. Bolshevik Party member since 1924. Engineer at Donbass. Since 1931 chief engineer at Gorlovka Nitrogen Fertiliser Works and deputy chief engineer at People's Commissariat of Heavy Industry, chemistry department. Arrested in connection with "wrecking". Confessed immediately and implicated his boss, Grigorii Piatakov. Sentenced to death and shot on February 1, 1937.

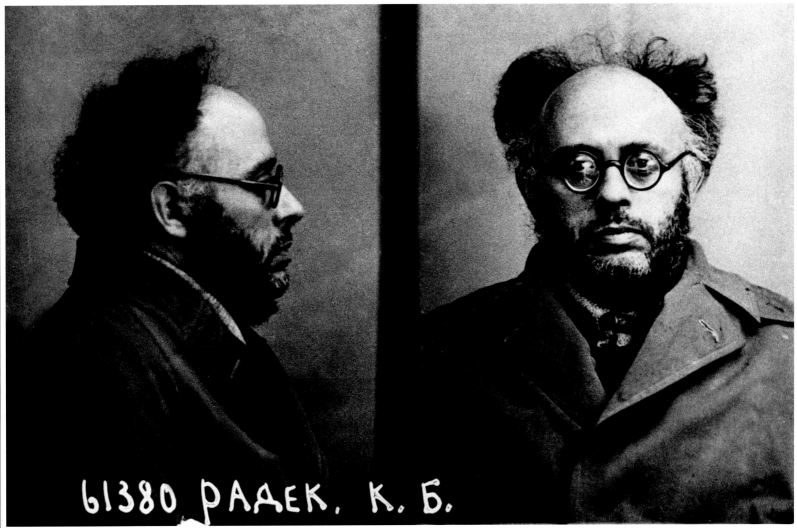

61380 РАДЕК, К. Б.

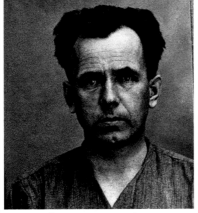

*Top:* Karl Radek. Born 1885. Party member since 1917. Left-wing communist. Member of the Central Committee, 1919–24. Comintern leader. Trotskyist. Talented journalist. Dean of Communist University for Far Eastern Peoples. Expert on Germany and China. Expelled from Party in 1927. Exiled to Siberia. Readmitted in 1930. Handed over personal archive on the Trotskyist Opposition to the OGPU. Helped draft the new (Stalinist) Soviet Constitution. Helped Yezhov prepare the second Show Trial. Found guilty of being in the "Anti-Soviet Trotskyist Centre" but "not having taken direct part in organising and carrying out subversive, wrecking, espionage or terrorist activity."

Sentenced to ten years imprisonment but murdered, either by another prisoner or the NKVD on May 19, 1939.
*Above left:* Ivan Grashe. Bolshevik Party member since 1917. Brilliant European and Asian linguist. Important roles in Comintern (with Bukharin) and Profintern (trade union organisation) from 1921–36. Follower of Trotsky in 1920s. Sentenced to death and shot on February 1, 1937.
*Above, second left:* Valentin Arnold. Small-time crook and adventurer. Born in Petrograd slums, he had three aliases by the age of seven. Travelled the world in his early teens; Finland, Germany, Holland, Norway and England. Conscripted, deserted and jailed in First

World War. Made his way to New York. Jailed again. Joined the U.S. Army, the Freemasons, the Communist Party of the U.S.A. All this came out in cross-examination at the trial and it sent his interrogators into a frenzy, not least in trying to find out from this strange and nervous man with almost no political convictions, what his real name was. Accused of trying to assassinate Molotov by driving him into a ditch. Unusually for these trials, the event in question had actually happened but it was nothing more than a minor accident. Arnold was sentenced to ten years imprisonment. He was shot in 1941.
*Above, third from left:* Ivan Knyazev. Left-wing Socialist Revolutionary (S-R) until

1918. Worked in People's Commissariat of Transportation. Arrested as former Trotskyist. Testified at the trial that many catastrophes on Soviet railroads happened because the system was old and badly maintained – not as a result of "wrecking". This, apparently, made Stalin furious. Knyazev was sentenced to death and shot on February 1, 1937.
*Above right:* Stanislav Rataichak. Bolshevik Party member since 1919. German prisoner of war who joined the Red Army, 1917–20. Deputy People's Commissar of Heavy Industry, 1932–34. Friend of Piatakov. Accused of "wrecking" and attempting to assassinate Molotov. Sentenced to death and shot on February 1, 1937.

271

*Top left:* Alexei Shestov. Party member since 1918. Trade Unionist. Played an important role in the mining industry. Arrested as a "wrecker" in 1936. Sentenced to death at the second Show Trial and shot on February 1, 1937.
*Above left:* Grigorii Piatakov. Born 1890. Party member since 1910. Leader of Left Communists in Ukraine in Civil War.

Left Oppositionist in 1920s. Expelled from Party in 1928. Reinstated. Deputy director of Heavy Industry. Sacked in 1936. Sent letter to Stalin pleading that he was not an enemy of the people (Piatakov's former wife had been tortured by the NKVD and denounced him), that he would die for the Party and Stalin. Became mentally unstable. Told

Yezhov that he was willing to "represent justice" at the next Show Trial. Prepared terrible letter saying he would shoot his former wife, that she was the real enemy of the people. He was arrested the next day. Sentenced to death and shot on February 1, 1937.
*Top right:* Boris Norkin. Bolshevik Party member since 1917. Director of

Kemerovo Construction Combine Trust, 1932–36. Arrested as a "wrecker" and for plotting to kill Molotov. Shot on February 1, 1937.
*Above right:* Iosif Turok. Bolshevik Party member since 1918. A director of Sverdlovsk Railroad. Arrested in 1936 as a "wrecker". Sentenced to death and shot on February 1, 1937.

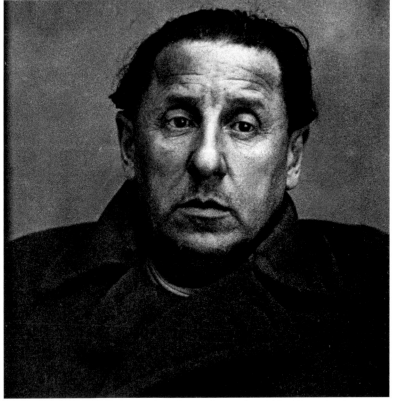

*Top left:* Nikolai Muralov. Born 1877. Bolshevik Party member since 1903. Left-wing communist. Civil War hero. Close friend of Trotsky. Agronomist. Expelled from Party in 1927. Wrote to Stalin requesting re-admission. Stalin told his secretary, "Don't bother to reply." Arrested and tortured for many weeks. Sentenced to death at the second Show Trial and shot on February 1, 1937.

*Above left:* Yakov Livshitz. Bolshevik Party member since 1917. Unskilled worker who became Deputy Commissar of Transportation. Trotskyist. Arrested in 1936. His boss, Lazar Kaganovich was upset. So upset he told Lipshitz's wife: "He was in the tsarist secret police, he was an S-R terrorist, a wrecker. Divorce him and I will give you a job." When she refused she was also arrested. Livshitz was shot on February 1, 1937.

*Top right:* Yakov Drobnis. Shoemaker. Revolutionary (surviving three death sentences) and Civil War hero. Friend of Trotsky. Arrested in 1936. Sentenced to death and shot on February 1, 1937. His wife was brutally tortured in prison.

*Above right:* Mikhail Boguslavsky. Bolshevik Party member since 1917. Tailor. Close friend of Trotsky in Civil War. Secretary of Red Army Political Department. Expelled from Party with Trotsky. Director of Sibmashstroi, 1932–36. Arrested as "wrecker". Sentenced to death and shot on February 1, 1937.

The third and final Moscow Show Trial (officially known as the Trial of the Anti-Soviet Bloc of Rightists and Trotskyists) took place at the House of Trade Unions in March 1938.

There were twenty one defendants. All of them were tortured (both physically and mentally) into signing confessions admitting the most absurd allegations. Eighteen of the defendants received death sentences at 4am on March 13, 1938. The other three were given long gaol terms but were later retried and shot in Orel Prison in September 1941.

Three of the main figures on trial were Nikolai Bukharin, Alexei Rykhov and

Nikolai Krestinsky. Bukharin (*above left*) was a popular Bolshevik, who edited *Pravda* throughout the 1920s before falling out with Stalin over the collectivisation of agriculture. He was arrested in 1937. The investigators apparently used Bukharin's passport photograph for their files, making a prison mugshot unnecessary. Rykhov and Krestinsky were both former members of Lenin's Politburo, Rykhov becoming head of the government after Lenin's death. Like most of the other defendants at the third Show Trial, their mugshots have yet to come to light. Also in the dock was the Bulgarian,

Christian Rakovsky (*above, second left*), one of Trotsky's closest friends until he was forced to recant in 1934; and Genrykh Yagoda (*third from the left*), the sinister secret police chief who oversaw the preparations for the first Show Trial in 1936. Stalin deposed him shortly afterwards, accusing him of being "four years behind in unmasking the Trotskyist–Zinovievist Bloc."

The photographs of Rakovsky and Akmal Ikramov (*above right*) both seem to have been taken in a prison courtyard. Ikramov had been Party boss in Uzbekistan. He had unwisely made a speech warning of "self conceit". Stalin

didn't like that and Ikramov was arrested in 1937.

Of the fifteen others accused, three were elderly and highly-distinguished physicians, D.D.Pletnev, L.G.Levin and I.N.Kazakov. Pletnev received a gaol term at the trial but was later shot. His tragic face is recorded in the mugshots (*top*) taken in Orel Prison in 1941 when his health was rapidly deteriorating.

All the defendants, with the exception of Yagoda, were rehabilitated in 1988.

*Opposite page:* Filming Chief Prosecutor Vyshinsky's speech: "Mad dogs must be shot – everyone of them must be shot."

*Overleaf:* An NKVD execution squad.

Mikhail Tukhachevsky rose to fame as a brilliant military strategist in the Civil War. Stalin called him one of the Red Army's most talented commanders. But in 1920 there was a major policy dispute between them, and Stalin's praise turned to hatred.

Even so, from the mid-1920s, Stalin found it necessary to make use of Tukhachevsky's genius. He was put in charge of modernising the Red Army which he did very successfully, equipping it with the latest tanks, aeroplanes and rockets. In November 1935, when his career was at its peak, Tukhachevsky was made a Marshal of the Soviet Union and received the Order of Lenin.

He was attractive, famous, smartly dressed and he had many lovers. He was a patron of the arts, giving advice to the young Shostakovich and others, guiding them through the cultural minefields of Soviet life. But Stalin had a long memory and wanted to settle old scores. He nursed deep suspicion and jealousy of all those able and popular people in his inner circle.

Mikhail Tukhachevsky was arrested on Stalin's orders with other high-ranking officers on June 10, 1937. A false confession was beaten out of him and after a secret trial of the "Anti-Soviet Trotskyist Military Organisation", all the defendants were shot.

*Right:* Tukhachevsky with his wife, Nina, and their eleven year old daughter, Svetlana. Terrible things happened to his family. Nina was shot in October 1941 in a Moscow prison, said to have gone insane. Svetlana was considered to be "socially dangerous" and spent years in the camps. Tukhachevsky's mother, Mavra, his sister, Sofia, and his brothers, Alexander and Nikolai were all annihilated. Two former wives and three more sisters were also sent to the Gulag.

The Tukhachevsky trial precipitated a terrible bloodbath in the Red Army. More than 25,000 high-ranking officers were wiped out by Stalin's secret police between 1937 and 1941, leaving the Soviet military decapitated at a very dangerous time.

*Above:* Marshal Vasilii Blyukher (right) in discussion with Yan Gamarnik (left), chief political commissar of the Red Army, and Marshal Alexander Yegorov at the All-Union Congress of Soviets, Moscow, December 10, 1936. Photograph by Emmanuel Yezverikhin. Seven months later Blyukher was on the military tribunal that decided the fate of Tukhachevsky. Yan Gamarnik would also have been there – but on the other side of the table. Certain that Stalin's dragnet was closing in, he preempted his arrest by committing suicide in May

1937. Blyukher himself did not escape. Endorsing the death of Tukhachevsky wasn't enough to save his own skin and he was soon arrested and killed. Yegorov was another victim of the military purges. He was denounced to the NKVD for complaining that all the Red Army's victories in the Civil War were "nowadays being ascribed to Stalin." He was tortured to death in the Lubyanka in 1938.

*Left:* Moisei Nappelbaum's portraits of the two most hated secret police chiefs of the entire Stalin era, Nikolai Yezhov (*far left*) and Lavrentii Beria. Their combined cruelty killed millions of people, whether close to the reins of power or simply ordinary citizens. Yezhov's rule was short but drenched in blood, Beria's was much longer; both of them came to a sticky end.

279

Stalin considered the possibility of having a fourth show trial of eminent Soviet writers and artists who had been arrested as part of his war on the cultural front. Isaak Babel would almost certainly have been one defendant and the avant-garde theatre director, Vsevolod Meyerhold, also would have been targeted. Meyerhold (prison mugshot, *right*) was arrested on June 20, 1939, after a defiant refusal to accept the doctrine of Socialist Realism. He was tortured in the Lubyanka by the same interrogators as Babel.

The investigators' file on Meyerhold contains a letter that he wrote to the Foreign Minister Vyacheslav Molotov on January 13, 1940. It is unknown whether Molotov actually saw the letter. It makes extremely harrowing reading. Here are some extracts:

"...The investigators began to use force on me, a sick, 65-year-old man. I was made to lie face down and then beaten on the soles of my feet and spine with a rubber strap. They sat me on a chair and beat my feet from above, with considerable force... For the next few days, when those parts of my legs were covered with extensive internal haemorrhaging, they again beat the red-blue-and-yellow bruises with the strap and the pain was so intense that it felt as if boiling hot water was being poured on these sensitive areas. I howled and wept from the pain. They beat my back with the same rubber stamp and punched my face, swinging their fists from a great height...

"When they added the 'psychological attack', as it's called, the physical and mental pain aroused such an appalling terror in me that I was left quite naked and defenceless. My nerve endings, it turned out, were very close to the surface of my body and the skin proved as sensitive and soft as a child's. The intolerable physical and emotional pain caused my eyes to weep unending streams of tears. Lying face down on the floor, I discovered that I could wriggle, twist and squeal like a dog when its master whips it. One time my body was shaking so uncontrollably that the guard escorting me back from such an interrogation asked: 'Have you got malaria?' When I lay down on the cot and fell asleep, after 18 hours of interrogation, in order to go back in an hour's time for more, I was woken up by my own groaning and because I was jerking about like a patient in the last stages of typhoid fever. Fright arouses terror, and terror forces us to find some means of self-defence.

"'Death, oh most certainly, death is easier than this!' the interrogated person says to himself. I began to incriminate myself in the hope that

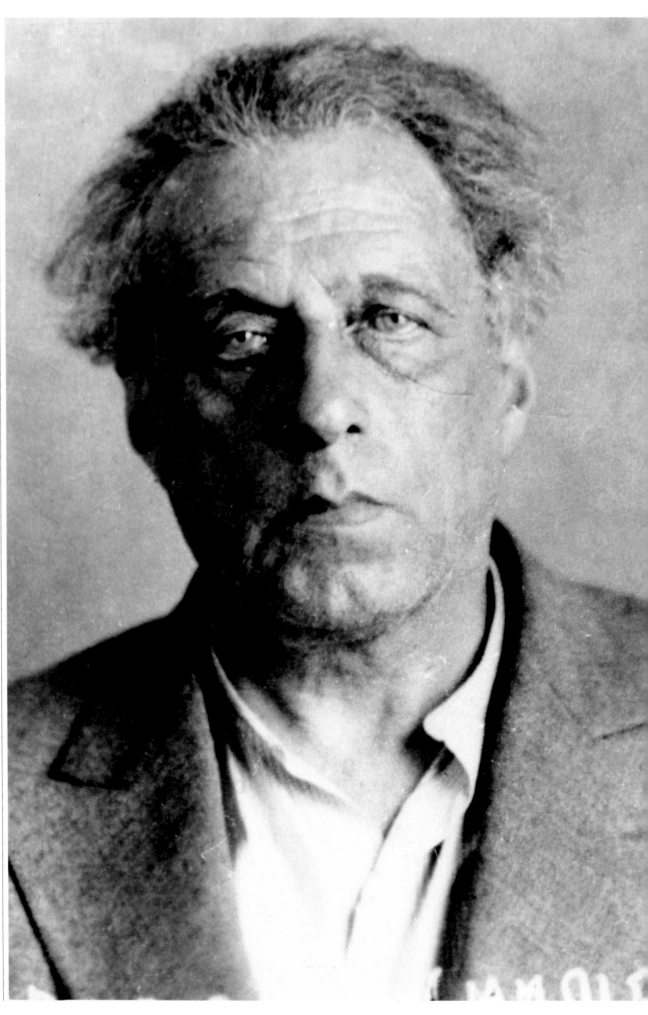

this, at least, would lead quickly to the scaffold...

"... There was one other terrible circumstance that contributed to my collapse, and total loss of control over myself... Immediately after my arrest I was cast into the deepest depression by the obsessive thought, 'This is what I deserve!' The government thought, so I began to convince myself, that the sentence I had received... was not sufficient... for my sins... and that I must undergo yet another punishment, that which the NKVD was carrying out now. 'This is what I deserve!' I repeated to myself and I split into two individuals. The first started searching for the 'crimes' of the second, and when they could not be found, he began to invent them. The interrogator proved an effective and experienced assistant and, working closely together, we began our composition. When my fantasy started running out, the interrogators took over... they prepared and revised the depositions (some were rewritten three or four times)...

"I still could not think at all clearly because a Damoclean sword dangled over me: constantly the interrogator repeated, threateningly, 'If you won't write (invent, in other words?!) then we shall beat you again, leaving your head and your right arm untouched but reducing the rest to a hacked, bleeding and shapeless body'. And I signed everything..."

One week after Meyerhold's arrest his wife, the actress Zinaida Raikh (*left*) was found murdered with her eyes gouged out in their flat in the centre of Moscow. It was the work of the secret police.

There was to be no fourth show trial. Poor Meyerhold was eventually shot on February 2, 1940.

*Top:* Meyerhold standing in front of a portrait of his wife, Zinaida, in the study of their Moscow apartment.

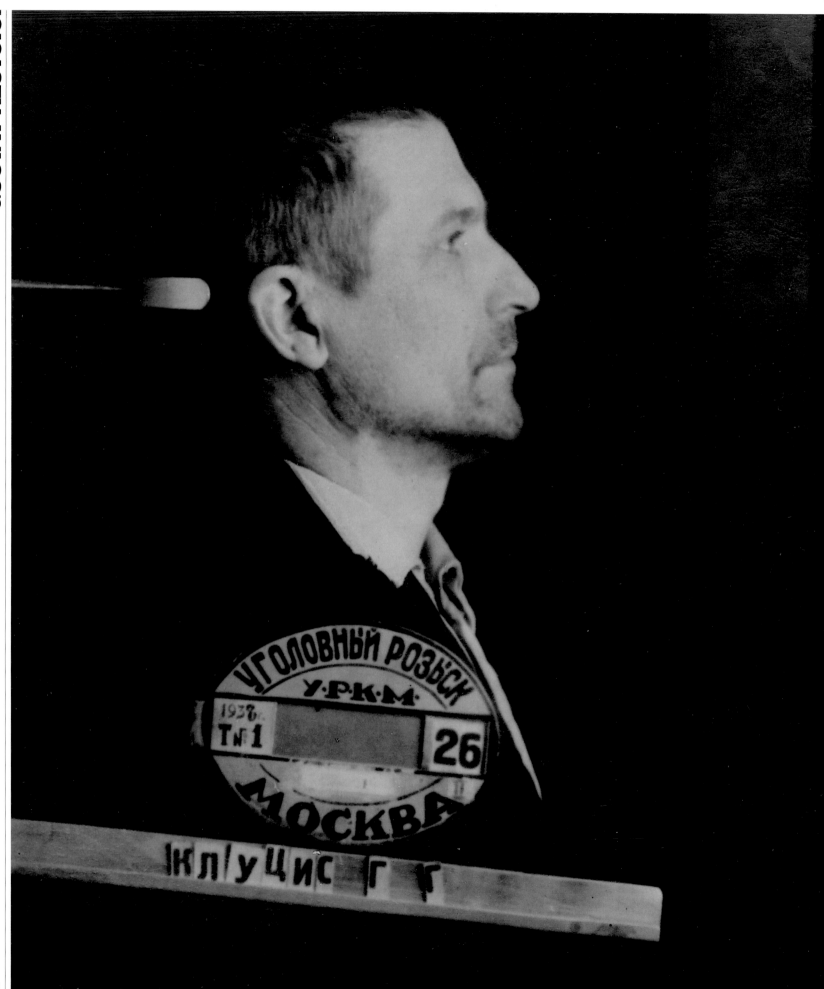

Another fine practitioner of the Soviet avant-garde to be arrested was the Latvian Gustav Klutsis, the great suprematist painter turned political poster designer, some of whose work can be seen in this book.

In his photomontage posters, Klutsis employed to the full his unique ability to visualise in the most dynamic manner the headlong rush towards industrialisation and collectivisation, and no designer contributed more effectively to the Stalin Cult.

For his trouble, Klutsis was arrested on January 17, 1938. The Great Purges struck as many as 70,000 Latvians living in the USSR and Klutsis was accused, wrongfully of course, of belonging to an "armed gang of Latvian terrorists".

*Left:* Klutsis was incarcerated in the notorious Butovo prison in Moscow where these mugshots were taken on his arrival. On February 26, 1938 he was shot along with sixty three other Latvian artists and intellectuals.

*Top:* Klutsis in 1922 with one of his constructions.

*Above:* Klutsis' hand photographed in 1930 for his famous photomontage (reproduced on page 209).

His widow, the distinguished artist and designer Valentina Kulagina died in 1987, never knowing the correct dates and circumstances of his death.

"Long Live Stalin, The First Marshal of Communism!" A poster from 1939 by B.Lebeshev in old-style Azerbaijanian.

The cover of an Intourist guide to cruise tours in the Soviet Union (first, tourist or third class) for 1939.

Ни одной пяди чужой земли не хотим. Но и своей земли, ни одного вершка своей земли не отдадим никому. /Сталин/

*Top:* Vyacheslav Molotov, the Soviet foreign minister, signs the Nazi-Soviet Non-Aggression Treaty in the Kremlin, Moscow, late at night on August 23, 1939. Ribbentrop, the Nazi foreign minister, Stalin and their respective aides look on contentedly.

Spheres of influence were also settled. Invasion, occupation or annexation for Poland, Estonia, Latvia, Lithuania, Finland and Romania by the armies of either Stalin or Hitler soon followed. Communist parties around the world did their best to justify all this as being in the interests of world peace. World War Two began two weeks later.

*Above left:* A typographical poster, circa 1939, with text by Stalin: "We do not want one inch of anyone else's land, but we will not give up one inch of our land to anyone else."

*Opposite page: USSR in Construction* magazine's interpretation of how the Red Army was greeted when it invaded and annexed eastern Poland, including most of Polish-held Belorussia.

*Above:* Viktor Koretsky's illustration was also published as a poster (seen in an October Revolution anniversary demonstration in Red Square, Moscow, 1939). Its original slogan was a quote from Stalin: "Our army is the army for the liberation of the working people."

USSR in construction

XXIIIrd YEAR OF THE GREAT OCTOBER · No. 2—3 · FEBRUARY MARCH 1940 · STATE ART PUBLISHING HOUSE
SOCIALIST REVOLUTION «ISKUSSTVO» MOSCOW—LENINGRAD

*Above, left and right:* Two gigantic sculptures by Sergei Merkurov ruling the centre of Moscow in the late 1930s. Stalin has seized the square in front of the Bolshoi Theatre, where famously Lenin and Trotsky once made speeches to soldiers departing for the Polish front in 1920. The Metropol Hotel is in the distance. The imperious Lenin, meanwhile, is positioned nearby with the Gosplan (State Planning Committee) building behind him.
*Right:* "Them... Us". The tragedy of Viktor Koretsky's huge double-image poster is in its timing. On the left is a scene of defiance amid devastation echoing Guernica, bombed by the Germans in the Spanish Civil War. On the right we can see Soviet Woman with her well-fed son, also looking to the skies, giving thanks to Comrade Stalin for the immeasurable riches that he has bestowed upon the Motherland. Within six months of the publication of this hideously self-satisfied comparison, the German army had invaded Russia.

*Opposite page:* A maquette, possibly for an enormous monument or piece of sculpture, from the late 1930s. Artist unknown. The theme is "Socialism in One Country". A myriad of scenes from the triumphs of industrialisation are acted out under the watchful gaze of Stalin, while border guards calmly defend Soviet territory.

Trotsky and Natalya Sedova, comrades for nearly forty years, had been living in exile in Coyoacán, Mexico City, since 1937. On August 20, 1940, Trotsky was attacked in his study by a Stalinist assassin with an ice-axe. He died of his wounds in hospital the following day. Stalin had finally succeeded in annihilating his most hated political opponent.

*Top:* The American Trotskyist press reports the crime. Over the next five days an estimated 300,000 people, mainly Mexico's poorest, filed past Trotsky's open casket to bid their last farewells.

*Right:* Trotsky's body entering the furnace, August 27, 1940.

Some months earlier, Trotsky had written his last testament:

"For forty-three years of my conscious life I have remained a revolutionist; for forty-two of them I have fought under the banner of Marxism. If I had to begin all over again I would of course try to avoid this or that mistake, but the main course of my life would remain unchanged. I shall die a proletarian revolutionist, a Marxist, a dialectical materialist, and consequently an irreconcilable atheist. My faith in the communist future of mankind is not less ardent, indeed it is firmer today, than it was in the days of my youth.

"Natalya has just come up to the window from the courtyard and opened it wide so that the air may enter more freely into my room. I can see the bright green strip of grass beneath the wall, and the clear blue sky above the wall, and sunlight everywhere. Life is beautiful. Let the future generations cleanse it of all evil, oppression and violence and enjoy it to the full."

L. Trotsky,
Coyoacán, 27 February 1940.

*Overleaf:* Stalin – the gravedigger of the Revolution.

"… in the opinion of Soviet circles, rumours of Germany's intention to break the pact and begin hostilities against the USSR are totally without foundation… rumours that the USSR is preparing for war with Germany are lies and provocations…"

On June 22, 1941, just eight days after these reassuring words had been published in *Izvestia*, the German Army invaded Russia over a vast front without warning. Stalin's initial disbelief in the seriousness of the attack is shown in a defence directive, given within hours, ordering Soviet forces to fight back but limiting air activity. The Luftwaffe was therefore able to destroy most of the Soviet air force while it was still on the ground. A Red Army wireless operator in an advanced position desperately signalled his headquarters: "We are under fire. What shall we do?"

*Left:* "Don't Chatter", Nina Vatolina's famous 1941 poster on the subject of careless talk costing lives. The small text reads: "Be alert. In days like these, the walls have ears. It's a small step from gossip to treason."

*Far left:* "Everything for the Front! Everything for Victory!" El Lissitsky's last poster before his death in 1942. In a gigantic undertaking, the Soviets organised the evacuation of factories and equipment from their industrial heartlands to safe locations east of the Urals. War production was then stepped up to unprecedented rates to replace equipment destroyed by the enemy, as well as to design and build new weapons with which to kill him.

*Above:* Nazi troops on Soviet soil, Vitebsk, July 1941. By the middle of July the Germans had taken Riga, Minsk, Vitebsk and Smolensk, and were heading towards Leningrad in the north and Kiev in the south. In early August, twenty Soviet divisions were cut off in southern Ukraine, resulting in the capture of 100,000 troops. Over 300,000 men and 3,000 tanks were captured near Smolensk and 600,000 prisoners were taken in the German advance across Belorussia. But as the beleaguered Soviet armies suffered such terrible losses, wave upon wave of reinforcements were marshalled in by the Soviet High Command to regroup or replace them. By September, the Nazis themselves had started to suffer substantial casualties and their first worries about new supplies of manpower and equipment began to surface. But Hitler, dizzy with the success of the campaign so far, decided that the fall of Moscow was now imperative.

*Opposite page:* Nina Vatolina's 1941 poster, "Fascism – The Most Evil Enemy of Women. Everyone to the Struggle Against Fascism." Vatolina used her neighbour (whom she would often see queuing in her local bakery, always wearing the same red head scarf) as the model for this heroic poster.

*Overleaf:* "Somewhere in Ukraine" is the wartime caption on this photograph of women discovering their loved ones, victims of the Nazi firing squads.

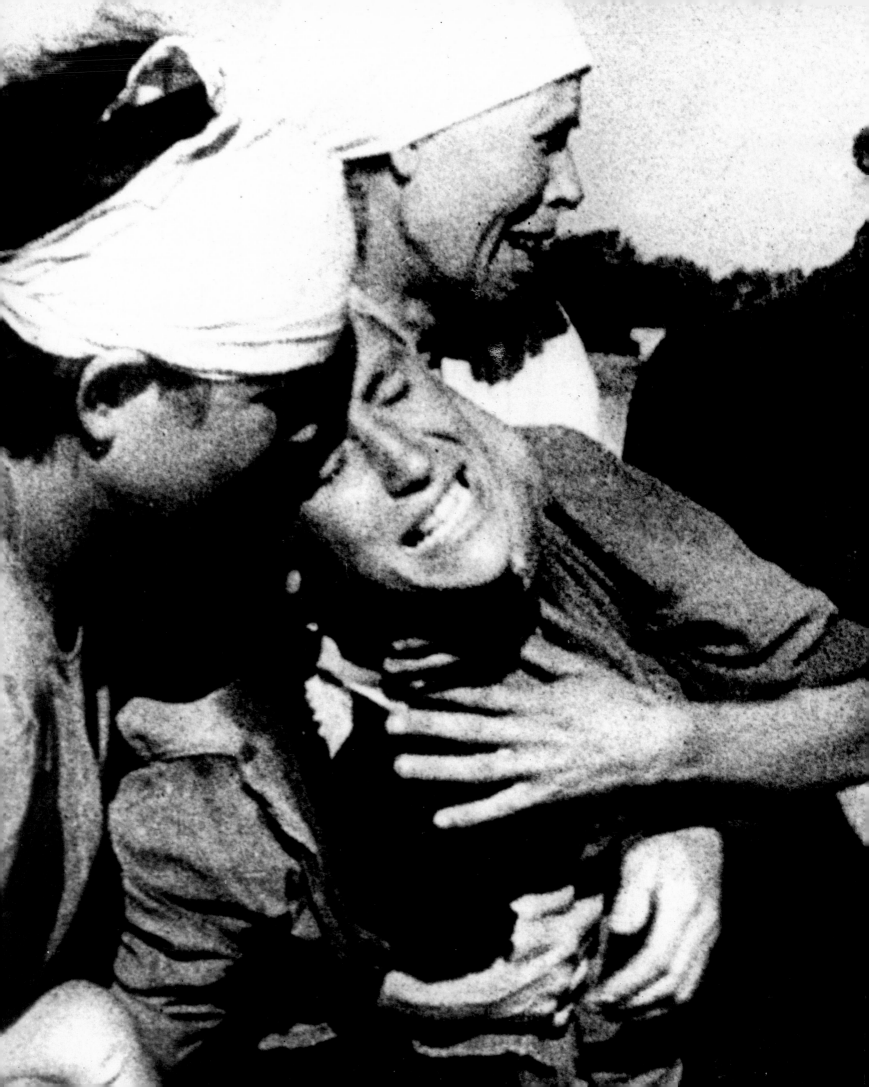

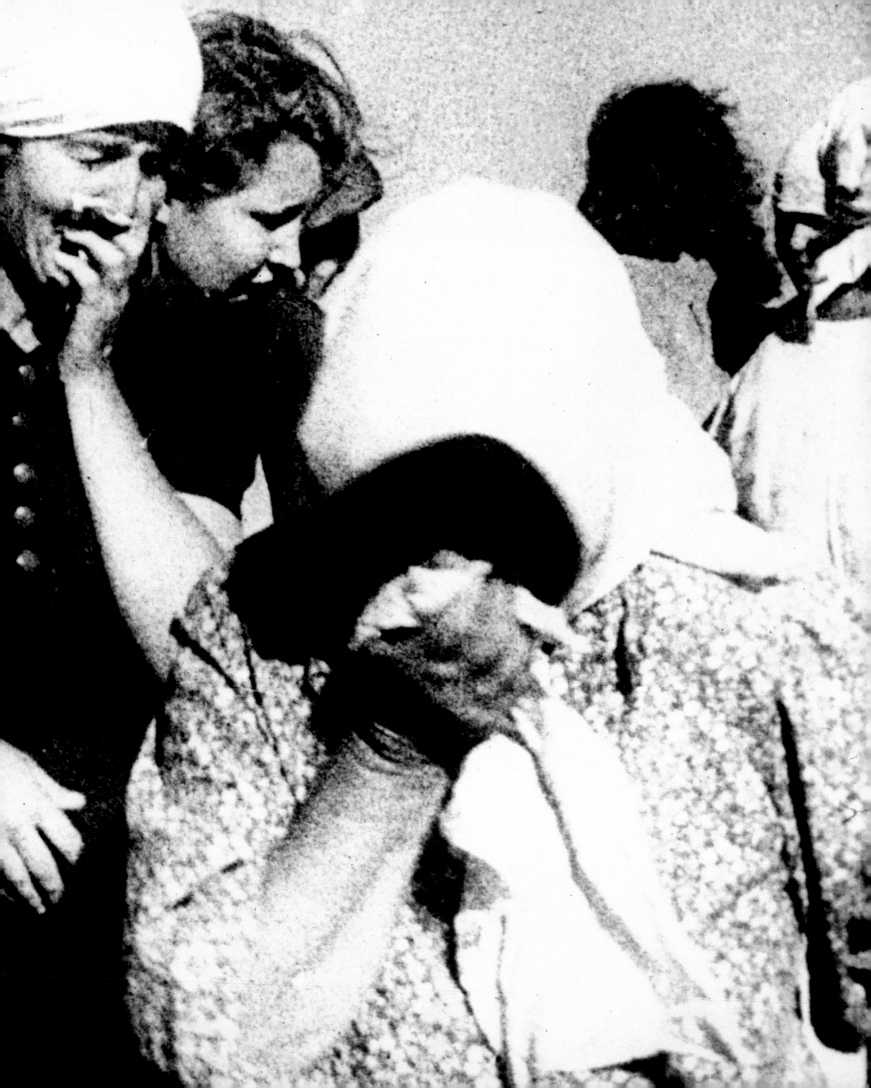

*Above:* Murmansk, December 1942. Photograph by Yevgenii Khaldei. The Arctic sea port was used in the war as a landing base by American and British convoys supplying the Soviets with huge quantities of military equipment, including aircraft. Murmansk had therefore been an obvious target for bombing since the war started but on June 22, 1942 Hitler ordered its total destruction. In twenty four hours of non-stop aggression, the Luftwaffe dropped 350,000 incendiary devices on the town's mainly wooden buildings, more than fulfilling the Fuhrer's wishes.

*Right:* Yakov Dzhugashvili, Stalin's eldest son, surrounded by his Nazi captors near Vitebsk, July 1941. Yakov's mother, Ekaterina Svanidze, married Stalin in 1903, giving birth to Yakov the following year. She died

of tuberculosis in 1907. Yakov trained as an engineer and volunteered for the front when war broke out. He served briefly as a lieutenant in an armoured division before his captivity.

In 1942, the German High Command offered to exchange Yakov for Field Marshal Friedrich Paulus after the defeat of the Nazis at Stalingrad. Stalin famously refused, reportedly saying, "There are no Soviet prisoners of war, only traitors." On April 14, 1943, Yakov was killed, shot by a guard at the electric fence surrounding Sachenhausen concentration camp, either trying to escape or in an act of suicide.

*Opposite page:* Nazi iconoclasm, Western Russia, August 1941.

*Opposite page:* Viktor Koretsky's famous poster, "Red Army Warriors, Save Us!" published in many sizes and huge editions throughout the war from 1942 onwards, also as postcards, leaflets and other printed matter.
*Right:* A large format, hand-painted version of the poster dramatically positioned over a tank production line in an armaments factory located east of the Urals. The slogan on the wall reads, "More Tanks For The Front!"

*Above:* Russian refugees fleeing the battle zone in the first days of the war. The photograph was taken by Max Alpert, a pioneer of Soviet reportage photography who covered the war as a correspondent for TASS, the Soviet news agency.

301

*Top:* The plight of the evacuees. A photograph by Mikhail Trakhman, a special war correspondent for TASS who often photographed behind enemy lines with the help of the partisans. His photograph of one of them, Alexei Grinchuk (*above left*), was taken at six in the morning on the Leningrad front. Grinchuk said to Trakhman, who was lying beside him, "Take a picture of me." Trakhman did so and this is the photograph. Shortly afterwards, the enemy opened fire and Grinchuk was killed.

*Above right:* A poster by Viktor Koretsky and V.A.Gitsevich from 1941 entreating Soviet citizens to "Join the Ranks of the Friends of the Front." The text continues, "The Volunteer is the Friend and Helper of the Soldier."
*Opposite page:* Ivan Shagin's photograph of a badly wounded political commissar directing the fighting.

Stalin had been warned more than once about the Nazis' plans to invade Russia. Richard Sorge, the Soviet agent, warned the Kremlin at the beginning of May and even predicted the exact date. The Soviet spy network in Western Europe known as "The Red Orchestra" also supplied accurate information. The British tried to share what they had learned. Stalin ignored them all; the Germans were just carrying out manoeuvres on Russia's borders, the pact was sacrosanct.

On being woken at 3.30am on the night of June 22nd by General (later Marshal) Zhukov and informed that it wasn't, Stalin appears to have gone into a period of indecision caused by panic.

It was not until June 30th that he formed a State Committee of Defence and he failed to make his first speech to the Russian people until July 3rd.

In this speech he invoked the famed scorched earth policy – the burning of crops and the removal or destruction of anything that could be useful to the Nazi invaders. He also summoned, for the first time, the people to fight in what he termed "The Great Patriotic War".

The reasons for this nationalistic and very un-Soviet slogan were manifold. Vast sections of the Russian people had suffered such terrible losses throughout the 1930s from famine, terror and the Gulag, that words like "communism" and names like "Stalin" and "Beria" were not universally appreciated. But tolerating the presence of "German child killers" on Russian soil was a different matter.

*Right:* Ill equipped for the Russian winter, December 1941. Photograph by Galina Sankova.
*Opposite page, top:* Forty degrees below zero, Moscow, December 1941. Photograph by Ivan Shagin.
*Opposite page, below:* "Long Live Our Motherland, Her Freedom, Her Independence! Death to the German Invaders!" A wartime typographical flier quotes Stalin. The German army had moved to within 40km of Moscow by the end of November but the harshest winter, interrupted supply lines, and sheer exhaustion stopped them in their tracks. Inside Moscow there had been panic. The government had moved to Kuibyshev but Stalin stayed.

On December 5, Zukhov ordered a massive counter-attack. A million men from the Far Eastern Command drove back the Nazis and Hitler's hopes of a blitzkrieg on Moscow were crushed.

# ДА ЗДРАВСТВУЕТ
# НАША СЛАВНАЯ РОДИНА
## ЕЕ СВОБОДА, ЕЕ НЕЗАВИСИМОСТЬ!
## СМЕРТЬ НЕМЕЦКИМ ОККУПАНТАМ!

### (СТАЛИН)

*Opposite page:* Three German soldiers gratefully surrender to the Red Army, "somewhere on the Western front" in this press photograph from 1942. The original caption to the picture tells us that the Germans had decided to give themselves up after listening to Stalin's May Day speech. Whether they had known enough Russian to understand it is open to doubt but in any case their future was bleak.

Eight million men and women of the Soviet armed forces were killed in the Great Patriotic War and, according to figures given at the 1946 Nuremburg trials, nearly ten million more Soviet civilians died during the German occupation, including some four million Jews. The Nazi commitment to massacre has been well documented.

Neither the Nazis nor the Soviets were interested in the Geneva Convention. One and a half million German POWs died in the Gulag during the war, mainly of typhus, starvation, frostbite or ill treatment, many others were put to work in the mines, construction and forestry. After the war, in order not to lose a skilled workforce, 35,000 German workers were charged with crimes such as plotting to invade the Soviet Union and given long sentences to rebuild the cities, roads and railways they had destroyed.

*Above:* Four posters designed by the English artist Reginald Mount in 1942 for display on the crates containing trucks, tanks, aircraft and other supplies heading for Russia. The slogans read: "From The British People. To Victory! We Are With You!"

*Top:* A pilot of the Royal Air Force (right) shakes hands with his Soviet counterpart at a Russian airbase, celebrating the delivery of another fully assembled Hawker Hurricane fighter aircraft.

COMRADES IN ARMS !

BRITAIN AND THE U.S.S.R.

*Above:* Churchill and Stalin meeting in the Moscow Kremlin, August 1942. British Foreign Office documents have left no room for doubt how much Churchill had hated the very idea of the Russian Revolution. As Secretary of State for War he had sent in British troops to support the White armies in the Civil War, branding Lenin's new government as the "foul baboonery of Bolshevism... a pestilence more destructive of life than the Black Death or the Spotted Typhus." But in June 1941, as Russia felt the full force of the Nazi invasion he "had not the slightest doubt where our duty and our policy lay." Britain and the United States remained allies with Russia for the duration of the war.

"Churchill hoped that he had established a genuine personal relationship with Stalin," noted the late historian, A.J.P. Taylor, "He was probably wrong." Stalin could not forget the past; but he also realised that Churchill's qualifications as an anti-Hitlerite were unquestionable.

*Top:* A British Ministry of Information publication from October 1941 encouraging British workers to build the tanks and aircraft bound for Russia with speed and efficiency.

*Right:* "Thunderbolt". TASS window poster No.504 hand-painted by the Kukriniksy, a famous Soviet trio of caricaturists. TASS windows were used for propaganda displays in the same way as Rosta windows had been back in the Civil War.

ОКНО ТАСС № 504

ГРОМОВОЙ УДАР

ХУДОЖНИКИ КУКРЫНИКСЫ

ОКНО ТАСС №469

# МОЛОДАЯ ПАРТИЗАНКА

КАК ЧАПАЕВСКАЯ АНКА,
И УПОРНА И СМЕЛА
МОЛОДАЯ ПАРТИЗАНКА
ИЗ СОЖЖЕНОГО СЕЛА.

НАШУ КРАСНУЮ КУКУШКУ
ФРИЦ БОИТСЯ, КАК ОГНЯ,
КТО ПОПАЛСЯ ЕЙ НА МУШКУ-
ТОТ ПОКОЙНИКАМ РОДНЯ!

ЗРЯ, БЕЗ ТОЛКУ, НЕ РИСКУЕТ,
ВЫБИРАЕТ, СМОТРИТ, ЖДЕТ,-
А УЖ ЕСЛИ „ПРОКУКУЕТ"-
ВРАГ, КАК КОЛОС, УПАДЕТ!

И В РАЗВЕДКЕ И В ЗАСАДЕ,
НА ПРИВАЛЕ У КОСТРА
ВСЕ СУМЕЕТ, ВСЕ НАЛАДИТ-
ПОВАР, СНАЙПЕР И СЕСТРА.

ПАРТИЗАНКА БОЕВАЯ
УЛЫБНЕТСЯ НАЛЕТУ:
- „Я СБИВАЮ-НЕ СЧИТАЮ,
ПОБЕДИМ-ТОГДА СОЧТУ.

Я В ОТРЯДЕ НЕ ОДНА ВЕДЬ:
ЕСТЬ ДЕВЧАТА ПОСИЛЬНЕЙ!::
КАК ТАКУЮ НЕ ПРОСЛАВИТЬ,
ПЕСНЮ КАК НЕ СПЕТЬ О НЕЙ.

Худ. А.Бубнов

Текст-Вас. Лебедев-Кумач.

*Left:* "Young Partisan Woman". TASS Window poster No.469, hand-painted by Alexander Bubnov with a poem by Vasilii Lebedev-Kumach.
*Top:* "The People's Avengers". A monumental sculpture by Matvei Manizer dedicated to the partisans.
*Centre:* Partisans taking a break in the depths of the forest. More than 800,000 Soviet women served in the Great Patriotic War as partisans, pilots, machine gunners and many other roles. Some two thousand women were also recruited as snipers. Lyudmila Pavlichenko was one of many who became legendary; she registered 309 kills before she was wounded in June 1942.
*Above:* Jewish partisans, Belorussia, 1943. Up to 30,000 Jews joined partisan units in the war. The largest Jewish unit in Belorussia was led by the Bielski brothers in the Naliboki Forest. Another, led by Shalom Zorin, was hidden in the same forest and included clothing and shoemaking workshops, a kitchen, a bakery and a bomb making factory, all run by civilian Jews, as well as a school for seventy students and a hospital run by doctors from Minsk.

Сын мой! Ты видишь долю мою...
Громи фашистов в святом бою!

*Top:* "My Son! You See My Plight... Smash the Fascists in Sacred Battle!" A poster by Fyodor Antonov, 1941.

*Right:* Dmitrii Baltermans' photograph "Grief", one of a series taken by him in 1942 at Kerch in the eastern Crimea. Women are shown searching for the bodies of their loved ones, non-combatant peasants massacred in a barren landscape by retreating Nazis. Baltermans has written: "War is, above all, grief. I have photographed non-stop for years and know that in all that time I have produced only five or six real photographs. War is not for photography. If, heaven forbid, I had to photograph war again, I would do it quite differently. I agonise now at the thought of all the things I did not photograph."

A.J.P. Taylor said of the "Grief" series: "No photographs have penetrated more deeply into the nature of war."

*Above:* Peasant women labouring in the mud to move a wagon carrying the corpses of their relatives and friends. Kerch, 1942. Stalin ordered three major offensives in the spring of 1942, spurred on by the abrupt curtailment of the German army at the gates of Moscow. The plan was to drive the Nazis from Russian soil with the utmost speed. All three offensives failed. Outside Leningrad, the Soviets lost a whole army. In May, Kerch had to be evacuated with the loss of 176,000 men and 350 tanks. At Kharkov, Stalin refused his high command's pleas for a tactical withdrawal and the German army overran the entire front. They took 240,000 prisoners and more than 1,000 tanks were lost.

# СМЕРТЬ ДЕТОУБИЙЦАМ!

*Opposite page:* Another harrowing photograph by Dmitrii Baltermans from his "Grief" series, taken in Kerch, 1942.
*Above:* "Death to the Child Killers!" A poster by Viktor Ivanov and Olga Burova, dated 1942.
*Right:* The Kerch offensive by Anatolii Garanin, 1942.
*Far right:* Marshal Georgii Zhukov with Marshal Semyon Timoshenko (behind him) on manoeuvres. Zhukov was appointed Chief of Staff of the Red Army in 1941.
He assisted in the defence of Leningrad that October but was quickly recalled to take control of the defence of Moscow. He was made Deputy Supreme Commander of Soviet forces in 1942 and a Marshal in 1943. He led the Red Army's assault on Berlin in 1945 and received the German surrender. He was to be marginalised by Stalin after the war. Timoshenko, blunt and outspoken, was always a favourite of Stalin, who made him

Commander-in-Chief at the outbreak of war. He was soon relieved of his position. He was in charge at Kharkov when Soviet forces were cut to pieces by the Nazis in the spring offensive of 1942. His next appointment was in July as commander of the Stalingrad front but once again he was soon replaced. He ended the war with responsibility for Ukraine.

ВСЯ НАДЕЖДА НА ТЕБЯ, КРАСНЫЙ ВОИН!

Художник В. Иванов     Редактор Поволоцкая     Государственное издательство     Тип. «Красный печатник». Гос. изд-ва «Искусство».
Л30158 от 5/IV 1943 г. Изд. № 6069. Объем ½ п. л. Тир. 40 000. Цена 60 коп.     «ИСКУССТВО»     Москва, ул. 25 Октября, 5. Заказ № 810.
    Москва 1943 Ленинград

*Above, left and right:* Masha Bruskina and Volodya Shcherbatsevich are hanged in public on October 26, 1941 in Minsk, Belorussia, by officers of the 707th Infantry Division of the German army. Masha was a seventeen-year-old Jewish high school graduate who had lived with her mother in the Minsk ghetto before joining the resistance. Volunteering as a nurse, she helped wounded Soviet soldiers to escape by supplying them with civilian clothes and false identity papers. She was informed upon, arrested and tortured.

Masha, the sixteen-year-old Volodya (also a resistance fighter) and Kiril Trus (a veteran of the Civil War) were all hanged on makeshift gallows at the gates of a yeast factory on Voroshilov Street. Masha was the first of more than 4,000 women to be hanged by Hitler's invaders. Many more were shot or guillotined.

Zoya Kosmodemyanskaya was another partisan heroine. She was eighteen years old when she was arrested for setting fire to a stables used by the Nazis near Moscow. She was raped, tortured and mutilated by the Nazi interrogators who finally hanged her in public in Petrishchevo on November 29, 1941. Her last defiant words of courage: "You can't hang all 190 million of us!" Zoya's life was made into a powerful Soviet propaganda film in 1944 directed by Lev Arnshtam with music by Dmitrii Shostakovich.

*Top:* Viktor Ivanov and Olga Burova's poster, "All Hope Lies With You, Red Soldier!"
*Opposite page:* A mass hanging of Russian peasants by retreating Nazis, late 1943.

The battle of Stalingrad, the most terrible in human history, raged for 199 days from late August 1942 until the beginning of February 1943 when Field Marshal Paulus, twenty two Nazi generals and what remained of their exhausted and starving troops finally capitulated to the Red Army. The immense brutality of the Nazi assault on the city on the Volga had been met by fierce resistance from the Soviets who defended their city brick by brick, bullet by bullet, wound by fatal wound. Nearly two million people are believed to have lost their lives fighting over the city's charred and infested, bombed-out remains.

Vasilii Grossman, the Soviet war correspondent and (later) novelist, who covered the street fighting for four months, wrote that the German attacks were eventually blunted by "dogged, rugged, Siberian obstinacy".

Victory at Stalingrad was the first heavy defeat inflicted by the Russians on the Nazi invaders and is considered to have been the major turning point of the Second World War.

*Left:* Fighting in the Red October metalworks, Stalingrad. Photograph by Yakov Ryumkin. The Nazi assault on the factory district in the northern part of the city started at the end of September 1942. In his authoritative book, *Stalingrad*, the author Antony Beevor describes their reception:

"The Red October complex and the Barrikady gun factory had been turned into fortresses as lethal as those of Verdun.

"If anything, they were more dangerous because the Soviet regiments were so well hidden... In the Red October plant, detachments from the 414th Anti-Tank Division had concealed their 45mm and 96mm guns in the rubble, using lumps of discarded metal as camouflage and protection."

Beevor quotes Ilin, a sniper who operated in the Red October factory and had the deaths of 185 "Fritzes" to his credit: "Fascists should know the strength of weapons in the hands of Soviet supermen."

*Top:* "Stalingrad" by Viktor Deni, 1942. A suitably violent reworking of his 1921 poster, "The Third International" (*see page 85*).

# С ГОРОДОМ ЛЕНИНА– ВЕСЬ НАРОД, К ГОРОДУ ЛЕНИНА– ВРАГ НЕ ПРОЙДЕТ!

25-IX-1941 г.

On September 22, 1941, Hitler issued a directive: "St Petersburg (Leningrad) must be erased from the face of the Earth... we have no interest in saving the lives of the civilian population."

Six weeks later, in a speech in Munich he screamed, "Leningrad must die of starvation!"

The Nazis, helped by Finland, had succeeded in blockading the city since the start of September. Almost all links to the outside world had been severed. Stalin considered Leningrad lost. In November, the Nazis began a relentless bombardment of the city using heavy artillery and massive aerial bombing raids that caused terrible firestorms. The aim was to obliterate the city's civilian infrastructure – housing, food stores, schools and hospitals, energy supplies and transport – as well as its population. The siege was to last for almost 900 days.

*Above:* "All the People are with the City of Lenin, the Enemy will not Enter the

City of Lenin!" A poster dated September 25, 1941.

*Top left:* The Volkova Cemetery, 1942. At its worst, the monthly death toll from starvation, epidemic and bombing for those trapped in the blockade grew to 130,000.

*Above right:* Air raid, Leningrad. Both pictures by Boris Kudoyarov.

*Left:* A Soviet supply truck making its way along the ice road on Lake Ladoga as the spring thaw begins. Crossing the lake by truck in winter, boat in summer, was extremely dangerous but one of the few ways of breaking the blockade. By November 1941, the daily food ration in the city had been reduced to 250 grams for manual workers and 125 grams for other civilians, literally a starvation diet.

*Opposite page:* Boris Kudoyarov's tragic photograph, simply titled, "Nevsky Prospekt, 1941".

AUSSTELLUNG »DAS SOWJET-PARADIES«
BERLIN, LUSTGARTEN, 9. MAI BIS 21. JUNI 1942

320

*Opposite page:* Viktor Deni's caricature from 1942 of Hitler reading a despatch from the front: "Goddammit! The Red Army is crushing everything!!!" Soviet soldiers finally broke through the German blockade on January 27, 1944. In retreat, the Nazis destroyed or vandalised museums and old tsarist palaces, looting vast amounts of art and artefacts. But in Leningrad itself, the empty frames on the walls of the Hermitage (*above left*) testify how thoroughly the museum had spirited away its great collections.
*Above right:* Nazi iconoclasm. A postcard showing a headless and armless statue of Lenin on display in an

exhibition entitled, "Soviet Paradise" at the "Pleasure Gardens" in Berlin, May 9 to June 21, 1942. Before the war, Leningrad had been a thriving Soviet city of three million people. Approximately 1,300,000, and probably many more, perished in the siege. About the same number again were evacuated. Only some 300,000 Leningraders were left in the city at the time of its liberation, easily outnumbered by the 400,000 Soviet troops that had been brought in to help. Incredibly, some semblance of pre-war life continued during the siege. Stage performances and sometimes even symphony concerts were given by artists and

musicians risking their lives to lift the people's spirits.
*Top:* One such person was the great Leningrad-born concert pianist, Maria Yudina. She can be seen in this wartime photograph, seated fifth from the left in the second row in the company of officers and comrades of the Red Army. Living in Moscow at the outbreak of war, she trained as a nurse and refused to be evacuated as the Nazis closed in. She was flown into Leningrad in 1943 and stayed there for several months during the siege, as emaciated and freezing as everyone else, giving live concerts, broadcast over the city's radio, often with her recitals of poetry in the intervals.

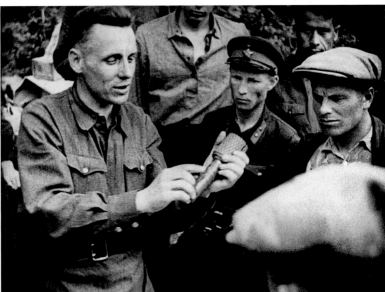

*Left:* Battalion Commander Alexei Yeremenko leading the attack. Photograph by Max Alpert. Yeremenko died in battle in 1942 and this photograph became a symbol of the Red Army's victorious struggle against the Nazi invaders.
*Top:* "A present for Hitler!" Top gunner Sergeant Korneiko of the Naval Air Wing of the Black Sea Fleet, April 1942.
*Centre:* Red partisans receive instructions on the correct handling of a grenade.
*Above:* Identity card of Konstantin Sherchenko, a Main Field operative of the counter-intelligence department, Smersh.

"Smersh" (literally "Death to Spies") was a branch of Beria's secret police, specially formed in 1943 to oversee military counter-intelligence operations. Smersh agents were widely deployed at the front to unmask suspected traitors and mutineers, interrogate prisoners of war and carry out executions of "anti-Soviet elements". Each Red Army regiment had its own penalty battalion made up of suspected criminals, oppositionists or dissenters who had been given the chance to "wash away their guilt with their blood". Smersh agents formed a sort of cordon behind the battle lines to shoot on sight deserters caught fleeing enemy fire.

The famed Soviet war photographer, Dmitrii Baltermans, was unlucky enough to have been wrongfully press-ganged into a penalty battalion at Stalingrad in 1942. The battalion was poorly trained and ill-equipped. Baltermans suffered a severe leg wound that put him out of action in 1943 but he was later allowed to return to the front, this time as a Red Army correspondent and photographer.

Belorussia had felt the full force of Stalin's secret police in the 1930s. The NKVD was everywhere – suspicious that the enemy was everywhere – interrogating, torturing and executing countless numbers of ordinary citizens.

So when the Nazis entered Minsk in the summer of 1941, they were welcomed with flowers by thousands of would-be collaborators dressed in their Sunday best and hoping for their liberation. The Nazi response was swift and predictable. Under their new General, Commissar Wilhelm Kube, they put into practice Himmler's master plan: kill 75% of the Belorussian population and condemn the rest to slavery. The ensuing genocidal brutality, aimed at the large Jewish population in particular, had the effect of creating the largest anti-Nazi movement of partisans, underground resistance fighters and their support groups in the entire war. Belorussian partisans are said to have wounded or killed over 500,000 Nazis and caused phenomenal damage to their military infrastructure, blowing up thousands of trains, trucks, military bases and bridges. Even Kube didn't escape their net. In September 1943, a young partisan woman by the name of Yelena Mazanik disguised herself as a maid and placed a bomb, planted inside a hot water bottle, in the General Commissar's bed whilst he was asleep. He was blown to bits; she escaped. The Nazis went berserk, murdering 1,000 Minsk citizens in reprisal.

*Right:* Viktor Koretsky's haunted poster published in 1943, "Soldier, Liberate Your Belorussia!"

*Opposite page:* Emmanuel Yevzerikhin's photograph of a wounded artilleryman and his comrades was taken in 1944 as the Red Army swept the Nazis out of Russia's blood-soaked territory. Surely no photograph, in its silence, has ever made such a deafening noise.

324

Following their great victory at Stalingrad, the Red Army went on to defeat the Germans in two further gigantic battles. The first was at Kursk in July 1943, in what became known as the greatest tank battle of all time.

For the first time in the war, Stalin stepped back from military planning in the Kremlin and allowed his generals in the field to make the important tactical decisions. This they did by dealing with the Nazi blitzkrieg at Kursk in a deliberately defensive strategic manner.

Receiving accurate information from the "Red Orchestra", the Soviet spy ring in Germany, the Red Army had time to position overwhelming numbers of tanks, aircraft and new troops in the front lines and lie in wait. Great use was made of camouflage and decoys, trenches and barbed wire, and millions of anti-tank and anti-personnel mines were laid to destroy the Nazis' dreams.

Both sides suffered huge casualties but the Nazis were unable to break through Soviet lines. The next great battle took place a year later, in June 1944, as the Red Army launched a major offensive to liberate blood-soaked Belorussia.

Operation Bagration (named after a Georgian prince mortally wounded at the Battle of Borodino in 1812) annihilated German Army Group Centre, causing a estimated 670,000 casualties, 300,000 of them mortal. It was the German Army's greatest defeat in the entire war.

At Minsk, 50,000 Nazis were taken prisoner and later marched through the streets of Moscow to humiliate them in front of the world. After the procession was over, the streets were ceremoniously washed clean.

*Right:* "Forward! Victory is Close at Hand!" A poster by Nina Vatolina, 1944.

*Above:* The Red Army magazine *Frontovaya Illyustratsia* (Frontline Illustrated) from June, 1943. Cover by Viktor Koretsky. The headline reads, "Soviet tanks are the terror of the German occupationists."

The Russian advance on Berlin began on April 16, 1945 with two million troops and 6,300 tanks. They entered the Nazi capital on April 30. Goebbels was still telling Berliners over the radio that not a single Russian soldier was anywhere near the city. Hitler obviously wasn't convinced; he killed himself the same day. *Opposite page:* The Soviet frontline poet and reporter Evgenii Dolmatovsky with trophy, Berlin, May 2, 1945. *Top:* Nazi helmets of no further use.

*Above left:* The Red flag is hoisted over the Reichstag, May 2, 1945. "How many millions had to die before that building was taken?" Evgenii Khaldei, the Soviet photographer who took these three iconic pictures, asked himself.
*Above right:* Generalissimo Stalin and his staff salute the Scots Guards as they arrive for a state dinner at Churchill's residence during the allies' talks on the future of the world at Potsdam, Berlin, July 23, 1945. Photographer unknown.

*Left:* The Soviet prosecutor, Lieutenant General Roman Rudenko (front row right, in military uniform) with his team at the first Nuremberg Trial following the Nazis' unconditional surrender. Twenty four of the most important captured Nazi leaders faced charges of war crimes and crimes against humanity. Ten were later hanged. The trial started on November 14, 1945, and lasted for almost a year. The International Military Tribunal was made up of judges and prosecution counsel from the United States, Britain, the Soviet Union and France.

*Above:* Nazis discussing the possible verdicts near the end of the first trial, late September, 1946. The photograph was taken by Evgenii Khaldei, who described the scene: "During a break, the defendants whispered to one another, 'What do you think? What kind of sentences are we going to get? Do you think a pardon is possible?' That's Goering, Keitel, Sauckel and Rosenberg. You can see the back of Frank, and Jodl is in the background. Frank was a real scoundrel, just like the rest of them. He had a diary that was bound in human skin. In it he'd written, 'The more Slavs we annihilate, the closer we will come to our ideals.'" All six seen in the photograph were sentenced to death. Five were hanged but Goering committed suicide the night before his scheduled execution. Nuremberg was chosen largely because it had been the main venue for the Nazis' rallies; the same city would therefore be associated with the Nazis' demise. More trials of Nazis followed at Nuremberg until 1949.

*Top:* "Glory to Stalin's Guards!" A poster by A. Gorgenko, 1945.

The minimum number of Russians who died in the Great Patriotic War is estimated at eighteen million, including eight million military losses. Some calculations have raised the figure to more than twenty-four million.

The tasks ahead for the postwar reconstruction of industry and agriculture were immense. The country's infrastructure was in ruins. Over 1,700 towns and 70,000 villages had been completely destroyed by the Nazis, and 65,000 kilometres of railroads. Hospitals, schools, libraries and museums all had to be rebuilt from scratch. Post-war propaganda more than emphasised Stalin's role in the great victory as well as appealing to the people's strong feelings of patriotism first invoked during the Nazi invasion. *Right:* "I will Vote for the Candidate's Bloc of Communists and Non-Party Members". Nina Vatolina's deliberately optimistic poster for the elections to the Supreme Soviet of the USSR, February 10, 1946. It was the first such election since 1937. Every candidate on the official list was returned.

Vasilii Yakovlev's "Portrait of Marshal of the Soviet Union G.K. Zhukov" from 1946. Yakovlev's overwhelmingly heroic portrayal certainly added to Stalin's postwar jealousy of his hugely popular wartime military leader. In 1941 Zhukov's tough tactics played a key role in the early months of the siege of Leningrad and he oversaw the counter-offensive that saved Moscow. In his role as Deputy Supreme Commander of the Red Army, he planned the great winter offensives of 1942–43, encircling the Germans at Stalingrad and the massive tank battles that would be the turning points of the war. It was at this time that Stalin started to become afraid of Zhukov's popularity. Zhukov went on to command the Soviet forces that took Berlin, and counter-signed for the Soviet Union the unconditional surrender of the German High Command. In 1946 Stalin tried to prepare with the aid of Beria, his secret police chief, charges of military conspiracy against Zhukov and others. The war hero's great renown in the eyes of the Russian people, however, meant that Stalin had to make do with expelling him from the Central Committee of the Party and sending him to military districts far from Moscow. After Stalin's death, Zhukov was quickly brought back to Moscow where for some years he would play an active role in government.

ЗА МИР, ЗА НАРОДНУЮ ДЕМОКРАТИЮ!

*Right:* Escorted by high-ranking military personnel, Lavrentii Beria, Anastas Mikoyan (centre) and Georgii Malenkov (right) show their faces at the annual May Day celebrations in Red Square, Moscow, 1947.

Beria and Malenkov had been elected members of the Politburo the previous year. Mikoyan had been a member since 1935. But in spite of their roles as Stalin's loyal henchmen, they all lived in constant fear of their ageing boss's unpredictable behaviour.

Beria had been Stalin's secret police chief since the downfall of Yezhov in 1938. His own reign of terror would last until after Stalin's death; he knew how easily Stalin succumbed to servile flattery in an atmosphere of mutual antipathy and distrust.

Mikoyan should be remembered chiefly for organising the sale of hundreds of priceless paintings and artworks (Rembrandt, Van Eyck, Titian, etc.) at knockdown prices to the Americans in the 1930s. At the same time he also oversaw, with Beria, the purge of the Party leadership in his native Armenia where thousands of "enemies of the people" were put to death.

Mikoyan's brother, Artem, co-designed several early versions of the famous MiG Soviet fighter aircraft and received many awards from the State.

Georgii Malenkov was a modest and unpretentious bureaucrat who cast himself as a "loyal servant of the State". So loyal that in the 1930s he had supervised, under Nikolai Yezhov, bloody purges of top Communist Party officials in both Belorussia and Armenia. At the time this photograph was taken, he was in charge of the dismantling of German factories and industrial plants and "relocating" them in the Soviet Union.

*Top:* Konstantin Ivanov's 1948 heroic poster, "For Peace, For People's Democracy", featuring Vera Mukhina's sculpture "The Worker and the Collective Farm Girl".

By 1947 the alliance between the Soviet Union and its wartime friends had disintegrated. Mutual distrust, the hatred of each other's political positions and above all the start of the nuclear arms race created an unnerving period of fear and paranoia on both sides, known as the Cold War. As Stalin turned the countries of Eastern Europe into a buffer zone to protect Russia from the threat of further invasion, the "iron curtain" descended across Europe. In response, the United States initiated the Truman Doctrine to come to the aid of countries that were threatened by a Communist take-over; the Marshall Plan to help rebuild war-torn Western Europe; and NATO to guard against any perceived Soviet threat. Postwar America indulged in a decade of Red baiting. Senator Joe McCarthy led a notorious campaign of witch-hunts against anyone suspected of Communist sympathies ("Are you or have you ever been...?"), whipping the country into a frenzy of anti-Communist hysteria. Aggressive investigations, blacklists, even prison – McCarthyism caused thousands of American lives to be destroyed.
*Right:* "Long Live the All-Union Day of Physical Culture". A poster by V. Khrapovitsky from Moscow dated 1947.
*Opposite page:* "New Techniques from Wall Street", Yulii Ganf's cartoon published in *Krokodil* magazine, May 10, 1952. An American soldier blasts "plague, typhus and cholera" into the upper atmosphere while Dean Acheson (US Secretary of State) and Trygve Lie (first Secretary-General of the United Nations) sing a duet: "The USA does not have biological weaponry". *Krokodil* and other Soviet magazines kept up a barrage of satirical propaganda, publishing thousands of pages of anti-American and anti-British cartoons and caricatures.

After the war the Stalin cult reached ever greater heights, culminating in the adoration the glorious leader was to receive on his seventieth birthday in 1949. In reality his health had been worsening since the end of the war and he gradually cut down on his excessive workload. This gave him time to tend the garden at his Black Sea dacha – and to concoct brand new schemes of cruelty and paranoia whilst he was doing the planting. One of these schemes would seriously backfire on him. In January 1952 Vladimir Vinogradov, one of his long-serving Jewish doctors, innocently suggested to him that, for health reasons, it might be time for his patient to consider retirement from political life. Stalin, prompted by his anti-semitic campaign against "rootless cosmopolitanism" that was in full swing, had all his well-meaning doctors arrested as "assassins in white coats". When he collapsed into a coma on March 1, 1953, his previously most-trusted doctors who had nursed him for decades were unavailable to help him; they were being tortured in the Lubyanka.

*Left:* Workers at the "Dinamo" plant in Moscow listen in sorrow to the radio announcement of their leader's death. Photograph by Emmanuel Yevzerikhin.

*Top:* Russian military in East Berlin, visibly shocked, anxiously await further bulletins from home.

*Above:* Official pass No.0716 issued to Comrade Trukhtanov for entry into Red Square for the funeral of the Supreme Soviet Minister of the USSR and Secretary of the Central Committee of the KPSS (Communist Party of the Soviet Union), Generalissimo Joseph Vissarionovich Stalin.

*Overleaf:* Stalin lying in state at the House of Trade Unions in Moscow, where the show trials of his political enemies had been acted out in the 1930s. Photograph by Dmitrii Baltermans.

339

The calculating, unpredictable and sadistic methods that Stalin used in his political life extended into his dealings with the entourage involved in his private life. But in his final years, as he grew more and more reclusive, his behaviour towards this inner circle became more like that of a madman. Not only did he send his own doctors to the cells, he also refused to take the medication necessary to improve his health and lower his very high blood pressure, even though he was known to be in great fear of dying.

He sacked his chief bodyguard, the loathsome Vlasik. He sacked his old Georgian bodyguards who had always served him faithfully and he even sacked Alexander Poskrebyshev, his long-time secretary who alone had the authority to interrupt his master at any time.

He also turned against his old comrades. He sent Molotov's beloved Jewish wife Polina to the Gulag for "over-praising" Golda Meir and he had Mikoyan's son arrested. (Much later Mikoyan admitted that this episode caused him to have serious thoughts about having "The Boss" assassinated). Beria, the secret police chief, also lived in dread, fearing that at any minute he might wind up in the place he had sent so many others.

On the morning of March 1, 1953, Stalin failed to summon the guards to bring his breakfast to his private room at Blizhnyaya, his dacha outside Moscow. This was unusual. The guards didn't know what to do. They were new. They were afraid to disturb him. They decided to wait. Better to do nothing than risk... But by 10pm, still no sign. They panicked. They banged on the door and entered his room.

The Generalissimo lay slumped on the carpet, barely conscious and drenched in his own urine; he had had a stroke. Malenkov and Beria, Bulganin and Khrushchev were the first high-ranking officials to be rushed to the scene. They lifted Stalin's groaning and gurgling body onto his bed and, incredibly (or more likely deliberately because they all hated him so much), just left him there. No one called for medical help until the next morning, March 2. When the doctors arrived they found him half-paralysed and he had been vomiting blood. Scared out of their wits at being face to face with the deteriorating dictator and unsure what to do, they telephoned the secret police to seek advice from his personal physicians who were incarcerated in the Lubyanka. They were told that little could be done.

On March 5 at 9.50pm, Stalin suffered a massive stomach haemorrhage and died; but not before his political fate had been decided. In the last hours of Stalin's life, his former disciples, Beria and Malenkov, Bulganin and Khrushchev, met together, dismissed the mass murderer from office and proceeded to divide up the political spoils.

*Left:* Kay Mapes and Alice Quessy (on the right with feathers in her tiara) toast Nikita Khrushchev, Chairman of the Council of Ministers and First Secretary of the Communist Party of the Soviet Union, at a first night party for the stars of the American spectacular, "Holiday on Ice", Moscow, May 1959.

Anastas Mikoyan, First Deputy Prime Minister and a key figure in bringing U.S.-style ice cream to Moscow after Stalin's death can be seen in profile, exiting stage left.

In the power struggle that followed Stalin's death, Khrushchev and Malenkov moved swiftly to block Beria's bid for the leadership. The secret police chief was arrested, held in an underground bunker in Moscow where he was tried in secret, found guilty and shot whilst pleading on his knees for mercy.

Khrushchev next ousted Malenkov, but in a more kindly way; the Prime Minister of the Soviet Union since Stalin's death was packed off to Kazakhstan in 1955 to manage a power station. Malenkov later returned to Moscow and lived quietly in retirement, dying in 1988. It is said that he became a churchgoer in old age.

The flamboyant Khrushchev, now in power, radically changed the culture of the Kremlin. His secret speech on Stalin's crimes, given at the Twentieth Congress of the Communist Party on February 25, 1956, deliberately set anti-Stalin Stalinists against the shocked and outwitted old guard of pro-Stalin Stalinists. The period of de-Stalinisation had begun. He made himself unpopular during the Hungarian revolution of 1956, and again during the Cuban missile crisis but he rehabilitated (even if posthumously) many of Stalin's victims and reduced the Gulag empire. Breaking with Soviet tradition he travelled to Yugoslavia, Britain and the USA. His humour and unconventional behaviour – banging his shoe on the table at a conference at the United Nations in 1960 for example – made him a great hit in the West. But in 1964 his agricultural policies failed him and he was removed from office, replaced by the conservative and grey Leonid Brezhnev. There followed twenty years of detente abroad and stagnation at home.

Mikhail Gorbachev was appointed Party General Secretary in March 1985. Six years later the Soviet Union had become the former Soviet Union and the capitalists of the world breathed a united sigh of relief.

First published 2009
by order of the Tate Trustees
by Tate Publishing, a division of Tate
Enterprises Ltd, Millbank, London
SW1P 4RG
www.tate.org.uk/publishing

© David King 2009
All photographs and artworks are from
the David King Collection, London
www.davidkingcollection.com
davidkingcollection@btopenworld.com
The author has made every effort to
contact the copyright holders wherever
appropriate, and apologises for any
omissions that have inadvertently
been made.

A catalogue record for this book is
available from the British Library

ISBN 978 1 85437 686 2

Designed by David King
Layout by Kate Tattersall at THS,
London
Colour reproduction by DL Interactive,
London
Printed in Hong Kong by Printing
Express

Translation credits:
Extract on p.105 from Isaac Babel: 1920
Diary, edited by Carol J. Avins,
translated by H.T.Willets. Russian text
© 1990 Antonina Nikolaevna
Pirozhkova-Babel. © 1995 Yale
University. Published by Yale University
Press, New Haven and London 1995.
Reprinted by permission.
Extracts on pp.280–1 from Vitaly
Shetalinsky, The KGB's Literary
Archive, translated, edited and
annotated by John Crowfoot. © 1993
Editions Robert Laffont, S.A., Paris
1993. English translation © John
Crowfoot, 1995. Published by The
Harvill Press, London 1995. The Harvill
Press is an imprint of Random House.
Reprinted by permission.

## ACKNOWLEDGEMENTS

It is more than four decades since I first
started collecting photographs, books,
posters and all kinds of graphic material
documenting the political and social
history of Russia and the former Soviet
Union, and communist movements
everywhere. During that time I have
been fortunate to meet many people,
worldwide, who have shared the same
interests and have contributed their
time, knowledge and enthusiasm.
I would particularly like to thank my
friends Valerie Wade, Judy Groves,
Francis Wyndham, Miklos Kun and
Agnes Gereben, Andrew Spira and
Susannah Clapp. Without their great
help and encouragement this book
would not have been possible.
Special thanks are due to Matthew Gale,
Head of Displays (Tate Modern) and to
Chris Stephens, Head of Displays (Tate
Britain) for their vision and support
with the continuing displays from my
collection over the last decade, from
which the idea for this book originated.
Particular thanks are also due to Kate
Tattersall at THS (layout), Clive Boutle
(editing) and Mark Fairman at DL
Interactive (scanning), for their
wonderful skill, intelligence and utmost
patience. I would like to thank
everybody at Tate Publishing for making
this project so exciting. In particular,
Roger Thorp, James Attlee, Tim Holton,
Beth Thomas, Sarah Tucker, Judith
Severne, and the Tate photographers
David Lambert and Rodney Tidman.
Many thanks are due to the following
people, in alphabetical order, who have,
over the years, also been so helpful:
Bruce Chatwin, Stephen Cohen, Igor
Dmitriev, Natan Federovsky, Robin
Fior, Alec Flegon, Jonathan Fishburn,
Pete Glatter, Walter Goldwater, Yoram
Gorlizki, Anita and Ronald Gray,
Dmitrii Gutov, Anthony C. Hall,
Charles Curtis and Wayne Seabrook at
Hanway Print, Pamela Hearn, Gertrud
Heartfield, Joanne King, Joseph and
Lucy King, Josephine King, Nina King,
Robin King, Vladimir Krichevsky,
Alexei Ladyzhensky and Galina Panova,
Harold Landry, Olga Lavrenkova,
Alexander Lavrentiev, Vladimir
Melnichenko and Tatiana Koloskova
(Directors of the Lenin Museum,
Moscow), Nina Lobanov-Rostovsky,
Sasha Lurye, Gerard McBurney,
Stephen Musgrave (who kindly gave
permission to reproduce four
photographs from his grandfather,
Walter Meakin's, collection), Svetlana
Palmer, Serge Plantureux, Howard
Garfinkel and Larry Zeman (Productive
Arts), Sasha Pyshakov, Michael Rand,
Doris Rau, Howard Schickler,
Alexander Snopkov, Pavel Snopkov,
Estaban Volkov, Ernst Volland and
Heinz Klimmer (collectors of the work
of Yevgenii Khaldei and other Soviet war
photographers), Kaiya Winnie Waerea,
George Weissman, and Erika Wolf.

*Above:* American Vice President
Richard Nixon with Castillo Armas
(left), President of Guatemala, at an anti-
Communist exhibition at the National
Palace in Guatemala City, 1955. They
are studying a "captured" portrait of
Georgii Malenkov. Another portrait,
this time of Ho Chi Minh, looms
ominously behind Nixon who was on a
"goodwill" tour of Central America,
trying to save it from communism.
*Above left:* Nikita Khrushchev showing
his disapproval at the United Nations,
New York, 1960.

## BIBLIOGRAPHY

Babel, Isaak. *The Complete Works.* New
York, 2002
_. *Konarmiya.* Moscow, 1927
–. *1920 Diary.* Translated by H.T.
Willetts. New Haven, 1995
Beevor, Antony. *Stalingrad.* London,
1998
Bonnell, Victoria E., *Iconography of
Power.* Berkeley, Ca., 1997
Boym, Svetlana. *Common Places.*
Cambridge, Mass. 1994
Cohen, Stephen F. *Bukharin and the
Bolshevik Revolution.* New York, 1973
Conquest, Robert. *The Great Terror.*
London, 1968
Deutscher, Isaac. *The Prophet Armed:
Trotsky, 1879–1921.* London, 1954
–. *The Prophet Unarmed: Trotsky,
1921–1929.* London, 1959
–. *The Prophet Outcast: Trotsky,
1929–1940.* London, 1963
–, and King, David. *The Great Purges.*
Oxford, 1984
Erickson, John. *The Soviet High
Command: A Military-Political
History, 1918–1941.* London, 1962
Fischer, Louis. *The Life of Lenin.*
London, 1965
Gabel, Paul. *And God Created Lenin:
Marxism vs. Religion in Russia,
1917–1929.* New York, 2005
Ginzburg, Evgenia Semyonovna.
*Journey into the Whirlwind.* New York,
1967
–. *Within the Whirlwind.* London, 1981
Glebov-Putilovsky, N. N., ed. *Lenin
Albom – Sto Fotograficheskikh
Snimkov.* Moscow, 1927

Gorky, M., et al., eds. *Belomorsko–
Baltiiskii Kanal imeni Stalina.*
Moscow, 1934
Grossman, Vasily. *A Writer at War.*
London, 2006
Heijenoort, Jean van. *With Trotsky in
Exile. From Prinkipo to Coyoacán.*
Cambridge, Mass., 1978
Kerzhentsev, P., ed. *Zhizn Lenina.* Illust.
by P. Staronosov. Moscow, 1936
King, David. *The Commissar Vanishes.*
New York, 1997
–. *Ordinary Citizens: The Victims of
Stalin.* London, 2003
–. *Propavshie Komissar.* Moscow, 2005
–, et al. *Trotsky: A Photographic
Biography.* Oxford, 1986
–, and Ryan, James. *Trotskii.*
Ekaterinburg, 2000
Krichevsky, Vladimir. *Obloshka.*
Moscow, 2002
Kun, Miklós. *Stalin: An Unknown
Portrait.* Budapest, 2003
Lunacharsky, Anatoly Vasiliievich.
*Revolutionary Silhouettes.* London,
1967
Mayakovsky, Vladimir. *The Bedbug and
Selected Poetry.* Bloomington, 1960
Medvedev, Roy. *Let History Judge: The
Origins and Consequences of Stalinism.*
New York, 1986
Montefiore, Simon Sebag. *Stalin: The
Court of the Red Tsar.* London, 2003
Olginskaya, Larisa. *Gustav Klutsis.*
Moscow, 1981
Rabinowitch, Alexander. *The Bolsheviks
Come to Power: The Revolution of
1917 in Petrograd.* New York, 1976
Rayfield, Donald. *Stalin and his
Hangmen.* London, 2004
Reed, John. *Ten Days That Shook the
World.* London, 1926
Rudiak, Ilya. *Twenty Thousand Faces of
Pasternak.* USA, 2004
Schapiro, Leonard. *The Communist
Party of the Soviet Union.* London,
1963
Service, Robert. *Stalin: A Biography.*
London, 2004
Shentalinsky, Vitaly. *The KGB's Literary
Archive.* Translated by John Crowfoot.
London, 1995
Sheridan, Clare. *Nuda Veritas.* London,
1927
Spira, Andrew. *The Avant-garde Icon.*
London 2008
Sukhanov, N. N. *The Russian
Revolution, 1917: A Personal Record.*
London, 1955
Taylor, A.J.P. *The Russian War
1941–1945.* London 1978
Trotsky, Leon. *Stalin: An Appraisal of the
Man and His Influence.* London, 1947
Tumarkin, Nina. *Lenin Lives! The Lenin
Cult in Soviet Russia.* Mass., USA,
1997
Tupitsyn, Margarita. *Klutsis and
Kulagina.* New York, 2004
Wyndham, Francis, and King, David.
*Trotsky: A Documentary.* London,
1972
Yakovlev, N. M., ed. *Stalin – Zhivopis,
Plakat, Grafika, Skulptura.* Moscow,
1934

# INDEX

Acheson, Dean 336
Adamovich, Mikhail 15
Akhmatova, Anna 204
Alexander III, Tsar 54
Alexandra Feodorovna, Tsarina 12, 24
Alliluyeva, Nadezhda 217, 250
Alliluyeva, Svetlana 217, 250
Alpert, Max 222, 301, 323
Altman, Natan 148
Amosova, Olga 38, 39
Andreyev 207, 258
Annenkov, Yuri 150
Antonov, Fyodor 172, 310
Armand, Inessa 160
Armas, Castillo 344
Arnold, Valentin 271
Arnshtam, Lev 314
Aseyev, Nikolai 188
Averbakh, Leopold 221
Babel, Isaak 18, 105, 280
Babel, Mikhail 105
Bakayev, Ivan 269
Baltermans, Dmitrii 310, 313, 323
Bedny, Demyan 68
Beevor, Antony 317
Berezinsky, A. 110
Beria, Lavrentii 247, 250, 279, 304, 323, 333, 334, 342, 343
Berman-Yurin, Konon 269
Bezymensky, Alexander 236
Bielski Brothers 309
Blok, Alexander 204
Blyukher, Marshal Vasilii 93, 279
Bogdanov, Sergei 172
Bograd, Izrael 256
Boguslavskaya, Xenia 61
Boguslavsky, Mikhail 273
Borisyuk, M. 236
Brezhnev, Leonid 343
Brik, Osip 190
Brodoty, Lev 35
Brodsky, Isaak 50
Brugière 124
Bruskina, Masha 314
Bubnov, Alexander 309
Budenny, Field Marshal Semyon 105
Bukharin, Nikolai 160, 271, 275
Bulganin, Nikolai 342
Bulla, Alexander 33
Bulla, Karl Karlovich 33
Bulla, Viktor 23, 33, 47, 117
Burova, Olga 313, 314
Chaliapin, Fyodor 204
Chekhonin, Sergei 12, 50, 62
Cheremnykh, Mikhail 167
Cherkes, Daniil 232
Chernov, Mikhail 258
Churchill, Winston 124, 308, 329
David, Fritz 269
Deni, Viktor 85, 88, 90, 96, 101, 113, 317, 320
Denikin, General Anton 68, 93, 102
Deutscher, Isaac 137
Dolmatovsky, Evgenii 328, 329
Dreitzer, Yefim 269
Drobnis, Yakov, 273
Dutov, Ataman 93
Dybenko, Pavel 93
Dzerzhinky, Felix 124, 134, 160
Dzhugashvili, Ekaterina 250
Dzhugashvili, Vasilii 217
Dzhugashvili, Yakov 298
Dzugavey, T. 236
Ehrenburg, Ilya 193
Eisenstein, Sergei 28, 183
Eliseev, K. 163
Emirov, Vasilii 42
Engels, Friedrich 58
Ermilov, Vasilii 110
Esenin, Sergei 204
Evseyev, Sergei 28
Firin, Semyon 221
Fitzmaurice, George 185
Frank, Hans 331

Frentz, Rudolf 28, 46, 171
Galadzhev, Pyotr 146, 147
Galer, Itska 105
Gamarnik, Yan 279
Ganf, Yulii 336
Garanin, Anatolii 313
Gerasimovich, Josif 181
Gelfreykh, G. 28
Ginzberg, Evgenia 17
Gitsevich, V.A. 302
George V, King 24
Glik, M. 247
Goebbels, Joseph 329
Goering, Hermann 331
Goldshtein, G.P. 214
Goltzman, Eduard 267
Gorbachev, Mikhail 18, 343
Gorgenko, A. 331
Gorky, Maxim 131, 221, 222, 225, 240, 256
Gothon-Lunion, Joseph 163
Grashe, Ivan 271
Grinchuk, Alexei 302
Grossman, Vasilii 317
Groves, Judy 16
Guminer, Yakov 210
Gushchin, V.D. 240
Heartfield, John 50, 190, 213
Himmler, Heinrich 324
Hitler, Adolf 213, 286, 294, 298, 304, 318, 320, 329
Ho Chi Minh 163, 344
Hoover, Herbert 131
Humbert-Droz, Jules 113
Igmunov, Sergei 263
Ikramov, Akmal 275
Ivanov, Konstantin 334
Ivanov, Viktor 313, 314
Ivanova, Tamara 105
Jodl, Alfred 331
Kaganovich, Lazar 207, 258, 273
Kahlo, Frida 263
Kalinin, Mikhail 105, 207, 249, 256
Kalmykov, Comrade 236
Kamenev, Lev 42, 124, 163, 266, 267, 270
Kameneva, Olga 124, 266
Kamenskaya, Tonya 14, 254
Kamzolkin, Evgenii 62
Kazakov, I.N. 275
Keitel, Wilhelm 331
Kerensky, Alexander 33, 34, 35, 42, 54
Khaldei, Yevgenii 298, 329, 331
Khayutina, Evgenia 105
Khmurii, Vasil 110
Khodasevich, Valentina 222
Khrapovitsky, V. 336
Khvostov, O. 110
Kibardin, Georgii 214
Kirov, Sergei 207, 248
Klutsis, Gustav 160, 187, 206, 207, 209, 213, 214, 240, 254, 256, 283
Knyazev, Ivan 271
Kochergin, Nikolai 121, 159, 178, 180
Kogout, Nikolai 138, 195
Kolchak, Admiral Alexander 68, 93
Kolli, Nikolai 61
Koonen, Alicias 148
Koretsky, Viktor 286, 288, 301, 302, 324, 326
Korneiko, Sergeant 323
Kornilov, General Lavr 35
Kosmodemyanskaya, Zoya 314
Kossior, Stanislav 207
Kostelevskaya, Maria 167
Kovalev, Lev 213
Krassin, Leonid 124
Kravchenko, Alexei 177
Krestinsky, Nikolai 275
Kruchenykh, Alexei 188
Krupskaya, Nadezhda 150, 153, 156, 160
Krushchev, Nikita 18, 342
Kube, Wilhelm 324
Kudoyarov, Boris 247, 318
Kuibyshev, Valerian 207
Kukriniksy (caricaturists) 308
Kulagina-Klutsis, Valentina

188, 283
Kun, Bela 18
Kun, Miklos 18
Kustodiev, Boris 121
Kuvshinova, Shura 17, 254, 256
Lashevich, Mikhail 12
Lavinsky, Anton 190
Lebedev, Vladimir 72, 144
Lebedev-Kumach, Vasilii 309
Lenin, Vladimir Ilych Ulyanov 14, 17, 18, 28, 34, 40, 42, 47, 48, 49, 50, 54, 58, 62, 68, 71, 72, 80, 85, 98, 113, 117, 124, 131, 134, 137, 140, 144, 150, 153, 154, 155, 156, 159, 160, 163, 178, 190, 197, 200, 204, 206, 213, 214, 239, 247, 256, 266, 288, 345
Leonidov, L. 85
Levin, L.G. 275
Lie, Trygve 336
Lissitsky, Lazar "El" 61, 144, 186, 191, 193, 197, 208, 222, 225, 294
Litvinov, Maxim 124
Livshitz, Yakov 273
Loskutov, S. 250
Lubetkin, Berthold 61
Lunacharsky, Anatolii 42, 58, 62, 137, 144, 171
Luyre, Moisei 268
Lurye, Nathan 268
Lyutov, Kiril (see Isaak Babel)
McCarthy, Senator Joe 336
Makhno, Nestor 93
Malakhov, V. 221
Malenkov, Georgii 334, 342, 343, 344
Malevich, Kazimir 193
Mamontov, General Konstantin 102
Mandelstam, Nadezhda 16
Mandelstam, Osip 16, 192
Manizer, Matvei 309
Mapes, Kay 343
Marenkov, O. 110
Markov-Grinberg, Mark 254
Marx, Karl 58, 85, 121, 193
Matveyev, Alexander 58
Mayakovsky, Vladimir 101, 137, 148, 183, 186, 188, 202
Mazanik, Yelena 324
Mdivani, Polikarp 178
Meir, Golda 342
Melnikov, S. 17, 128, 191
Menjou, Adolphe 185
Merkurov, Sergei 150, 213, 288
Meyerhold, Vsevolod 148, 204, 280
Mezentsev, S. 58
Mikoyan, Anastas 249, 258, 334, 343
Mikoyan, Artem 334
Mileeva, Liubov 192
Mindlin, Yem 189
Moholy-Nagy, László 188
Molotov, Vyacheslav 207, 249, 256, 258, 271, 272, 280, 286, 342
Moor, Dmitrii 35, 66, 88, 90, 93, 98, 167
Mount, Reginald 307
Mrachkovsky, Sergei 269
Mukhina, Vera 334
Munzenburg, Willi 189, 190
Muralov, Nikolai 273
Nappelbaum, Moisei S. 42, 132, 204, 279
Naumov, Alexander 185
Negri, Pola 185
Nguyen Ai Quoc (see Ho Chi Minh)
Nicholas II, Tsar 12, 23, 24, 25, 56
Nikandrov, Vasilii 28
Nixon, Richard 344
Norkin, Boris 272
Oistrakh, David 204
Ordzhonikidze, Sergo 178, 207, 248, 249
Orosz, Istvan 345
Otsep, Fyodor 185

Otsup, Pyotr 40, 213
Padalka, I. 110
Pasternak, Boris 204
Paulus, Field Marshal Friedrich 298, 317
Pavlichenko, Lyudmila 309
Peters, Yakov 160
Petlyura, Symon 101, 102
Petritsky, Anatolii 110
Petrov-Vodkin, Kuzma 171
Petrusov, Georgii 105
Piatakov, Grigorii 270, 271, 272
Pichugin, Sergei 154
Pikkel, Richard 267
Pilsudski, Marshal Jósef 98
Pletnev, D.D. 275
Polonsky, Vyacheslav 171
Popova, Liubov 142, 144
Poskrebyshev, Alexander 342
Prakhov, Nikolai 243
Protazanov, Yakov 185
Puni, Ivan (Jean Pougny) 61
Pushin, Gavriil 270
Quessy, Alice 343
Rabichev, I. 156
Radek, Karl 271
Raikh, Zinaida 281
Rakovsky, Christian 266, 275
Rand, Michael 15
Rasputin, Grigorii 24
Rataichak, Stanislav 271
Razin, Stepan 214
Reed, John 50, 124, 159, 183
Reingold, Isaak 269
Ribbentrop, Joachim von 286
Rivera, Diego 171, 263
Rodchenko, Alexander 18, 144, 182, 189, 192, 222, 225
Rodzianko, Mikhail 23
Romm, Mikhail 214
Rosenberg, Alfred 331
Rothstein, Andrew 15
Rothstein, Theodore, 15
Rozenel, Natalya 137
Rozhdestvensky, Vasilii 171
Rudenko, Roman 331
Rudzutak, Yan 207, 249
Rykov, Alexei 153, 267, 275
Ryumin, Yakov 317
Samokhvalov, Alexander 197
Sankova, Galina 304
Saryan, Martiros 174, 175
Sauckel, Fritz 331
Sedlyara, V. 110
Sedov, Leon 163, 263
Sedova, Natalya 163, 263, 290
Serebryakov, Leonid 270
Serebryakova, Zinaida 172
Shaduntz, Suren 258
Shagin, Ivan 302, 304
Shaw, George Bernard 222
Shcherbakov, A. 189
Shcherbatsevich, Volodya 314
Shchuko, Vladimir 28
Shchusev, Alexei 152, 153
Sherchenko, Konstantin 323
Sheridan, Clare 124
Shestov, Alexei 272
Shkiryatov, Matvei 258
Shkuro, Andrei 102
Shostakovich, Dmitrii 314 278
Shteinberg, Yakov, 12, 18, 23, 35, 51, 54
Shumolov, Sergei 134
Simakov, Ivan 129
Sokolnikov, Grigorii 270
Sokolovskaya, Alexandra 263
Sololov, Anatolii 270
Smirnov, Ivan 266, 267
Spiridonova, Maria 266
Stakhanov, Alexei 240
Stalin, Joseph 17, 18, 50, 93, 105, 110, 113, 153, 154, 155, 159, 160, 163, 171, 179, 188, 193, 200, 204, 206, 207, 217, 218, 221, 225, 230, 235, 239, 247, 248, 249, 250, ,256, 258, 263, 265, 266, 268, 269, 270, 271, 272, 273, 275, 278, 279, 283, 286, 288, 294, 304, 307, 308, 310, 318, 324, 326, 329, 331,

332, 334, 336, 342, 345
Staronosov, Pyotr 28
Sten, Anna 185
Stenberg Brothers (Georgii and Vladimir) 182, 185
Stepanova, Varvara 144, 192
Strakhov, Adolf 110, 156, 164, 165, 187, 210, 213, 240
Stranich, Vladimir 200
Stroilov, Mikhail 270
Sukhanov, Nikolai, 28
Svanidze, Ekaterina 298
Sverdlov, Yakov 12, 42
Tairov, Alexander 148
Tal, Boris 258
Tatlin, Vladimir 16, 144, 204
Taylor, A.J.P. 308, 310
Tearle, Conway 185
Telingater, Solomon 222
Ter-Vaganian, Vagarshak 267
Timoshenko, Marshal Semyon 313
Trakhman, Mikhail 302
Tretyakov, Sergei 188
Triva, V. 189
Troshin, Nikolai 222, 225
Trost, David 105
Trotsky, Leon 12, 14, 15, 16, 34, 35, 40, 42, 62, 67, 98, 113, 124, 137, 154, 155, 156, 163, 167, 183, 190, 263, 265, 266, 267, 269, 270, 271, 290 273, 288, 345
Trus, Kiril 314
Tukhachevsky, Marshal Mikhail 113, 278, 279
Uritsky, Moisei 12
Uspensky, E. 236
Usupov, R. 236
Vatolina, Nina 294, 326, 332
Vertov, Dziga 182
Vesnin, Alexander 144, 148
Vilde, Rudolf 132
Vinogradov, Viktor 80, 128
Viskovsky, Vyacheslav 181
Vlasik, Nikolai 250, 342
Volkova, Zinaida 263
Vorobiev, P.V. 153
Voroshilov, Kliment 207, 217, 249, 258
Vyshinsky, Andrei 270, 275
Wilhelm II, Kaiser 25
Wrangel, Baron Pyotr 68,102, 113
Wyndham, Francis 15
Yagoda, Genrikh 221, 275
Yakovlev, Captain 105
Yakovlev, Vasilii 333
Yakovlev, Yakov 258
Yegorov, Marshal Alexander 279
Yeremenko, Alexei 323
Yevdokimov, Grigorii 268
Yevzerikhin, Emmanuel 279, 324
Yezhov, Nikolai 105, 258, 265, 271, 272, 279, 334
Yudenich, General Nikolai 68, 93
Yudina, Maria 17, 18, 320
Yuon, Konstantin 172
Yurovsky, Yakov 56
Zbarsky, B.I. 153
Zeiler, G.F. 70
Zelensky, Alexander 140
Zhemchuzhina, Polina 247, 256, 342
Zhukov, Marshal Georgii 304, 313, 333
Zinoviev, Grigorii 12, 34, 42, 121, 124, 163, 265, 266, 267, 268, 270
Zorin, Shalom 309
Zys, David 105

*Above:* Istvan Orosz's poster "Comrades, The End!" marking the withdrawal of Soviet troops from Hungary in 1989. Published by the Hungarian Democratic Forum.
*Below:* Khrushchev in London, 1956.

*Overleaf:* Hall No.3 of a gigantic exhibition held in Moscow to celebrate Stalin's seventieth birthday in 1949. The ideals of Socialist Realism are eerily displayed: Lenin is dumbstruck, Trotsky is not even a ghostly presence and the marble Stalin is invulnerable to the assassin's bullet.
*Pages 348/9:* The destruction of Kistaludi-Strobl's hated 60 foot high monument to Stalin in Budapest during the Hungarian revolution of 1956.
*Pages 350/1:* Leaving the Iron Curtain. The extinct border control posts at Helmstedt/Marienborn where Eastern Europe (in the shape of the former German Democratic Republic) once met the West.
Photograph by David King.
*Page 352:* "Workers of the World, Unite!" Gouache on paper by the same artist ("N.Sh") who painted the work on page 1. Leningrad, mid-1920s.

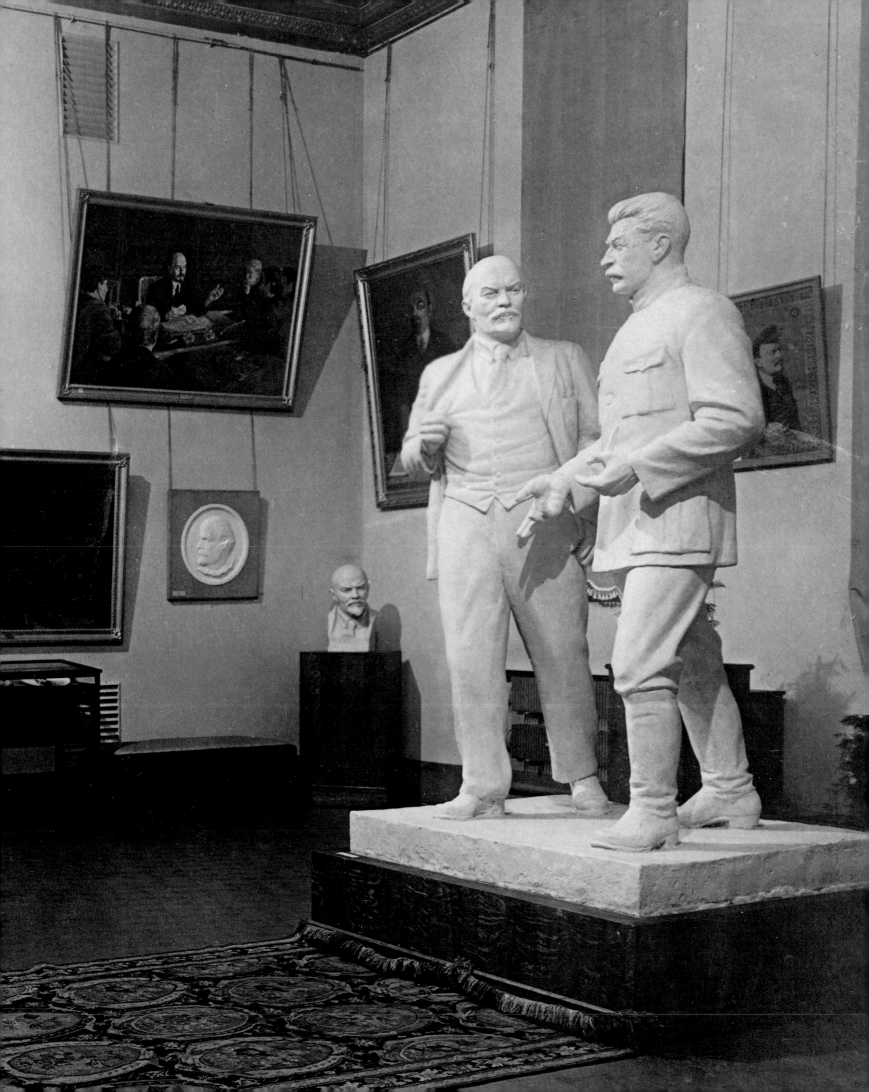